CRITICAL ACCLAIM FOR TWO BROADS ABROAD

"From the starting line to the finish line, a laugh-filled sprint!"

DON SCHWARCK, RETIRED TRACK COACH,
SOUTH LYON SCHOOLS

"This book provides the answer to the age old question: which is tougher, achieving world peace or trying to deal with a European bathroom at age 65?"

DAVID B. LANDRY, MAYOR CITY OF NOVI

"Karen was always a good writer. I remember when she wrote all over her bedroom dresser!"

IRENE RAYNER, KAREN SCHWARCK'S MOM,
NAPLES FLORIDA

"I don't know how well she writes, but she still has her own teeth."

PETER W. LAZARCHUK, D.D.S.

"She wrote a book? Are you kidding? About the UK? Is that where she was for so long?"

HUGH D. CRAWFORD,
MICHIGAN STATE REPRESENTATIVE - ELECT

"Despite the trauma of their encounters with the devils of the British countryside, they have managed to write the magnificent tome that you are about to read. Bill Bryson wrote of England in his "Notes from a Small Island", but it was nothing like this. Shakespeare inspired by centuries of English culture penned fine sonnets, but they were nothing like this. Churchill wrote his "History of the English Speaking Peoples", but I can guarantee that it too, was nothing like this. I can say without fear of contradiction, without any regard for the strait jacket of truth, and with a confidence born of complete ignorance of the text, that there has never been anything quite like this."

NIGEL PONSONBY SMYTHE, ENGLISHMAN

"Hilarious, witty, insightful and often times downright touching to the very bottom of the soles of your feet! Actually, haven't read the book, just sucking up because Kathy is on City Council and her husband Hugh is on his way to the Michigan State House of Representatives!"

BLAIR BOWMAN, SMALL BUSINESSMAN
ROCK FINANCIAL SHOWPLACE

Two Broads ABROAD

Kathy S. Crawford &
Karen Schwarck

SNACKBAG PUBLISHING
Novi, Michigan

Published by Snackbag Publishing

First Edition: December 2008
10 9 8 7 6 5 4 3 2 1
ISBN: 0-9743614-0-2

Manufactured and distributed in the United States of America by:
Impact Media Professionals
POB 113
Novi, MI 48376
info@impactmediapro.com

For more information about the Two Broads:
www.snackbagpublishing.com

This book is dedicated to all the adventurers out there who have chosen to do something out of the ordinary in order to grow into something more, rather than recede into something less.

~~~~~~

We are profoundly grateful to our husbands, Hugh and Don, for their love and support in most everything we do and also our children, siblings and other family members who have encouraged and inspired us. A special thanks to all of our girlfriends who persistently believe in us and always provide us with enriching experiences, along with gigantic doses of humor.
~~~~~~

Dear Reader,

If you picked up this book you may be wondering what's so special about two over-fifty women going on a trip.

What's special is the journey itself.

For one broad, the journey began with a decision to take a chance and change her life. For the other broad, it was an opportunity to fulfill a livelong dream to write a book about one of life's great adventures, friendship.

Once the trip was over, our real adventure began. How could we write one book from two very different perspectives? Should we each write alternate chapters in a "she said, she said" style, or should we write together as an omnipotent onlooker?

After several incarnations, we decided to write the book so that the reader could enjoy the journey through the eyes of just one of us, the one known by many to possess the most amazing sense of humor, my naturally comedic friend, Kathy Crawford.

It is with great pleasure we present this story to you.

The other broad,

Karen Schwarck

CONTENTS

Trek of the Two Broads

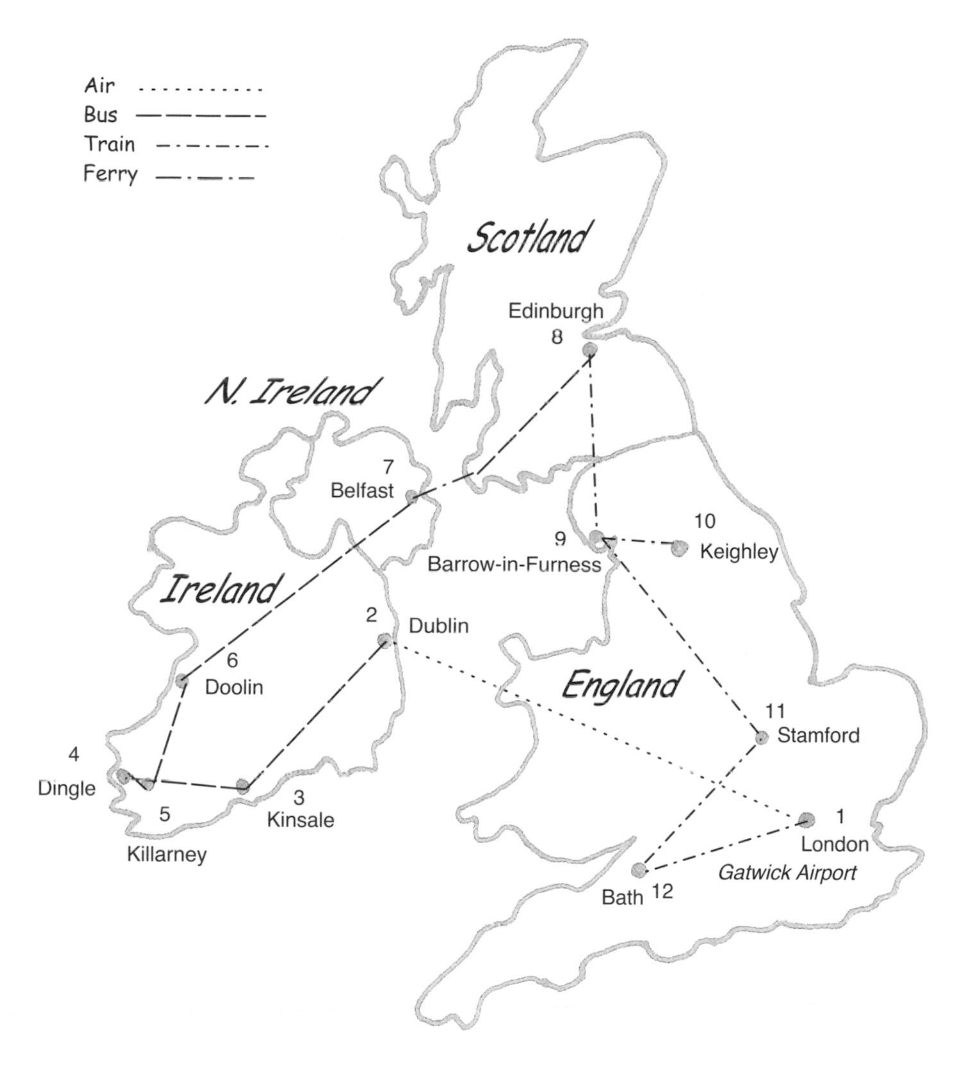

CHAPTER 1

I AM A STRANGER HERE

I caught myself tucking a used tissue up my sleeve. Just imagine ….tissue that had already been used….saving it, when there was a lifetime supply of new ones on my desk. Then the family Chihuahua ran by, wearing the spongy medicinal pads that refused to adhere to my throbbing bunion and hammer-toed feet. I began to wonder, "What… the hell….. is goin' on?"

To my mind, one day I was wearing a full skirt with a crinoline and flashy red spiked heels, then almost overnight, it became a polyester muumuu and navy orthopedics with gel inserts. I have been so doggedly distracted by my job and family that I have been totally oblivious of merging into a geriatric phase.

My profession for the past thirty years involves management of a Senior Citizen Center and all of its programs. I believe I know almost everything about aging and older adults, but I am not ready to be one myself!

There were a few signals and clues I should have heeded:

Clue #1: Our young grandson gleefully played with the flab under my upper arm whenever I read him a story. When did those flappy wing things appear?

Clue # 2: Decades of yo-yo dieting, as well as a propensity for submitting my fluffy torso for medical weight loss experimentation, caused me to be hospitalized for the removal of my abused, nonfunctioning gall bladder.

Clue #3: I traveled across the border to Canada for cheap Lasik surgery in order to eliminate the necessity for the ugly thick glasses I had worn since childhood. The surgery was a miracle, and people began to comment on my extraordinarily expressive eyes and long lashes. My days without glasses lasted for two glorious weeks and then my vision waned, dispatching me to an expensive ophthalmologist. The doctor announced that I needed immediate cataract surgery in both eyes and jovially reported that he would also keep “a close eye” on my macular degeneration.

Clue #4: My arthritic middle finger locked in the dreaded upright position. Periodic injections became necessary. Unfortunately, this did nothing to arrest the bumpy hardening of all of my fingers, which now only point around corners and can no longer grip change, or catch small flying objects.

Clue #5: Showering began to present an unforeseen hassle; the necessity to lift and/or move body parts around in order to adequately clean or dry them.

The above mentioned clues were grievous but, sadly, just the “ribbon-cutting” of my personal initiation into slowdown and ruin. They also triggered a whopping landslide of abnormalities such as skin tags, elongated nose and ear hair, foot and shoulder spurs, polyps, deviant moles, and a healthy fear of impending blindness.

For years, I was the perky President of the local Optimist Club and have a plaque and gold ID card to prove it. Regrettably, motivational speeches and enthusiasm only go so far when you are relegated to pulling up your underwear with a hooked stick. The unexpected deaths of younger friends and family members added into the woeful mix and necessitated my need for optimism. All of these events caused me to hunger for solutions and seek critical information to make sense of my life.

My quest began with a search for all-important papers… do we have any? Burial insurance? 401K? What's in my pension? Where are our birth certificates and the husband's honorable discharge from the Marine Corp? Do we still have to keep his moth eaten woolen uniform in case he gets called up? Why, oh, why, did I drift off during Human Resource's benefit presentations? What if I go into a spiraling decline, will insurance let me live out my days in one of those delightful, cheery, assisted-living homes? I presented these questions to my spouse of 42 years.

The husband reported that all-important papers might be shielded in his gun safe. This monster is so imposing and colossal, it should be housed in a financial institution. It is 3x6x4 feet of sparkling, shiny, black metal and features a Herculean four-spoke wheel with three combination tumblers. A flourish of gigantic gold letters identify the maker; "National Security Safe Co." I vaguely recall two years back, right after the safe's delivery; he fanned a huge document in my face. It professed the safe's capacity for surviving explosions, a blazing inferno, and a drop from a seven-story building. He stated that he would search for all important papers the next time he went in.

"Well, why can't I go in, now?" I queried.

"Do you remember the combination?" he countered.

"Uhm.....Nooohh!"

There was some grumpy muttering on his part. It seems he had given me this critical information, but now the hockey game was on and I was an unwanted interruption. Grudgingly, the husband continued:

"If you don't remember the combination, the numbers are written on a card inside the closet wall safe and also in a file marked "Jack" inside the smaller file safe on the floor. The small safe combination is on a paper inside the cabinet in the dining room. Once you get the combination, twirl it, find the file and get the big safe combination, then twirl that on the door tumblers. Get the keys off the keychain in the bedroom, put the key in the lock, turn it, and it opens right up."

"What? You- have- got- to- be- kidding! Are you saying that I have to remember a combination to one safe, in order to get into another safe, so I can find that combination, and then I have to get keys to open the huge safe after I twirl the right combination?"

He emitted a slight snort. "Well, you have to keep guns locked up, so kids can't get to them."

"Yeah.... but we don't have any kids here! Shouldn't I be able to get in there? Geeze, when you die, I'll have to rent a trailer to get this thing to a ten story building and shove it off, hoping it'll crack!"

Don't you think it's freakish and abnormal to have three safes in one minúte bedroom? There are no family jewels or booty from shipwrecks. He has a few guns, plus the rifle I won at a NRA dinner he dragged me to, but that's it!

I have now lost all interest in going in for the papers. I am resigned to waiting, until he goes in!

I begin to examine my domicile in a new light. As I do a little survey, I ascertain that absolutely no room here is mine, except maybe the pint-size kitchen. The husband knows very little about the cooking room, but has great expectations for food items to appear from it daily. He occasionally twirls around in there and asks if there is any milk or do we have any forks. The refrigerator and the utensil drawer have been in the same location for well over 30 years.

When did my seldom-quiet little nest become so unfamiliar? When was it transformed into an impregnable bunker without my knowledge or approval? Apparently, while I have been doing important government work for the past thirty years, life has gone on here, without my taking part. This house, my husband, and my personal deterioration, have become unsatisfactory, baffling, and totally alien.

I am a stranger here.

CHAPTER 2

TO GO OR NOT TO GO. . .THAT IS THE QUESTION

My tumble from the usual and predictable cannot be blamed on some inexplicable depression or change-of-life, but is the direct result of an alarming encounter with my own aging and the surprising evidence that I have become a stranger in my own home. My major life-shift was just around the corner and was introduced during a one day outing with an old friend.

Long time girlfriend, Karen Schwarck, has always provided innovative distractions and frequently offers excellent counseling. Her prescription for the doldrums was a lively one day adventure to nearby Canada. "We will play hooky all day and into the night," she pronounced.

Neither of us are sure when or why it happened, but early into our thirty year friendship, we began calling each other by our last names; Crawford and Schwarck, yours truly being the former.

Schwarck is hardly a girl, since she is post menopausal, fluffy, and rapidly spiraling toward sixty. Her naturally curly, graying locks are reminiscent of spun cotton candy. She is an organic, casual type, rejecting makeup and dressy attire, particularly sequins. Though eight years her senior, I invariably become child-like in her presence. She exudes wonder and enthusiasm for virtually everything, along with a big dose of charming airy-fairy obliviousness.

I, on the other hand, am more practical and oftentimes cynical. I see and accept things as they are, but find humor in almost every situation. I am known for dressing in bright colors, sparkles, and oversized earrings to match the ensemble. My earrings have become so notorious that when I am laid out at the funeral home, a creative friend has been charged with assuring my earrings match the outfit. She will also be trusted with laying a wide belt and a size ten dress, with size tag showing, on top of my deflated corpse. I have never been able to wear a belt nor size ten anything, including shoes. The viewing will be astounding.

When “hooky day” to Canada finally arrived, Schwarck and I approached it with unbridled eagerness, assured of a full day of fun and frivolity. We just recklessly abandoned all responsibility and departed for the day. I called in sick, with no explanations to the office or family members.

Schwarck pulled up to my house at 9:00 A.M. and I suspected that something was up. She was amped to the gills, which is an indication that driving, particularly lane changes, will be a two-person operation. When she has exciting news to impart, such as spotting a distant crop circle, then I must be extra vigilant as co-pilot. She’s a very cautious driver, but easily distracted by things like deer at the edge of a forest, or the rare sighting of a

Piliated Woodpecker. Her eyesight is astounding. I never see these things, for I am too busy waving around the guy who is laying on the horn and giving us the finger as he passes us on the shoulder.

Our first stop of the day was the bakery. The luscious aroma was apparent a mile away and our morning mouths were watering as we pulled into the drive and entered the front door. After much vacillation, we selected fifty, yes, fifty, delightfully assorted, but very expensive, tea sandwiches. I would have been completely satisfied with a BLT and chips, but Schwarck, the accomplished artist, felt a mere sandwich was too boring and unsuitable for today's jaunt. Food presentation is a highlight of her activities; eating is mine. We made another short stop for drinks and chips, then headed north to our favored foreign destination.

Canada is splendidly alien and feels so much further away than the actual short hour from home. Canadians worship an honest-to-God queen and they are protected by red festooned Royal Canadian Mounties, the RCMP. Canadians seem more enlightened than us. They comprehend kilometers, liters, temperatures in celsius, and they have beautiful shiny lines across their paper money.

Our first objective, after negotiating the no-nonsense border crossing, was to head for the pristine park underneath the Blue Water Bridge where, according to Schwarck, we will enjoy an early spring picnic while gazing out at the southern tip of Lake Huron as it empties into the St. Clair River.

"Crawford…look! Those two benches closest to the water are perfect!"

"Doesn't it bother you a little that we should be wearing leather gloves and mukluks while we sit and gaze and have our little picnic? Oh my God, it looks like the bathrooms aren't even open yet. That's gonna be a problem!"

I point out the frigid temperature hoping to stay in the warm car and eat. That bridge is so colossal and the water so vast, both are easily enjoyed from the car. Undaunted, she unloaded the food and eagerly headed toward the bench closest to the most spectacular of the water views.

My pal is enthralled with any large iron edifice, particularly steel bridges. She gestured broadly and babbled on about the immense armored girders while I peeled back layers of wax paper from the bakery's delicacies. It's all about the food for me, and how many of the stupid little sandwiches it will take to actually make a meal. I was gnawing my way through tea sandwich number six and had broken open the huge bag of sour vinegar chips when she began her investigation.

"Crawford, did you really look at the egg salad?"

"Uhm, no."

"How do you think they cut the eggs up so small? Did you know those chips are real potatoes and homemade? What kind of potatoes do you think they use?"

I peered at her egg salad and inspected two of the biggest chips before popping them into my mouth. It immediately became apparent that I would need to alternate sips of water between each potent, welt-raising chip. "Geeze, these take my breath away and make my eyes water! I bet it doesn't make any difference what kind of potato you use, if you let' em sit in vinegar for a couple a' years. Are my lips starting to swell?"

"Crawford, just look at that cucumber decorated with purple cream cheese! Isn't it beautiful?" she chortled as she peered worshipfully into the box teetering on her lap.

"Yep, it's beautiful alright, but you're going to have to eat about 30 of the little buggers to get a full size sandwich."

There was a considerable amount of munching and quiet contemplation of the lake's sparkling blue-green water. I was contemplating and calculating the distance between me and the bathroom and how long she would sit here before we could get back in the toasty car.

"Crawford, don't you feel sorry for women our age who don't have little adventures in their lives like we do? I mean….here you are, fresh off bunion and cataract surgery, your mother has Alzheimer's and is bedridden at home. If you don't have a little distraction once in awhile, you'll go crazy! Your job is a killer, too! You take care of people 24/7!"

"Well, thanks for reminding me of all the catastrophes! You better give me another five sandwiches 'cause I'm starting to feel miserable."

"These little outings are fun, but I believe we should think bigger. I mean really big! Have…. you ever considered going to another country for a long time; say, at least a month? We should go far, far away, and then I see us writing a book about it. We could take laptop computers and digital cameras. After the book is done, we could go on a book tour. I even see us on Oprah!"

"Well, do you also see me getting in the car right now and driving to the bathroom?" There was a long pause. "You know what, though? You might be right! I should go somewhere far, far away. I have been married to Hugh Crawford for over 42 years and I could sure use a little five week hiatus!"

"I'm serious, Crawford. We are natural storytellers, you especially. People tell us that all the time and they would love to read about our hilarious adventures. It would inspire older women who are afraid to do things like that. We shouldn't make any reservations; we'll just show up somewhere overseas. I think the UK would be far enough away. Five weeks would be perfect!"

I gave her my reality-check squint, but it was evident that she was in earnest.

"Are you kidding, Schwarck? We could barely get out of town today! How could we ever get off work for five weeks? Also, can you imagine how expensive a five-week trip would be? There is no way I could do it! You should go, though. Take your sister."

We both sank a little lower on the bench as we thought of all the things we hoped to accomplish in our remaining lifetime, but time and money are among our highest hurdles. I tried not to sound sarcastic as I stated the obvious, "Don't you think another little snag might be that we don't have laptop computers or digital cameras?

We also don't know how they work. Money could be a problem, too, since neither of us have any and that's why we work all the time! Here's another small thing: shouldn't we actually take a writing class or perhaps read a book or two before we write one and head out on a book signing tour, prior to the Oprah show?"

Let me say right here that it is truly uplifting and wide-eyed wonderful, when someone believes, without a doubt, that you can do something so astonishingly beyond your capability. We should limit our associations solely to the extraordinary people who prod and push us up to a place we never could have attained without their urging. My zealous friend, Karen Schwarck, has been that person for me. She perpetually has a knack for advocating my participation in out-of-the-ordinary enticements and endeavors that would have never occurred to me without her insistence.

Last year, Schwarck got it in her head that I would be an excellent artist. She appeared with armloads of mysterious containers, two complex looking easels, and several blank canvasses. For an entire summer she and I were obsessed with preparing to paint. We purchased acrylics and watercolors, took pictures of subject matter and got so… ready. She, being an art teacher by profession, began to impart her knowledge and after only two months, I was able to produce a coffee brown tree stump suspended from the sky. She believed it was a magnificent start. That painting is in the garage.

Then came the quilting phase. Apparently, we are still in this period, as we continue buying expensive "fat quarters" everywhere we go. Sadly, it turns out I am incapable of sewing, due to my frozen arthritic fingers. Digits, I discovered, are critical to the traditional quilting process. There is also a sizable amount of a lack of quilting interest, on my part. Schwarck never gives up on this, however. She is convinced that I have a smaller, more artistic quilt within me. A wall hanging, if you will, that will not be sewn at all. It'll be taped or glued or some such and people will come for miles around just to view and admire it.

On our way home from a meeting a couple of years ago, Schwarck got the notion that she and I should start a spirit circle with approximately four of our closest friends. "Crawford, who do you think would be good in our circle?"

"Well, that depends on what we are going to actually do… when we get in a circle."

She went on to explain that someone she knew was a part of such a circle. There were numerous articles, tapes, and books on the subject. The idea was to get together weekly and each member would keep a journal. Discussion would take place as to what each member would want to work on that week. All members would take time each day thinking of their spirit partners and focusing positive energy in their direction.

We selected four special friends to be in our group and they enthusiastically agreed to take part. We met once a week, journalled, sent the positive vibes out, lit candles, meditated, drank herbal tea, and ate pound cake. Changes did occur. All six of us gained a monumental amount of weight. One friend suffered and cried nonstop because of a painful divorce; another quit her Michigan job, sold her condo and moved to Arizona; my fifty year old sister was pink slipped from her long time insurance job; another's father went blind; and my mother died. With a "thank-you" to the spirit gods, we quit meeting, before anything else happened.

Yes, Schwarck is impossible for me to resist when she suggests creative, but oftimes, peculiar schemes. This UK five-week, book-writing, picture-taking, book- signing, Oprah show plan is, without a doubt, the most bizarre of all.

Schwarck told her family of her plans to travel to the UK. She will be the only family member to visit the town where her father was born. Her goal is to meet her father's relatives that her mother just uncovered via the Internet.

"Crawford, if you went with me, we could find your Irish relatives! Doesn't anyone in your family know where your grandfather's family lived in Ireland?"

"Well, Granddad always said that the Cotters came from an island, but now that I think of it….that could have been it, Ireland. Why don't you just get your sister to go with you? Bet she'd love to meet the relatives."

"Crawford, you are the only person I could ever spend five weeks with in the same room and that includes all my immediate family."

Schwarck owns and operates a tour business and many of the seniors from my Senior Center travel on her unique, fun-filled excursions. Weeks after hooky day, I heard from tour travelers that Schwarck had been announcing that she and I were considering a long journey, which would culminate in an uproariously amusing description of our travels in book form. She later reported that virtually everyone on her trips couldn't wait for us to write THE BOOK!

I needed to call a firm halt to this snowball she had started rolling. Schwarck knew government employees just couldn't take off for a month. There is important work involved, not to mention a dependant husband, three adult children who are sometimes homeless, and two grandchildren who desire clothes and toys. There is no way I could ever go overseas on an amusing month long frolic. In addition, just because I write notes on most of my Christmas cards, doesn't mean I am adequately prepared to write a book!

About a month later, my left knee decided to cave in. I saw the doctor who recommended a large brace which I was to wear constantly. Next, there were injections to relieve pain and finally, a knee replacement.

Thankfully, I breezed through the knee replacement surgery without contracting some gory flesh-eating infection. Recovery included long periods of being prone and plugged in to a machine that continuously bent my knee, whether I wanted to or not.

My down time was enhanced by visits from girlfriends toting dark chocolates, smutty novels and soup. There were hours of watching Oprah and Dr. Phil while under the influence of powerful mind-altering drugs. It was a forced time of contemplation and self-awareness.

I began to ponder what would actually happen if I told my boss that I must go on a five week sabbatical of great consequence, just like noted professors. He's from Indiana and has probably never heard of this. I reflected on all that had occurred in the past twelve months: Mother's Alzheimer's and death, my cataracts, the knee surgery, and physical therapy. Life is, without a doubt, uncertain. According to recent statistics, at age sixty-two, my life is more than three quarters over. How do I want to spend my last quarter?

I resolved, with great barbituated certainty that I want to live a life that matters, leave a magnificent legacy, and do something significant and maybe "out of the box"!

I'm running out of time here. Hell, I'm not going to ask for a sabbatical, I'm going to quit work work entirely, buy a laptop, and travel with Schwarck to the UK. We will search for people that look like us and then…take their picture… and……yes, why not…write THE BOOK!

CHAPTER 3

THE SIGN

The decision to retire seemed plausible while under the influence of a morphine drip, but it was slightly scary after the drugs wore off. Okay. I think, yes, I believe, I am kind of positive that I must quit work, retire, and go on a five-week UK adventure. Yep! That's it! I'm goin'!

"Schwarck, I've decided to go with you to the UK. When do you think we should go?"

"Oh, my God! Really? That's great! So your boss liked the sabbatical idea? What did he say? More importantly, what did husband Hugh say?"

"Well, I haven't told the husband yet. I didn't tell my boss either about the sabbatical thing because I have decided to just completely quit work. I'm going to retire."

"What? You can't be serious! Are you still on the morphine? I never meant for you to quit work. How can you do that? You love your job!"

"Well, yeah, I know, but I can't go on forever here. In March I can start collecting Social Security, plus, I can get my pension from the city. My Dad died at 55 and I'm 62. Now, what does that tell ya?"

"Oh, my God! This is terrible. I don't want to be responsible for you leaving the Senior Center. I don't think you should do it. People are going to kill me! It's my fault for suggesting the sabbatical thing."

Well, yes, it was her brainstorm, but the idea was a sign that now is the right time for me to move on. "Go ahead and book us on a flight after March 15, when I get my first Social Security check!"

"Well," Schwarck paused befuddled. "Okay, if you are really sure. What if Hugh says you can't retire? "

I initiated a brave "well, he's not the boss of me attitude", knowing full well, that my retirement and travel announcement would more than likely be met by fierce resistance on the home front.

Truly, there is something unnerving and spooky about retirement, especially when you consider that you have never in your entire married life been at home alone with your spouse for longer than the occasional snow day. Retirement could mean that you'll be incarcerated for years with a roommate who has a myriad of annoying tics. Most women I know, have expressed a deep sense of dread and foreboding as they contemplate entering the retirement phase with their spouse. What will we do all day? Will there be an expectation of three cooked meals? Will I ever hold the remote? Will he grow a beard and refuse to shower because he has no plans or places to go?

Aging and retirement allows too much time to cogitate and be bothered by little personal things you never before observed. For example, Hugh has a big toe that is singularly ugly and is starting to point to the toe next to it. And, there's the bed vibrating snores. Also where the hell did his chest hair go? Did it depart with the hair that used to be on his head?

Despite trepidation, I plan to enter the retirement valley of the shadow of death and I will fear no evil.

There was a great deal of thought put into how I would trumpet my imminent retirement to Hugh who had already retired and been at home marking his territory for years. I know him well enough to believe he'll agree to the retirement, but expect that the notion of a five-week trek through England, Ireland and Scotland is utterly preposterous!

Therefore, I decided to appeal to his practical nature and introduce the trip as a money-making venture. THE BOOK thing is a new slant. That might be so novel, unusual and queer, that he will go for it.

I began with little daily announcements, usually during halftime of the football game, when he might be more lucid.

DAY ONE: "You know, I'm going to be 62 in March."

DAY TWO: "You know, I can get a pension from the city because I have worked full-time for over twenty years."

DAY THREE: "Well, I've decided to retire from the city in March, so we can finally be together everyday."

That statement was met with a suspicious glance.

LATER ON DAY THREE: "Here's what I'm thinking; Schwarck and I are great storytellers and we are going to write a book that will be so popular, that we believe we'll end up on Oprah. The research is going to take five weeks. We have to go to England, Ireland, and Scotland where we will photo journal our relatives, question them about our ancestors, record their interviews on a laptop computer and go to the local colleges to further research.

I must say that he took it all quite well but had a lot of questions: "Have you seen my brown shoes? Did you kick them under the bed again? Are you going to make dinner soon?"

I predict my retirement messages will reach his brain when he sits down to eat dinner. sit….rhymes with quit and also shit! That should trigger something and get him going!

"Geeze!" he spouted while falling on a pork steak. "What did you say you wanna do? Quit work? You wanna go to England? And you're gonna write a book? Where did you get that idea? Geeze! I don't know if you should do that? Geeze, I don't know!"

Most of his questions are actually statements of frustration, not requiring an answer. I leaned forward in order to appear to be actively engaged in his concerns. I highly recommend this strategy.

His biggest complaints seemed to center around the length and destination of the trip.

"Why do you need to go to England for five weeks? Why don't you just go somewhere around here and write a book? That'd be a lot cheaper and you wouldn't have to quit work."

Now, I needed a thought-provoking answer. I chose a moderate tactic with a goal of diverting his attention away from retirement.

"Well, you are right." They love to be right. "It would be cheaper to stay around here, but we are going to places where we can discover our ancestry.

We are going to see if we have relatives who look like us and then we're going to take their pictures and write the story of the whole adventure. This will require time and a great deal of research."

"Well, my grandparents are the ones from Scotland. I should be going!"

"I do think you should go someday and I'll go with you, but this is work. We are writing a BOOK."

That declaration was beginning to find a place in his brain, and being a semi-professional photographer, he found a way to regain control and, unknowingly, approve of the plans.

"Well, our camera is not that great. The new digital cameras with at least four megapixels are a lot better. They do all kinds of stuff now. You could put your pictures on a computer, print them out, make postcards, movies, whatever!"

"Yeah". I could see he was buying this! That would be so much better, but we don't have any of that new stuff. It'd probably be pretty expensive, too. The trip will cost a lot, but maybe I can have a big retirement party and people will donate for a camera and computer equipment."

By this point, I was emotionally drained, but yes, the seeds were planted.

The retirement announcement to my boss was surprisingly traumatic. He thought I was meeting to ask for another van driver and had already dug in his heels. This news was totally unexpected.

"What? You can't do this! You're a legend! You told me you'd give me at least five more years!"

I never said any such thing to anybody! My doctor won't even give me six months much less five years. His words were flattering, and I had the distinct feeling that if I hit him with the notion of a sabbatical then he'd buy it in a heartbeat! I felt a little sorry for him, but I was enlightened now. Retirement is my destiny.

The Senior Center was visibly rocked by the news. There was whining, real crying and a lot of hugging. I reminded them that they had retired once, why couldn't I? I'm not leaving town, or dying, just changing direction a little. I'll still be involved in senior citizen programs. I am one myself for God's sake!

Things at home swiftly started to erupt. Hugh became a research analyst as well as my personal shopper for all technical stuff. Every time I entered the house he had something new to show me that required me to make choices. The dining room table became the repository for stacks of brochures and flyers proclaiming the special capabilities of the various digital cameras and computers. He was making it his life's work. I just wanted him to pick something and bring it home! He interpreted that as a lack of care and concern on my part. Uh, he was correct!

The decisions he wanted me to make were microscopic compared to the gigantic ones I was in the throes of; writing a job description for my successor, preparing a budget and goals for the upcoming year at the Senior Center, filling out all necessary retirement documents, filing for Social Security, and a butt load more.

I found myself actively looking and alert for signs and signals affirming that my life is on the right track and that the retirement decision is a good one.

There it was….an impressive signal, a guaranteed sign. While casually flipping pages in the local community education booklet, I discovered a new writer's class. It was a compelling omen! Participants would be taught how to self-publish their literary works. Schwarck and I registered immediately and could barely wait to attend the class.

On the big evening, we entered the classroom with twenty young scholarly looking types. Schwarck and I were bristling with anticipation. We struggled to slide our roly-poly bodies into the dwarfish high school desks and glanced uneasily about the room.

A short, middle-aged, rumpled, and rotund guy introduced himself as our instructor. His credentials were startling; a card-carrying member of Mensa, concert pianist, teacher, attorney, travel guide, chef, inventor of a dried cookie mix in-a-jar and self-published author as well owner of a publishing company. How did this guy have the time to get so huge?

He started the class by asking class members to introduce themselves and tell where their writing project was in the publishing process.

The first fledgling author, noisily slurping some liquid yogurt from the largest dairy container ever created, arose from her desk and embarked on a tale of living in the shadow of the Fermi Two Nuclear Plant. She was convinced that she might have been affected by radiation poisoning, as her body was perpetually nutrition deprived. She unfurled a canvas bag to exhibit a plethora of hard cover books she had not only authored, but also illustrated. They were science fiction. She, herself, had printed the cosmic works at considerable expense and was here to discover how to get published nationwide.

Schwarck and I locked eyes and nodded in appreciation. This was already an utterly exciting evening. We scooted to the very front of our seats in absolute admiration for every person who stood and explained what they had achieved.

The most riveting introduction of all was from a tall, exotic, darkly tanned woman, who emotionally told of her desire to write the true account of surviving the Andrea Doria shipwreck. She had been a passenger with her aging Italian grandparents on this state-of-the-art Italian ship.

They had sold all of their worldly possessions in order to bring her, at age six, to the land of the free. What few precious possessions they brought on board, were lost at sea, when the ship sank.

Our turn was next and we unsteadily arose together, like Siamese twins, and I nervously explained:

"Uhm. Schwarck here....Karen, that is.... and I haven't written anything yet, but we are going on a five week adventure, overseas, and once we do, we are going to write a hilarious book about it, and maybe appear on Oprah."

There were no gasps of awe, just questioning frowns and a few sympathetic nods.

We slowly squished back into our little seats feeling somewhat like kindergartners in a college chemistry class. How lame could we be?

No weighty, colorful, examples of our completed works or dramatic story of a painful childhood or near death experience.

What we do have, however, is total validation and certainly a sign that we are where we should be at this very moment. We instantly loved these artistic types and are as much engaged in their success, as we are our own.

They are witness to the pupa of our metamorphosis.

CHAPTER 4

READY. . .OR NOT

What is splendidly dismaying to me is the amount of acceptance and outright validation we receive implying that Schwarck and I are superb author material, despite our undeniable lack of experience. Friends and family members were positively giddy with the notion that they are acquainted with or related to authors.

Schwarck has written numerous mystery plays that I, along with whomever else she could coerce, performed in as actors. I did prepare a cookbook for the Methodist Church's fundraising efforts back in 1968. I hardly think that either of those projects makes us certified literary geniuses. But there you have it, proof positive that you can assume a title, such as "author", and eventually, everyone will accept it as truth. This naive acceptance may be particularly dangerous in fields such as medicine and nuclear fission.

Several years back, our then 15-year-old daughter, Kelly, announced that high school was a total waste of her time. She wanted to shovel crap at the local doggie daycare and after working there awhile would automatically become a veterinarian. So, hence, if I were you, I would peruse a heap of credentials before I let someone in a white coat cut through my breastbone or clip little Fluffy's testicles.

Schwarck booked our UK flights, generously using her personal air miles as a thank you for accompanying her on this adventure. She also made the surprising announcement that we were to travel in first class, an unimaginable treat! There was no wimping out now. The enormity of my life altering decision was burdensome.

Four weeks before the trip, I began to experience meltdown. The dreadful "what-ifs" materialized hourly. What if my other knee gave out and I had to be hospitalized in some forbidding antiquated clinic? What if I ran out of my blood pressure meds or more frightening, lost my hormone replacement therapy and became a screaming naked bitch cavorting down cobblestone lanes?

My meltdown continued as my work schedule became staggering, and I was shadowed incessantly by a jittery successor, who was also overwhelmed. In addition, I became dubious of turning over my life's work to a tall, bejeweled, too-tan woman, that I could easily see, wore thong underwear and had a tattoo. This is clearly inconsistent with senior citizen programming,

Any spare time I had was consumed by appointments with Social Security, Municipal Employees' Retirement training, doctors, and retirement party planning. These activities did not allow sufficient time to sit down with the husband for the hours of evaluating the astounding properties of the various technical gadgets and gizmos he has so unselfishly researched and purchased for me.

Another pressing concern was what to pack for five weeks. Buoyant buddy Schwarck initiated daily advice regarding the travel essentials required for our expedition, with fervent cautions regarding the necessity to "travel light".

The "travel light", while pulling over hill and dale, notification sent the spouse into increased frenzy. He visited numerous luggage shops on a mission to purchase the most indestructible and feather light model in existence. He brought home two examples, because he was unsure which color I would prefer; midnight navy or black. Any difference between the two escaped me.

He reported that this suitcase brand is unparalleled in its sturdiness. The salesperson proclaimed that flight attendants would kill to have one of these. Hugh relentlessly demonstrated the ease of pulling and twirling as well as yanking up and down staircases until I thought I might burst into flames or at a minimum experience one of those hideous "fits" my grandmother had warned me about years ago.

Then came another caution from Schwarck: the backpack and fannypack must be chosen with great care, for it will be worn daily and should be lightweight and comfortable. She uses a backpack everyday instead of a purse, while I have never even tried one on.

I'm going to suggest that in the future, Schwarck keep these recommendations to herself, because this time, I was obligated to accompany the spouse to "Dick's", which, by the way, is the most extraordinarily perfect name for that store. You would have thought we were choosing a private school for our genius child instead of a backpack. Several salespeople fearfully backed away from our aisle as the intense questions and observations about the styles were debated. Hugh launched into a kind of game-show prize display activity, hoisting bags above his head and demonstrating the ease of slipping hand and fingers into mysterious little crevasses.

He strapped, jiggled and buckled me into several hefty models before lobbying for his choice. He had selected several bags as well as neck bags and belly bags, which included secret pouches for other bags designed to hang somewhere else on my person. He would share his plan for what essentials should go where when we get home. At that very moment, there was a complete realization that I did not give one whit about those items or any other item featuring a sturdy belt that would constrict my midsection, which thrived on freedom.

"My clothes barely fit me now without all this crap hanging around my neck and waist. Do you really think I need all of this?"

He was incredulous.

"You have got to protect things like your money and passport. They have to be hidden on your body at all times. The rest of the stuff you have to protect because it is priceless and electronic. These things are stolen all the time. Muggers go to the airports just to get this stuff! You can never let them out of your sight."

Honestly, I am confident that my sagging boobs and floppy midriff could pretty much conceal all documents, as well as stacks of money, but whatever floats his boat I will attempt to tolerate.

I nudged him toward the exit. “Okay….okay! Let’s get outta here!”

We walked out to the dimly lit parking lot, lugging four large bags containing bags, with him peering apprehensively back over his shoulder. I looked behind me, too. His paranoia is contagious. I’m becoming uneasy.

Not only did Hugh want to help me prepare adequately for this venture, but my three siblings were also anxious to get involved. Sister Barbara, in particular, had advice because she had worked for and with Brits for years. She initiated an influx of emails featuring names, addresses, as well as personal and business phones of her counterparts in the UK. “These numbers are good to have in case of emergency. You have met all of these people before. Remember at the cottage when some of them came up and we drank all those Margueritas?”

“I’m thinking that’s why they aren’t ringing a bell at all!” I stated matter of factly.

She urged that I contact each Brit prior to leaving, insisting they would love to pick us up at the airport, take us touring, and would be delighted for us stay with them.

Now I am beginning to get it! Sister Barb has been obligated to hostess all of these English types in the States, off and on for years. They had invaded her privacy countless times and now, it’s payback time.

I took all the advice to heart and managed to find fun in the mini-parties, farewell luncheons, and the magnificent final retirement celebration featuring two chocolate fountains, piles of shrimp, open bar and a harpist. It was a magical event with several hundred friends in attendance.

No time to bask in the glow of parties and farewells when piles of provisions were stacking up in the living room fanned out for inspection and falling over. Yards of cords connected Hugh to computer geniuses all over the world. He continually muttered, remained unshaven, and wore his robe for days at a time. At times he appeared to be speaking in tongues. There were some things that just wouldn't install properly and he couldn't get a grip on the East Indian accents of the "techies". He was also ticked that they addressed him as Mr. Huge.

With only one week to go and my life in a frenzied state of trip preparation, an absolutely unimaginable event occurred: my 56-year-old sister appeared on our doorstep toting paintbrushes and paint. It seems she had been pink-slipped at work and would soon become homeless. She had spoken to Hugh a couple of weeks ago and he didn't see any problem with her moving in with us temporarily. She was here now to decorate the back bedroom, which had been intended as my new office for writing THE BOOK. She and sister Jan cheerily began hauling in giant garbage bags full of clothes and set them in the dining room until the painting was completed.

Hugh was not even mildly perturbed by this predicament. It was so out of character that I was convinced he had been afflicted by some baffling disease.

"Well, Nancy is the easiest person in the world to get along with," he stated assuredly.

"What? You've never lived with her! This won't be temporary. She moves like a three-toed sloth! Besides that, she has a surprising temper. I saw that first-hand when she ate an entire yard full of grass because Mother and I wouldn't take her with us to the movies! When I was in high school, she and her little friends would wait till I got on the bus, then they'd steal my clothes. They would wear my niftiest things around all day. I'll never get over her tying my fur balls in a knot around her neck and then she had her friend's mother cut the little velvet ties in half to keep them from strangling her. That was my all time favorite accessory."

"Well, geeze! All that kid stuff happened over fifty years ago. Besides, she just needs a place to stay for a little while till she gets organized."

"I predict that this is gonna get ugly! We have only one bathroom, remember? And you are always in it."

The truth was dawning on me. Old Hugh was thinking of his immediate future. If the accomplished gourmet-cooking sister were here while I'm gone for five weeks, she would prepare fabulous meals for him, wash his clothes, and clean house. Of course he was more than satisfied with the arrangement!

We only recently escorted our youngest child out of the house, who, by the way, was almost 30 years old. None of our friends have had their parents, children, grandchildren, or siblings live with them. Most of them have kicked their own spouses out, if not completely out of the house, they are definitely out of the same bedroom. Here I am, entering the last quarter of my life, ready to retire and depart on a thrilling book writing adventure and right here at home, there's an excess of kick-ass peril.

If we were still attending our spirit circle, I would petition the gods, What…. the hell….. is happening? There is no doubt about it; I am so anxious and ready to leave here!

CHAPTER 5

DECLINE THE SPOTTED DICK

I am hopelessly ignorant of the colorful nuances of the British English, according to sister Barbara who stopped by to give me some last minute tips. According to her, if I'm going to "get along across the pond" I must be cautious when speaking and interpreting.

"They're English, right? How hard can it be?"

"Well, you're gonna find out, that even though it's English, it could mean something totally different than what you think. Order lager, not dark beer; remember that an elevator is called a lift, the toilet is called the loo, never order "Spotted Dick", and do not under any circumstances, make reference to your "fanny pack"!

This was the extent of her advisements. The "fanny pack" statement was befuddling. According to her, a British "fanny" does not describe buttocks at all. It is, instead, slang for the female genitals, and I should never be overheard making any reference to "my fanny" or its "pack."

This news, while splendidly helpful, did nothing to assist with my immediate need for packing since I am only one glorious day away from escape. Today's to-do list will begin with a visit to Linda's Hair and More for a shorter haircut, followed by a visit to the mystical Asian nail salon where, according to my three younger female siblings, I will be treated to "the works".

Linda, CEO of Linda's Hair and More has been my personal hairdresser and good friend for over 30 years. Her mod attire often includes shiny skintight leather pants yanked over her extraordinary long legs and a skimpy stretch tube pulled in place to expose her svelte bare midriff. Her adornments usually include jingling bracelets, sparkling necklaces, and colossal hoop earrings. At one point, Linda was the proud owner of the most monumental bosom ever displayed in our quiet suburb. Her gigantic orbs were notorious, but interfered with virtually everything she did, particularly motorcycle riding and her aerobic program which included vigorous leaping about the living room. She had them whacked off and her husband divorced her.

I trust Linda implicitly with my golden graying locks. She has encouraged me through the helmet hair days and on to the Shirley Temple curly locks years. As I nestled down into her chair this morning, I reminded her that I was leaving for the five week UK adventure tomorrow. She had perused numerous European hairstyle books and swore that what she was going to do to me, would not only be up-to-date for over there, but would also be a cinch to maintain. The "Sissorhand" pruning was launched on my already short do, and I could clearly comprehend why her hands were so severely scared and often bleeding profusely. She's the crowned queen of multitasking. Linda was on the phone to one client, pointing to another indicating where to sit, and offering coffee to me all while merrily chopping away on my head. Suddenly, there was silence and she whipped the chair around nodding in smug approval of her masterpiece. She whirled me back around and handed me the giant mirror. As I gaped in astonishment, I was reminded of the aggressive bantam roosters we used to have on the farm.

"Wow! That's really different. Are you sure this look is in?"

She ignored my comment and began to demonstrate the ease of using the special stiff taffy guaranteed to stand every hair at attention, which was the look she said everyone in London would have. Linda also began her squinting inspection of my ears and multiple chins in search of old people hairs. She trimmed my eyebrows with a razor and cautioned me seriously about energetic plucking, as if it were one of the world's most critical problems. Addressing me very seriously she stated, "Now that you're over 60, they won't come back anymore and you'll have to pencil them in."

Yikes! This news awakened memories of something Schwarck said recently on an overnight trip, "Crawford, we've got to go down to the Lost and Found. I've got to see if they have my eyebrows down there. When I went to bed, I had them and now they're gone." Guess she'll be using the pencil from now on. That thin line eyebrow is not a good look for older women. You can never get them even and they always have too much arch. I've seen women laid out at the funeral home that looked totally surprised to be lying there!

Linda has considerable experience with funeral makeup and frontal hairdos, which she has rendered for friends who have departed. She wants everyone to look natural while lifeless. I have attended many viewings where visitors have expressed how wonderful the deceased looks. It is my personal goal to look better alive than dead, and Linda will gladly assist whether I'm standing up or lying down!

My mind snapped back to the present and I said my goodbyes at the salon. I resolve to be very accepting of my new permanently startled look that is much like the "frightened family" in the old Saturday Night Live skits.

From Linda's, I met my three sisters at the Asian nail salon. They have had numerous nail sessions and I, the oldest, had never been to one, so it was high time. They introduced me to the diminutive salon ambassador who led me into the pedicure room. There was a lot of pointing because English wasn't even the second language here. There is no logical explanation for it, but I speak louder to those who do not speak my language. I do this for blind people, too. As I was lowered into the tub chair, two older Lilliputian Asian ladies each roughly yanked down a tender foot and I felt like the turkey wishbone at Thanksgiving. The sisters were laughing out loud and enjoying my discomfort immensely. They had come along just for amusement, much like when mother attended my Saturday ballet lessons when I was a chubbo ten-year old positioned for the running arabesque.

I had believed there would be soft classical music and gentle massaging action on my 62-year-old bunioned feet, but Noooo ooooo! It was like a tool and die shop in there. Staffers wore lab coats and thick goggles. There were loud grinders, whirling razors, sanding tools, pokers, prodders, and bolt cutters for the biggest jobs. Nails and nail dust were flying in all directions. This was not the relaxing afternoon I had pictured. It was a great relief to hobble out of there two hours later.

The sisters then presented me with a complete travel wardrobe that was guaranteed wrinkle free, could be swished clean in a sink, and was touted as drying in only minutes. One clothing article, a black knit miniskirt, will be left behind for the Chihuahua to wear on holidays. I never wear skirts and they bought me two: one that would drag on the floor and another of astounding minuteness. They also gifted me with special Space Age bags, which would allow me to pack twice as many clothes, if I could mash all the air out of them!

I am so much older than my three Boomer siblings that I seldom feel comfortable wearing what they pick out. The baby, 12 years my junior, emerged from the "smoke dope, jump rope, cantaloupe" era as a yoga-posing vegan. She would love for me to get enthused about following her into the yoga positions called "Downward Dog and Reverse Warrior" while wearing wicking spandex. Great God above! I'm just happy to eject myself from a recliner.

When I arrived back home, there was a cheery message from my health insurance provider stating I would not be covered by medical insurance while in the UK. They seemed to delight in telling me I shouldn't go on this trip.

A phone call was in order to Schwarck.

"Schwarck? Guess what? My insurance company says I won't be covered over there. That is scary! I shouldn't even go."

Let me just say right now, old buddy Schwarck is infinitely more sympathetic and genuine, unlike me who is prone to feigning concern. If a friend reported to me that they found blood in their urine that morning, I might issue a quiet, "Oh, wow." Then I'd go on to ask them if they thought these pants made my butt look big. Not her though. Every concern is a puzzle, requiring evaluation, answers, and solutions.

"Oooooooo, geeze! Are you sure they won't cover you at all? That's just terrible! Well, you know they have socialized medicine over there, so if something major happens; they'd have to get you in. Besides, we'll take some antiseptic cream and some band-aids. I've had CPR too!", Schwarck exclaimed.

"Oh right, that should certainly cover anything that'll go wrong with me. Hey, remember when we were at that conference banquet right after you had the CPR class? You heard something and leaped over two tables to give that guy the Heimlich maneuver and he was just clearing his throat. His table was pretty shocked. None of them could even touch their cheesecake after that little episode. You were sure quick!", I replied.

"He had all the classic signs of choking. His face was all splotchy and red!", Schwarck added.

"I bet his face was red from all of the wine he consumed before dinner and the splotchyness came while you were exuberantly squashing his mid-section."

The more I thought about first aid and taking a few band-aids, the more I was reminded of the last time I saw my own bleeding. A band-aid or even pressure applied by an enormous maxi pad could not have stopped it. It was a hemorrhage likened to a geyser due to my penchant for aspirin consumption to ward off heart attacks.

I headed back out to the store in order to purchase a slick little First Aid Kit that included a tourniquet, as well as to choose some small travel containers for medical necessities. I became incensed, as I sorted among midget travel items and noticed the outrageous cost. The Attorney General should be alerted immediately! Companies that make toothpaste, for example, reduce the contents by more than two thirds and charge twice as much. Is there some sort of factory retooling involved that would cause such giant price gouging for fewer ingredients? They do the same thing with diet foods. Take out all of the sugar, carbs, and fat and you will be left with a food item that has nothing in it, but you will pay an arm and a leg more. Where is the justice in that, I ask? And where is the plain old vaseline? I finally found nursery jelly. Is this the same stuff?

All this frustration was starting to wear on me, so I decide to just leave the store, not do anything else except head home to continue packing. I also needed to call my children and the two grandchildren to say "so-long, farewell". Who knows when or if I'll ever see them again?

After that, I'm going to eat chocolate ice cream with nuts and hot fudge, a peanut butter jelly sandwich, and go to bed. Precisely in that order! I'll probably need something for indigestion, but I will be comforted.

Guess what, Houston?

Tomorrow we have lift-off!

CHAPTER 6

WHY CAN'T I JUST LIFT OFF. . .RIGHT NOW?

Something was smacking my feet.

"Don't forget the travel iron and I've put your money in five separate stacks here on thc bcd, along with copies of the Traveler Checks. There's the manual for the computer and camera as well as the battery packs. All of that has got to go in your backpack."

Hugh had been up all night messing with and preparing my equipment for travel. He isn't considerate in the least about the large lumps still sleeping in the bed, which were the Chihuahua and I!

"What'd you say? Don't forget what? What time is it anyway? It doesn't even look like it's light out yet!"

"I said, don't forget your travel iron here, and there's all your stacks of money. I've put them in five different piles. You need to keep them all in separate places in case you lose one. I've rolled up all the cords and here's the special UK plugs."

In all of my sixty-two years on this earth, I have never lost money, particularly, stacks of it. In the unlikely event that I am jumped by some berserk derelict who performs an intense pat down and threatens great bodily harm if I don't give up all valuables, I will easily hand over piles of money, as well as anything else he wants because I am not keen on pain and suffering.

Here's something else you should ponder: if you rarely perform some activity when you are at home, like read a thick manual or iron, why would it suddenly become imperative to take these items with you on vacation? I grumped out of bed and headed for the cherished coffee pot.

Yay, this is the big day….liftoff! I choose to be oblivious to the rude awakening, the jumbled mess and piles of my sisters' belongings, as well as the mounds of boxes and bags throughout the house. Hugh has an affinity for retaining every box and wrapping of anything we have purchased in our lifetime "in case we need to send it back." The garage is overflowing with these piles to the extent that we have never in our over forty years of marriage, put a vehicle in there, nor have we ever sent anything back! I am enormously aggravated by stores that put their merchandise in spiffy, sturdy, and unique containers of such perceived usefulness that we will never ever dispose of them. They will be kept forever in closets, basements, and garages long after the item that came in it, is broken or obsolete.

After dry cereal and a refreshing shower, I make a daring attempt to spike my hair as Linda had demonstrated. She did say it was supposed to look messy like I just got out of bed. I believe I have successfully recreated that look.

I wish she could see me right now, or better yet, put me on display at the Manhattan Club where she and other gyrating botoxed Boomers could praise my hipness.

I am now mentally prepared to energetically tackle the final trip preparation. Phone interruptions were numerous, as friends called to say good-by and wish me well. There was a bit of a "funeral" feeling to it all. Niece Carrie and our new roomer, sister Nancy, stop by to bring more garbage bags and measure for blinds. Oh, yes, and to also say "bye-bye"!

These little diversions were starting to rub Hugh the wrong way. He was doubtful that I could ever be ready when the Schwarcks arrived in the early afternoon, due to my excessive "dilly-dallying".

I decide to utilize the funky new see-through bags, designed to take all the air out of my clothing, allowing more space in the suitcase. I love how tiny my floppy-leg underwear looks when the air is sucked out of them. In fact, all my clothes will look a lot like freeze-dried beef, but at least I can get' em all in my luggage.

Hugh held up some gadget and began a last minute drill. "Do you know what this plugs into?"

"Uh….mmmm. The wall?"

"That's right! You plug this in first. It's your surge protector and then you plug this other thing into it and then this."

Oh my God! He's holding up stuff that I have no idea what it is or what orifice it should go into. As he rattles on, I drift off to my happy place. With any luck at all, the Schwarcks will be picking us up soon and we will have our last supper with the men before entering the airport's alluring revolving doors. I try desperately to keep my heightened eagerness under wraps.

Difficult choices are immediately mandatory. Would it be necessary to pack those miniature travel toilet paper rolls sister Barbara gave me? She has been to England countless times and always takes a toilet roll. There must be some logical explanation for her insistence. Maybe toilet paper is still in short supply due to WWII. All factories along with everything else were leveled, and I saw the National Geographic pictures of Churchill walking over the piles of debris. I think I'll just live on the edge and only take one roll. I could understand it if I was going to a Third World country where someone is stationed outside the ladies room to parcel out rice-paper sections of toilet paper for five cents, but to carry my own to a place where people speak English seems uncalled for.

I am abnormally obsessed with packing my precious toiletries, unsure if they can be replenished in a far off land. I don't know about you, but my personal stuff has become impossible to replace when I am away from home. I use specific color make-up, which can only be purchased at my beauty salon. My particularly thin panty liners have to be a certain brand and must be excruciatingly soft and extra, extra long. My shampoo and rinse are purchased annually from a booth in a Florida flea market. It is the only product my tinted thinning hair can tolerate. In spite of the extra weight, I insist that my precious toiletries and medications fit into the backpack. The suitcase could be hopelessly lost by the airline or, at a minimum, be pulverized by that gorilla that jumps up and down on luggage after it is slammed on the conveyer belt.

As for the medications, I should do what Schwarck does. She sorts out each day's dose of vitamins and meds and puts them into tiny zippered snack bags. Problem is, I'd have to use five weeks worth of quart-size for all I consume. Next come the various arthritis ointments. In as much as Schwarck is extremely sensitive and oft allergic to odors, I vow to take the least odoriferous, but I most assuredly will take them and pray they won't trigger the onset of her debilitating migraines.

My two new pairs of size eleven-wide expensive, rugged hiking shoes, occupy a flabbergasting amount of space, therefore I decide to take only the black pair and sadly, must leave the brown behind. These shoes are indestructible and could be safely worn while working in a steel factory or on safari. The salesman proudly declared that large heavy objects could fall on them and never even leave a dent. Well, that "heavy object" that falls will probably be me! I am quite confident, however, that if a ferocious critter were to attack my feet, I would be well protected and if the nutty little character would sit still long enough; I could squash out its savage life with one peppy stomp. It could happen.

Okay, the suitcase is all packed and ready for take-off. When it thumped down off the bed onto the floor, I felt the earth move. It began to twirl all by itself as if possessed and then laid down on its back like a turtle. Holy crap! Should I take something out of it? It's like a rolling glacier!

"Where did you put your five piles?" questioned Hugh.

"Five piles? What five piles? oohhh, yeah! I've got' em! They're all in here." I began to pat my waist, thighs, chest and neck to a sort of Macarena routine.

"Remember.......cords and transformers should be kept with the computer. Other cords and battery packs have to stay in their pouches in the camera bag. Here are all the 800 numbers to call for assistance and all the manuals. Where are you going to put the numbers?"

Uh, oh. It will be necessary to demonstrate a logical location for his approval. It is also imperative to give proof that everything is safe and in its proper place. I quite honestly wanted to demonstrate how he should just shut up!

At that very moment, the Schwarck's called. They're rolling!

And it will very shortly be time for the last supper!

Thank-you, Jesus!

CHAPTER 7

FEMALE WITH A WAND

"Hugh! When are you coming out of the bathroom? Hurry up! Schwarcks just pulled up. Are you still in your robe? Come on!"

He never answers questions when he's in the bathroom, but at least some aggressive and earsplitting nose blowing has commenced, which is the signal for the thunderous toilet seat drop. There is rarely any variance in his bathroom routine, therefore I know he will emerge in precisely two minutes and will say what he always says when I rush him;

"Geeze! Why didn't you tell me what time it was?"

This is one of those annoying questions not requiring an answer; therefore, I glare and add a little head-shake-eye-roll. There has been an oversized wall clock in the bathroom for years and it keeps excellent time.

Inwardly, I am rejoicing at the thought of how he and the sister are going to coordinate their considerable bathroom activities and adjust to each other's various eccentricities.

When the Schwarcks got up to the porch, I greeted them warmly with hugs and proudly displayed my corpulent suitcase for shock and awe.

Don Schwarck, Schwarck's husband, eyes blinked and his mouth gaped. "Wow! Your bag looks more like a cube than a rectangle."

"Well, that's because it has all of these handy expandable sections and I have already expanded every freakin' one of them. I don't know how a person can go away for five weeks with only one bag, but your wife says one bag is all I can handle along with the backpack."

Schwarck gleefully exclaimed; "I don't have hardly anything in my suitcase. I'm going to buy whatever clothes I need over there."

She has a very practical approach to travel. Don't take clothes or money, just preload a credit card and go to the ATM two or three times a day and buy whatever you need. I, personally, have no faith in this system for a variety of reasons. I can hardly find clothes to fit me when I'm home, so what do you think the chances are that there will be an abundance that will fit me in another country? What size am I in another country anyway? What if we are in a country of little people and they don't make anything but tents to fit me? Also a wretched ATM in San Juan sucked up my credit card two years ago and refused to give me my own money which was vital for food and shelter.

"Look at this travel rain coat Hugh ordered for me on line. Have you ever seen this many pockets on anybody except a fisherman who ties his own flies?"

Hugh's interest and overactive involvement in our adventure is in sharp contrast to Don Schwarck's, who doesn't really remember where we were going or for how long. He has also reserved his opinion about THE BOOK and Oprah thing to see if anything actually materializes. As a science teacher, he requires proof.

Schwarck is slightly envious of my spouse's helpfulness and concern. To my way of thinking, Hugh's interest is way beyond helpful and profoundly weird. She should walk a mile in my steel-toed shoes; she would then embrace Don's apathy.

Hugh finally appeared fully clothed but unshaven and greeted Schwarcks, who were surveying the depths of chaos in both the living and dining areas of our home. I followed their eyes as they took in the stupefying piles of electronic refuse, then I shrugged. "Well, I'm ready. Let's get this stuff in the car and head for dinner."

The two husbands grabbed my luggage and backpack and threw them in the back of the car. They took the two front seats and immediately initiated plans for golf outings. Schwarck and I took the back seat and nervously searched for all critical documents like passport, drivers license and credit cards, seriously hoping we had not forgotten anything.

We stopped at Bob Evans for a hasty "Last Supper" with the men and expected that they would be gloomy and woebegone. Instead they were overly jovial and exuberant. Schwarck and I were the ones who should be giddy. All of us ordered food items smothered in gravy, even though we girls would soon be enjoying a fabulous four courses dinner while flying in first class. Schwarck gave Don a last minute drill about running her travel business while she is absent. He assured her that all would be handled with great efficiency, but her recollection of the number of times this week that he had lost his glasses, car keys and wallet, made her uneasy. I have no instructions for Hugh.

We were only a short ten-minute ride from the airline terminal. The boys pulled up to the curb and hurriedly dumped our suitcases onto the sidewalk. There were little pecks on the cheek and off they went into the sunset, with us numbly waving as they drove out of sight. I don't even think they looked in the rear view mirror.

"Come on, Crawford, let's get checked in."

Then came my moment of reckoning. I had never actually put on the loaded backpack, fanny pack nor lifted my suitcase. Everything was profoundly weighty and the backpack caused me to lean forward much like overburdened water carriers in Zimbabwe. Yikes!

I was forced to build up speed in order to propel myself forward. Schwarck was yards ahead and fairly skipping up to the check-in counter. She easily lifted her feather light suitcase onto the scale. When I arrived shortwinded at the desk and slammed my ponderous bag onto the calibrating equipment, I expected horns to blast and alarms to erupt. The attendant's eyebrows shot up as she attempted to hoist it onto the conveyor. Thank God she is wearing one of those weightlifting girdles.

Free at last of at least one bag, I hitched up the backpack and stumbled behind Schwarck to the security checkpoint.

It took a considerable amount of time to remove the heavy steel-toed shoes, computer, camera, fannypack and all the secret bags, then limp through the little archway. Apparently, I aroused a great deal of suspicion because the conveyor came to a screeching halt and the overhead mics blared; "Female with a wand!"

Part of the distress among the uniformed types, was a direct result of Schwarck's gleeful endeavor to photograph my pat down. It seems photography is not allowed under any circumstances in the secured area. I made an attempt to display the official card certifying me as a prosthetic wearer but this was an effort in futility as a burly wand-carrying woman curtly declared; "We don't care about those cards, ma'am. Anybody can get one."

"Well, the doctor gave it to me." I reported sternly. "He told me to carry it with me at all times and show it at the airport. I have one for cataracts too."

She was superbly controlled and enormously indifferent to my declaration.

"We have a new policy and I must examine each of your legs and under your breasts. I'm going to pat you in the chest area now."

Well, good luck with that. My breasts could be anywhere right now because for comfort's sake, I am wearing the oldest stretched out bra I own and suspect it is laying inert, on top of my saggy boobs at this moment. A glance to the right gave me a good view of Schwarck being escorted outside the gated area by an armed guard. My bags were unattended and prime for theft, as Hugh had so correctly warned.

When my personal inspection was complete, I gave "wand woman" my best glare of displeasure and searched for a chair in order to retie the steel toes with my stiff arthritic fingers. Schwarck could be overheard chatting up everyone nearby about writing THE BOOK.

I tersely remind my good buddy; "See? This is what happens at airports. You are distracted at security and someone grabs your stuff and runs. We've got to be more careful. Look at your backpack over there. You better get it, quick." We collected all of our belongings and ambled away from security.

I entered the first gift shop I came to and eyeballed the brightly colored magazines and paperbacks. I treasure reading materials. Schwarck wandered off to explore.

"Hey Crawford! Guess what?"

I turned too quickly, jostling an old lady on a cane with my prodigious fannypack and completely swiped a shelf clean of plastic Motown mugs.

"Crawford, I just signed up for an Aromatherapy Oxygen Massage. You should do it too. I picked Rosemary for $15. We have plenty of time."

"What? What are you talking about? A massage? Now? At the airport?" I was astounded.

"Yeah, aromatherapy massage, over there. I had one of these in California two months ago and it was so relaxing. It'll be part of the adventure. I'll take your picture. Come on, let's go."

I'm relatively dubious of massage in general, but particularly skeptical of body kneading in a small dark room at the airport while under the influence of herbal oxygen. This seems offbeat. Schwarck, however, is geeked at the prospect of spending a half hour with a stranger in a small confined space while prone and hooked up to inhalants. She carelessly dropped all her expensive computer equipment at my feet and happily trotted down a dimly lit hallway behind a tall Star Trek looking guy,

While I was contemplating Schwarck's risky behavior, I was approached by another male "Trekkie" type whose hypnotizing voice inquired; "Madam, would you like to see a menu?"

Inexplicably, I replied;

"Why….. yes, I would."

I have no idea what came over me, except my desire to open my mind for adventure as well as appear that I am so into New Age activities. This oxygen stuff is probably an enormous scam. How qualified can these airport massage artists be? Also won't increased oxygen wake you up more rather than relax you? At that very moment, a harried looking customer emerged from one of the little rooms and inquired about her bill. She looked as though she had been dropkicked through a wind tunnel. The very dramatic and sophisticated looking hostess replied that it would be $30 and the gratuity was not included. Figures. Schwarck was at least $20 off on the price of the massage.

My mystery man reappeared and asked if I had selected a fragrance. He launched into a monotone recitation regarding the special effects of each scent.

"I do love Lavender," I replied wistfully thinking that Rosemary, Schwarck's choice should only be rubbed on pork prior to cooking. Unfortunately, my frozen digits inadvertently pointed off in the wrong direction.

"Basil, excellent choice." His prosaic voice declared while at the same time yanking out an odd looking chair that may have been used for torture in the dark ages. There is no way I'm going to tell him this is all a big mistake. Why couldn't I point to Lavender? Basil is horrible! It goes on spaghetti doesn't it? I'm probably going to throw up!

There was no suggestion that he and I should proceed to a more secluded location. I approve of staying in the large open room since apparently I am the only responsible party for the priceless electronics in our backpacks.

His blasé hand motion indicated that I was to squat myself into the low chair. There was considerable grunting on my part as I began to squeeze my uncooperative body into the contraption. His bored voice requested that I plug in the oxygen tubing. Great God above, I don't know where to put it! How lame am I? His fake smile indicates that this is tiresome for him. He took the tubing out of my hand and gave me the correct end to put in my nose.

What commenced was painful in more ways than one. First there was immediate and forceful mashing on my delicate shoulders along with powerful tugging on my elbows. Second, my face was mashed into a donut pillow, which was merely inches away from his partially zippered pants. This was not relaxing by any stretch of the imagination, but there I stayed nose-to-crotch for a full 30 minutes of Basil induced pulverizing. I plan to bitch slap Schwarck if she ever returns. I'm not sure what that is exactly, but I recently read "bitch slap" in a romance novel and it seems like the very thing this situation calls for.

When my torture was over, I had great difficulty removing myself from the mini chair. Both knees had seized up and it took a few moments of standing erect to realign body parts.

A delighted Schwarck reappeared during the extraction process.

"Oh, I have a great picture of you, Crawford. Look! Wasn't it relaxing? What aroma did you get?"

I limped over to her side and informed her that the little aroma massage was not $15, but actually $30 plus tip.

"Oohhhh. I thought I saw a sign that said 'Aroma Therapy Massage-$15.'

"Don't speak to me again. Schwarck. I don't think I can walk anymore and I can't get the Basil smell out of my nose. I have already spent almost fifty dollars and I haven't even gotten to the gate yet!"

CHAPTER 8

THE FRILLS OF FLYING

First Class folks are allowed to board the plane ahead of withering decrepit people and screaming infants. This is exceptionally delightful. We were greeted warmly at the plane's entrance by a neatly uniformed and beaming hostess. She ushered us to ample leather seats up front, just behind what I imagine to be brawny armed pilots with velvety calming voices. This is the way all air travel should get underway. Riff-raff was guided down another aisle and could not be observed nor allowed to thump our shoulders with their carry-ons as they lumber past. As we deposited our belongings in our seats, a beautiful toothy attendant magically materialized and inquired if we desired any reading materials. She also recited a delectable list of beverage options.

"Schwarck, did you actually order a newspaper? You despise the news. And you asked for a Bloody Mary with extra celery? You know they put alcohol in it, right? Geeze!"

She is the only person I know who will nurse a beer all day and throw out half because it got warm. I'm surprised that she could even recall the name of a mixed drink. Bloody Mary! Egads! It'll be my luck if she doesn't go psycho on me and flight attendants have to stun her with a TASER.

"Well, it's the only exotic drink I could think of and I ordered the USA Today for you. Look at this cute little red bag they gave each of us. It's loaded with stuff-like cushy socks, aspirin, and earplugs. Oh! And look, even a little eye mask! They thought of everything. I just love this little bag. I'm going to keep it for my camera cords."

What is enormously intriguing is that Schwarck has spent thousands of dollars for our First Class flight and the most coveted part of it all turns out to be a little red nylon zippered bag of cheesy goodies.

Pint sized blankets and free ear headsets have been hermetically sealed in plastic and placed on all leather loungers in precisely the same location on each chair. Everything up here with the captain is so splendidly special.

I struggled to lift my ponderous backpack into the overhead and Miss Perky immediately appeared to take over this mundane task. Schwarck's equipment had been carelessly plopped in the aisle and there it remained. Drinks arrived, in real glasses, and we clinked them together in gleeful acknowledgement that we are officially launched into adventure land.

"Crawford, I've been thinking. I don't believe we should go on Oprah. We should go on Ellen instead. I don't watch Oprah anymore."

I took a big gulp of gin and looked at her askance. "Yeah, well, maybe we should just get our own talk show. Anyway, do you think we relate better to a gay liberal Hollywood celebrity that likes to dance over a table than we do to a fluffy black zillionaire who loves Dr. Oz and stiletto heels?"

"Well, I believe Oprah has lost touch with her audience, and I don't think it would be good for us to be on her show."

"Really? I have to tell you, when Oprah calls, I'm goin' on. I like Ellen, even though she did come out of the closet in a rather spectacular way. Hey, remember the woman from the bed and breakfast in Saugatuck who thought we were gay?" I quizzed Schwarck.

"Yeah, I hated her. She was terrible!"

Months earlier we had signed up for a writer's workshop and Schwarck wanted to stay in a Bed and Breakfast in Saugatuck overlooking Lake Michigan. I had never stayed in a B & B so I was game and she made the reservation. When we checked into the stately Victorian manor, the chatty amiable owner inquired as to why we were in town. We enthusiastically explained that we are attending a writer's workshop at one of the churches. There was a dramatic change in her demeanor. Her dark eyes narrowed as she looked up and hesitated in completing our registration.

"OOOoooohhhhhh…. is that the workshop in the church across the bridge? I was thinking about signing up for that, but I don't agree with their thinking, so I cancelled. Well, uh, here's your key. We have an unusually full house this weekend, so I am putting you two in the cottage out back."

Schwarck questioned, "You mean we aren't going to stay here in the main house overlooking the bay?"

The owner's insincere voice replied, "I'm so sorry, but we have a surprise wine growers conference and are completely full for the next few days. You can come in here for breakfast, though, if you come between 6:20 and 7:10 A.M... Just ring the bell outside."

A disappointed Schwarck persisted. "When I called to make the reservation, you didn't say anything about the wine conference. You told me that you had plenty of room."

"Yes, well, this is the way things happen in the B & B business," the owner insisted.

We reluctantly accepted the keys and went out back to enter the tiny cabin. It seemed clean enough, but the musty smell indicated it had probably been unoccupied for months. We had certainly expected to be in the picturesque main house. Unfortunately, the early short time frame for breakfast was not going to work with our schedule. "Breakfast" is a highlight in the Bed and Breakfast world and we felt cheated of "Breakfast" and our "Bed" wasn't even located in our "Bed and Breakfast".

As we unpacked, Schwarck was still perplexed. "What do you think she meant when she said she didn't agree with the church's views?"

"Ya got me. Let's get going or we'll be late to our first session."

The writer's workshop was not affiliated with the church at all. The church had merely provided space for the writing activity which was being conducted by an author friend of ours, Mary Blocksma. Mary booked the location because of its convenience and affordability.

We pulled up in front of the church to be greeted by a gigantic rainbow sign. The lettering underneath the sign proclaimed the congregation's acceptance: "everyone welcome". This underlined large-capitalized declaration seemed unnecessary. Shouldn't all religious organizations accept everyone? We entered the building and took seats. The chunky female minister came by to welcome our group; I took particular note of her brush cut, t-shirt, jeans and tattoo. She was accompanied by the choir director who was a "little person" i.e.; dwarf. Oddly enough, and I say this kindly, Schwarck knew the dwarf. This little person was an acquaintance of her son, Matt, who he had met while playing guitar at an "I Love Jesus" concert.

It wasn't until the very end of our short stay in Saugatuck that we "got it". There had been no tidying of our room, our beds were not made daily, and used towels were not replenished. We had been banished because of the owner's perceived notion that our lifestyle was not like her dour heterosexuality. I pictured her entering our cabin after we departed, wearing thick rubber gloves and a hazmat suit.

The memory made me rethink our upcoming Oprah Show appearance and I announced to Schwarck with conviction, "You're right, Schwarck! We should go on Ellen first. We should support diversity on all levels. But Oprah is pretty diverse too, and it would help if she promoted us, don't you think? I mean, getting the nod from Oprah is worth hundreds of thousands in book sales."

As my mind came back from picturing our first TV appearance, Miss Perky reappeared offering a printed dinner menu. The plethora of tasty sounding offerings was delightful, and I began to circle my choices and handed the menu back to our attendant, Miss Perky.

"Madam, this menu must be used again by other First Class passengers. Please just tell me what you wish to order from the menu." And then Miss Perky left.

Whoops! Obviously, I need to get out more and put greater distance between the medical community and myself. When hospitalized, my only pleasure each day was to circle what I wanted to eat. I made circling hospital food my life's work, but this is apparently not acceptable in First Class air travel, or probably anywhere else.

This First Class experience is enchanting but slightly disconcerting. Even the takeoff was odd. There were no warnings of any type. First Class passengers are apparently so highly evolved that they do not need the seat belt demo or a reminder that their seat cushion may be used as a flotation device. We were not instructed as to when we could walk about the cabin or where the exits doors were located. I already predict that there will not be any applause when we land. We in First Class are totally unregulated and assuredly above the rest.

Our dinner courses along with the correct wine with each was a culinary vision, remarkably delectable, and delivered with stunning precision. After dinner dishes were cleared away, warm, lemon-scented, wet-cloths were distributed and the lights were dimmed. We responded by whispering our conversations.

"Schwarck, when we land, where should we go first? Should we call Barbara's Brits and tell them we're crashing with them for a month? Schwarck? Are you sleeping?"

"ZZZZzzzzzzzzzz"

I figured out how to turn on my personal TV and watched The Last Samurai with over three hours of dashing barefoot over mountains and relentlessly hacking off human limbs. It was exhausting but I never get to watch anything but sports and Fox News at home, so I relish opportunities to see a movie. I needed a nap after all that blood and trauma, but the lights came back on for the delivery of hot face towels and breakfast. By the way, if someone uses tongs to give you a hot towel, I don't think it's because they are especially concerned about sanitation. Miss Perky uses tongs in order to avoid cremating her flesh, yet considered it completely safe for you to be awakened by laying this blistering item on your face.

A muffled sounding Schwarck leaned into my space. "Crawford, do you know how lucky we are. We are going to be landing soon in London and we are going to write THE BOOK. Millions of people would die to be in our shoes!"

There was some mumbling incoherence on my part as I struggled to relieve myself of the hot towel. "Schwarck, why would anybody want to be in my steel-toed shoes right now? I don't think so. I haven't slept in at least two days. We don't even know where we will sleep tonight."

"I've been thinking. Maybe we should go to Ireland first." Schwarck debated.

"What? Ireland!? Aren't we landing in London? Why didn't we just fly directly to Ireland if that is where we should start?" I was dumbfounded.

"Well, let's just see how we feel when we get in the terminal. Something will tell us what direction to take." Schwarck was steadfast.

"Really? I'm just a little curious. What do you think will let us know? Oh, my God! Did we just land? They didn't even tell us to buckle our seat belts. Look! My seat is not even in an upright and locked position." Now I was amazed.

"Let's go, Crawford. This is so exciting!" Schwarck's enthusiasm was increasing.

"Yeah, right." I countered sarcastically.

CHAPTER 9

DUBLIN YOUR PLEASURE

We disembarked from the plane and merged with thousands of harried travelers inside London's Gatwick Terminal. From the look of things, this week before Easter is a wildly popular vacation time. Brits relish their holidays and probably get more time off work than anyone else in the world. There were no unoccupied seats in the terminal, so we plopped our backpacks down on the floor and surveyed the perimeter.

I glanced over and said quickly, "Okay, Schwarck. Didn't you say we'd get a feeling when we got here that would tell us where to go next? Well…we're here and I don't feel a thing except exhausted. Hey! Look at that! There's a little booth giving free whiskey samples. That might help us think better. Let's go!"

"You go ahead. I'm going to go over to the Ryan Air counter and ask some questions. Maybe we should just get tickets to Ireland right now before we go to baggage claim." And then Schwarck was off.

I watched her weave through throngs of travelers and get into a long line while I then hustled over to the Jameson's Whiskey booth. All airports should offer free alcohol samples. Adults only, of course, and not enough to be over-served, just enough to take the edge off all the aggravation you're going to experience. Several samples later, I noticed she had reached the head of the line so I made my way over to the counter. Schwarck had been quizzing a painfully thin, stern faced lady in a green uniform.

"Crawford, they have two seats for a flight that will leave in a couple of hours. What do you think? Should we fly over to Dublin today? Same day air is very expensive."

"How expensive is it?"

Schwarck was clearly befuddled. "I don't know. I can't figure it out that quickly. We have to convert US dollars into Euros not pounds. But, actually, our money will go further in Ireland than in England, which is good.

"Didn't we hear that a flight from England to Ireland was only about $45 US?"

"Well, they didn't buy tickets the same day as going and it wasn't the Easter holiday. I just don't know…..let me see if I can figure this out."

There were no helpful suggestions offered by the pursed lipped airline representative. Schwarck's muttering was inciting those waiting behind us. Their eye rolls and sighs indicated their patience was wearing thin. I kept smiling and nodding to them offering little, "Oh, well…I don't know what she's doing" hand gestures and shrugs.

"Okay, Crawford. If I figured this out right, at least I hope I figured it right, we're going to pay $700 of our total $6800 on the card. So, if we buy these tickets, we're going to have to budget a daily allowance, or go home early."

"Just… get the tickets, Schwarck!"

I checked the crowd behind me to see if anyone wanted to enthusiastically pump my hand in gratitude for making a decision.

I am no help with calculations at all. Also, lack of sleep does not bode well for my thinking clearly about even the simplest of problems. Besides, I have never excelled with math formulas and if you throw in a few whiskey and rum samples, I'm hopelessly incompetent. All money calculations will be given over to Schwarck, who should supply me with an allowance and tell me where to go, just like Hugh does at home.

There is no way on God's green earth that I will slink home early. I'll get a job over here if I have to. Isn't this supposed to be the five-week adventure of a lifetime? How pitiful are we if we can only stay one week because we can't figure out the money!

"Let's not worry any more about it, Schwarck," I stated confidently. "We'll leave for Ireland in a couple of hours and when we get a good night's sleep, we'll talk again about budgeting. Let's go see if our luggage followed us to England, then get down to the gate so we can sleep sitting up for a few minutes."

Our entrance into the Dublin plane was nothing at all like the delightful First Class reception we enjoyed in Detroit. Even the gangway here is chaotic. The floor was jumping as tribes of screaming redheaded urchins raced up and down. Plane seating is first come, first serve, and due to our hesitation to strong arm the elderly and shove unattended infants aside, we were rammed through to the rear of the plane. We weren't swift enough to get seats together either.

The take off was deafening between the screaming kids and the loud whooshing air pressure in the tail section of this old, over-used aircraft. I don't remember seeing a flight attendant. I suspect they had locked themselves in with the captain.

As soon as the "Fasten Seat Belt" light was turned off, boisterous passengers leaped to their feet and ran to line up for the john. I was so fatigued, I conked out with my face mashed into my backpack. A blaring announcement rudely awakened me. A very high-pitched voice ordered passengers to immediately take their seats and fasten their seatbelts. We would be landing shortly and in between the static bursts, I distinctly heard a squeaky mention of "wind shears" and "extremely high gales".

I tightened my seat belt and got a death-grip on both armrests as we began a bouncy descent. I expected the overhead oxygen masks to drop any minute. I feverishly tried to remember all emergency instructions I had ever heard and sincerely hoped the aisle would light up. Flight attendants place great emphasis on lit up aisles… if there would still be an aisle if we unexpectedly dropped from the sky. I remember something about a whistle I should blow, but maybe the whistle was in the raft I must inflate in case of a water landing. Water landing my ass!

There were numerous heavy thumps up and down on the ground and cacophonous screeching of brakes, shopping bags scooted down the aisle, and a few overhead compartments sprang open and unloaded onto chortling passengers. No one but me seemed the least bit unnerved by all the landing drama.

We finally ceased moving and a calm lilting Irish voice welcomed us to Dublin.

I gratefully tumbled out the rear exit door onto a narrow, unsteady, and steep stairway leading to the tarmac. Forceful artic wind shears whipped my spiffy raincoat over my head. The frigid blast took my breath away. This was not even a bit like my imagined triumphant arrival on the soil of my Irish ancestors. I looked back to see a giddy Schwarck snapping pictures of me from every angle. She was clearly amused.

"God, Schwarck! I thought you said that April would be the ideal time to come here. Flowers would be in bloom. See this, I'm putting on gloves! This is ridiculous!" I burst through the tiny terminal's door in hopes of finding a roaring fireplace and my eyeglasses steamed up immediately. " Shhheeeze, Schwarck! That flight was terrible and so was the cold wind! Where does our luggage arrive…that is…if it wasn't blown out of the plane?"

"Here come all the bags…there's ours! Let's head down

the hall. There should be a Tourist Bureau desk. They are everywhere over here. They'll help us find a room and transportation." Schwarck added optimistically as always.

At the very end of a half-mile of hallway was a wee tourist desk and we wearily shuffled up to the counter. It was difficult to comprehend the advice the tourist lady was offering due to her thick accent, but with our sure fire system of speaking louder to people we can't understand, we managed to secure a hotel room in Dublin and learned that we could take a bus from here into the city.

What wasn't very clear is precisely which Dublin bus would take us the closest to our destination: the Drury Court Hotel in the Trinity College section. We had a plan. Every time a bus pulled up, Schwarck would run out and ask the driver if he was going to the Trinity College District. If she gave me the nod, I would spring forward, exact change in hand, and step onto the bus putting the coins into the box. Schwarck would give our desired destination to the driver and would grab the luggage and throw it up to me. I'd drag all the bags to a seat.

Eventually after about fifteen bus inquiries, we got the correct one and managed to get onboard even though my frozen fingers dropped several coins before they made it into the little coin box. It was a double decker bus and already packed on both levels. More people kept getting on at each stop and no one got off. We hugged our luggage closer and tried in vain to take up the least amount of space possible.

Exiting the bus was a going to be a crapshoot. We would be blessed by the Divine if we could claw our way to the exit door before the plucky driver rapidly closed the door and accelerated again. It was like a cat and mouse game for him. We had no clue which stop was ours. We began to interrogate riders closest to us. A young couple took pity on us and said they would give us a warning when our stop was approaching, but cautioned us to get off quickly as the bus "doesn't dally". well, no kidding! I watched a number of hapless passengers without baggage attempt to get off this bus.

When our new UK friends gave us the nod, we rumbled our husky luggage over toes and jammed shoulders in order to get in position. There would only be a second and one chance to jump off with all of our gear. My body staunchly resists leaping of any sort so this would be an incredible challenge.

It all happened so quickly. There we were, knees bent, luggage close at our sides, backpacks in place, and the door folded open and we leaped off simultaneously. It was like a synchronized Olympic event, but was also electrifyingly painful when our heels slammed down on the sidewalk. We had vaulted onto a sidewalk teeming with disheveled young people who were hell-bent on darting in and out of bookstores, coffee shops, alleyways and pubs. There wasn't enough room for our bags and bodies on the walkway. We began to plod forward through the hordes, with no idea which way was correct. Schwarck finally popped her head into a beauty shop and shouted in, "Excuse me, can anyone tell me where the Drury Court Hotel is?"

There was dead silence and Schwarck's face transformed into a hopeful version of Stan Laurel's. Finally, a young purple-headed stylist dropped her customer's head on the basin and came to the doorway, pointing her hairbrush back down the way we had just come.

"Sar-ree, luv, it took me a minute, I coon't understand yur accent, but there's yur lane, right dere!"

It is imperative now, for me to keep my body in motion or my lower torso will certainly seize up or perhaps just pitch forward onto the cobblestones. Has it only been three days since I slept in a bed? I also believe I'm losing my eyesight like that waif who took an hour to die in les Miserables'.

"There it is, Crawford! See the sign?"

" No. I can't see anything any more. I'm blind."

There was some stumbling, but I managed to pick up speed and remain upright.

I plunged through the door and thundered up to the meager Drury Court Hotel desk. A middle aged woman in a beige blazer was behind the counter. The place looked more like an elderly dentist's no frills waiting room than a hotel. Schwarck explained that we were the Americans who made the reservation from the airport, requesting the non-smoking room.

"Ooo, sor-ee, Mum, we dinna' ave nun-smoking rums. If ya wanna tek a peek in it, ya' kin."

"Crawford, do you want to see the room first?"

I was nearing mumbling delirium. I couldn't have cared less, even if ten old naked Irish cigar smokers were in residence up there. Somehow, I mustered up an overly loud reply, followed by a short sob, "We'll take it!"

CHAPTER 10

SOMETHING SMELLS ROTTEN AND WE'RE NOT IN DENMARK

We were given a large ornate metal key to a second floor room as well as coupons for an Irish breakfast. The prim desk clerk reported that this hotel features a lift, which is a rarity in this old section of town. She led us to the ancient lift and it was most assuredly beyond rare. This lift was possibly the first lift in existence in all of Ireland. It was gloomy and grungy and reluctantly jerked us up to the second level. I slid the squeaky hinged gate aside and we exited in grateful appreciation for our safe arrival.

We shuffled down a narrow, dim and dingy hallway leading to our room and Schwarck slowly unlocked and cautiously opened the door, with no small amount of trepidation. A bright light suddenly blinded us. We stepped over the threshold into a spacious fresh smelling room featuring pristine white lace curtains looped happily over unusually large windows. There were two fluffy looking twin beds with nightstands and nightlights, an overstuffed armchair and a highly polished cherry wood desk. There was an electric teapot on the desk as well as a tray containing a tea assortment, instant coffee, linen napkins, flowered china teacups, and packages of cookies.

The bathroom was exceptionally large and a toilet water tank was perched high on the wall with an attached four-foot pull chain. The toilet stool and bowl were a phenomenon. The stool was quite high, almost requiring a little jump to get up to it. I expected a toilet bowl with standing water like at home, but what I saw under the seat was more of a giant ceramic pipe. A small child could fit down in there and probably get flushed through to China. No one had ever warned me about foreign deviations in bathroom apparatus.

No matter how weird the toilet was, we were deliriously grateful. If it were physically possible, we would have done a lively dance in acknowledgement of our room's surprising magnificence.

"We've got to stay awake, Schwarck. Let's get unpacked and go downstairs to the pub and eat. I hope I don't fall face first into my chowder. We've got to at least try to stay up until 8 P.M."

In less than thirty minutes, we were downstairs, out the door, and entering the heavy mahoganied pub. There were only a couple other patrons in the bar and we chose a polished wood table near the window overlooking a narrow street. "Look at all the people in the street, Crawford. They're just standing out there. Do you think there's a protest?"

My explanation was interrupted by a white aproned waiter who reported that dinner could not be served for another half-hour, but we could order drinks. Uh-oh. What did Barbara say I'm supposed to get? Was it lager? Is Guinness a lager? We both ordered pints of Guinness and I began to relay what I knew of the current Irish news.

"Schwarck, if you ever read a newspaper or listened to the news, you would know that things are in turmoil over here because the government just passed a smoking ban in pubs. Today is the very first day of the ban. That is why so many people are in the streets puffing away."

Our frosted mugs arrived and we were beyond thirsty. After mug number three, we ordered fish and chips with mushy peas. The welcomed meal arrived featuring giant chunks of battered cod as well as a heaped mixing bowl full of fries. The bright green Irish peas were mashed into the consistency of baby food.

"Didn't I tell you how wonderful this fish and chips platter would be?" an appreciative Schwarck cooed.

It's my less traveled opinion that any fish and baby food cooked or not, would be considered gourmet, if preceded by three frosted pints of Guinness. After dinner we slowly ambled back up to our quaint little room and even though it was barely sunset, we prepared for a long awaited sleep.

Our window overlooking the main street exposed the front doors of no less than three pubs. My personal favorite; "The Hairy Lemon" had the biggest crowd of raucous smokers spilled out onto the sidewalk. Pedestrians were forced to navigate through murky clouds of smoke. Walking here was going to be iffy, as I am not accustomed to holding my breath for long periods of time while dodging traffic.

Tonight is our very first night sleeping on Irish soil. How amazing. Schwarck's eyes were already closed and she was making little puffing sounds.

My nighttime ritual, because of my numerous throbbing joints, includes the careful placement of sticky medicated pads called Salampas. I also might slather Ben Gay on my person which might be followed with a double dose of nighttime sleep aids. Unfortunately, due to my extreme exhaustion, I momentarily forgot that Schwarck couldn't tolerate heavy medicinal smells in an enclosed area. Oh, well. I'll just keep myself under the covers.

Normally I am capable of reading at least three paragraphs of steamy historical romance before entering my nighttime coma, but tonight I barely opened the book before starting to doze. Something startled me awake.

"Crawford, what the hell is that smell?"

CHAPTER 11

THIS IS DUBLIN, DUDE. . .WATCH OUT FOR THE BIG BANGER

After a mercifully long night of coma like sleep in a downy bed, we slowly came alive and prepared strong, hot cups of coffee. Schwarck said her sleep had been frequently interrupted during the night by shrieks and bellows from pub revelers on the street below our windows.

"I told you to take some of my nighttime sleep aids. Try it tonight. Trust me, you won't hear a thing. Aren't you starving? Let's get downstairs to find our Irish breakfast. Whatever it is, I hope there's a lot of it."

"I am starving, too, so we better hurry up because I don't think they serve breakfast after 10A.M. There are two things we must do today: go to the Tourist Bureau and the Internet Café. If we have time, maybe you'd like to go see the famous Book of Kells at Trinity College. I've seen it already. It's pretty impressive and not too far away, maybe ten blocks or so. In the 8th century, an Irish monk hand scribed four gospels of the New Testament and they have it under glass at Trinity College. They turn one page a day.

"Ten blocks? It's just a real old book, right? And…. you can only see one page of it? If it was Moses' tablet, then I'd walk the ten blocks over, but I think I'd rather go to the Tourist Bureau and leave off the trek to see the book. It's enough for me that you have seen it." I countered.

After only five minutes, Schwarck was completely ready for the day, while I was still evaluating which pair of black pants to wear. Following my clothing selection, there would be a hurried slathering of creams along with make-up application. I refuse to be seen without make-up. I never want to see me without make-up, and I am quite sure no one else will want to see me sans make-up either.

I have never known anyone who can get completely ready for any event faster than Schwarck. She can be showered, fully dressed for a formal occasion, and out the door in less than thirteen minutes. There have been many instances where she has not bothered to get dressed at all before appearing in public. When we have stayed at hotels without coffee service in the room, Schwarck will leap from bed in her jammies and head to the hotel lobby or cross the street to McDonalds, returning in less than four minutes with coffee for two, along with a bud vase containing a rose which she plucked off a room service tray. I would never do that.

After an abbreviated make-up application and hair-do prep, I was ready for the day, and we made our way downstairs. Breakfast was served in a small underground bunker. The café furniture was mismatched and rickety, but the odd tables were covered with white linen cloths and the silverware appeared to be clean.

The only waiter was a young Asian man who also might have very well been the cook and dishwasher. He was a man of no words and looked particularly serious. Breakfast service in his world consisted of collecting our coupon and pointing in the direction of bread and coffee. After about twenty minutes, he reappeared carrying two identical breakfast plates consisting of grilled mushrooms, fresh tomato slices, a giant sausage, two unidentified lumps, and one egg. Schwark explained that the lumps were black and white pudding and the big sausage was the Banger. I had hoped for at least two eggs sunny side up, plus thick bacon, but this is the Irish breakfast, and we don't get to order what we want.

Vittles of any type never frighten or disgust me, therefore if my hot Irish breakfast included two strange looking lumps called black and white pudding, I was willing to give em' a try, but what about that Banger? It was floating placidly on a little river of dark brown grease. Schwarck had already slid her Banger and puddings onto a saucer and proclaimed she had these once before and that was enough.

"What part of the animal do you think a Banger comes from, Schwarck? Look at these black and white things. They shouldn't be called pudding. They're meat, not dessert. Yuck! They taste terrible!" I exclaimed.

Schwarck was admiring several French Impressionist paintings hanging on the peeling gold cement walls, while gnawing away on a stack of Irish Soda bread slathered with Raspberry jam. I predict she'll be sucking seeds out of molars for the remainder of the day. I gingerly nibbled away at the black and white pudding and then tackled the Banger. I experienced some queasiness and I couldn't determine if it was due to the slippery Banger, the black and white pudding or the hotel's mildewed and oxygen deprived basement.

We managed to find more than enough breakfast to our liking, particularly the grainy Irish bread, and we left a nice tip on the table in hopes that tomorrow's service would be improved upon.

In my lifetime of dieting, I have observed a glaring difference between thin and fat people. Chubby folks like me will completely devour a food item and then declare it was unfit for human consumption, whereas thin people will move it all over their plate, maybe roll it over and say, "Yuck…I'm not eating that!" To make matters worse for me, I will actually eat more to get a nasty food taste out of my mouth.

I inherited many of my poor eating traits from my dad's southern–cooking mother, who easily weighed over three hundred pounds, but was exceedingly proud she could bend over and touch her toes. The only way I could ever touch my toes would be to sit down and pull my toes up to my hand. My Grandmother had another diet-killing habit; she would eat something sweet and then profess;

"Ooooh, that was so sweet! Honey, give me something salty to get that sweet taste out of my mouth. How about that big bag of chips! Good Lord above, weren't those chips salty? Gimme that chocolate pie so I can get that salty taste out of my mouth!" She would eat like that all day.

My giant grandmother was the same person who thought

if you didn't eat a lot, you would get cancer because every person she knew who had cancer was painfully thin and weak. My eating philosophy has been profoundly influenced by her throughout my life.

We departed the hotel for the Tourist Bureau and quickly discovered that the sliver of sunshine was deceiving. It was blustery, cold, and clouds were rolling in. Walking unburdened by luggage and backpacks, however, was tremendously freeing. I almost felt nimble.

I was troubled and uneasy about leaving all of our priceless belongings in the room. Hugh's "theft" cautions resounded in my head. I hid my backpack and camera equipment in the hotel closet, only slightly confident that they would escape a wily thief's detection. For an extra measure of safety, I unfurled my underwear that had been worn for three consecutive days, right on top of the bags. To my mind, a hotel safe couldn't keep my costly belongings more untouchable than that.

The show Riverdance and The Other Boleyn Girl novel, did not prepare me adequately for Dublin, Ireland. I had believed there would be more open jolliness and merriment. Where were the Irish Rovers, the brawny lads, "The Rose of Tralee" and where the hell are all the Irish Setters? That's the Ireland I had expected. There appears to be a glut of gloom here. Dubliners are suspiciously thin, chain-smoking, and pierced. What I am beginning to grasp is that this city is a college town, teeming with impoverished, unseasoned, academic types. We over-seasoned matrons are glaringly out-of-date and place, despite our adventuresome spirits.

On our way to the bureau, Schwarck sidled up to the ATM for the first of our daily allotments of cash. She began entering the code for "give us the money" and the display on the LCD said "Funds Not Available-Insufficient". In disbelief she anxiously thumped out the request again and was once again refused.

"What's going on? I don't get it. The credit card is preloaded with our $6800. How can it tell us there are insufficient funds?" Schwarck wavered.

"Well, I'm not normally one to say I told you so, but I did say never ever trust these machines. It's our money and they won't let us have it. Probably a complete stranger can get it easier than us. Good thing I have five piles of cash under my boobs so we can eat dinner!"

"I wonder what time it is in New York?" mumbled a confounded Schwarck. "We've got to call the credit card company and get this straightened out. I called them before we left, and I told a Ms. Smith that we'd be traveling in the UK, so the card company wouldn't get concerned or suspicious when they received invoices from over here."

Let me ask you....do people sincerely believe that if you converse with a Ms. Smith from a financial institution in a megalopolis like New York City and tell her you're going to be traveling in the UK, Ms. Smith will remember the conversation and actually be the same Ms. Smith you talk to again? I don't think so! In addition, while this $6800 means life and death to us, it is an inconsequential and paltry sum to Ms. Smith.

As we stepped away from the ATM, a piercing sleet/rain

combination began to pour down on us, making the five-block walk more than miserable. Being a steadfast optimist, I observed the positive effects of rain and sleet pelting sidewalks pervaded by litter and smelly refuse. I also noted the extraordinary length of each wet freezing block.

Our brains had descended into such a cold mind numbing fog, that once we entered the prehistoric building housing the Tourist Bureau, the first thing we did was search for a seat to plop down our cold waterlogged carcasses. I'm pretty sure we smelled a lot like wet Labradors. "I may have to sit here awhile, Schwarck, and hope my frozen fingers uncurl. What are we supposed to do here, anyway?"

"We should look through maps and brochures to figure out where we want to go next. Looks like we are supposed to get a number and wait to be called, then we go up the stairs and one of those tellers will make reservations for us. We shouldn't take a number until we know where we want to go." Schwarck explained.

Okay, that's the real crux of our situation here which is the real nitty-gritty. We need guidance and the travel spirits have not as yet spoken to us. Therefore, we are flummoxed, so I chose to step up to the Tourist Bureau souvenir counter to feel fluffy miniature lambs and purchase a chocolate Celtic cross for a snack. Schwarck opted to pour over a colorful assortment of travel brochures. After munching and browsing for a few more moments, I returned to my harried partner's side.

"I started to pull a number for us, but I'm…I'm so confused. Maybe we should just leave and come back here later after we find an Internet Café. I don't know if we'd be better off staying here for a few days or get out to the country. What do you want to do, Crawford?"

"I want to see green rolling hills and Danny Boy. I don't think we should decide right now. Let's come back here later." I was ready to rest awhile.

"Okay, but I feel a little disappointed that we can't decide anything. Maybe it'll be easier after we get the Internet connections going. You're going to love it!"

The Internet Café visit could be intimidating for me. I have never been in one, nor am I familiar with computer gear and lingo. Schwarck thinks we must use the Internet everyday to keep in touch with home as well as make on-line reservations for tours and housing. After we tramped down several blocks, I gently inquired, "Do you think the Internet Café is much further?"

I am adamantly opposed to unnecessary strolling of any kind. Mindless ambling for no purpose causes me needless pain and suffering, even though I'm confident that the exercise would be greatly beneficial. Friend Schwarck is an ardent proponent of daylong oblivious sauntering, greeting small critters and admiring the flora and fauna. If I don't offer some suggestions, this mosey will continue indefinitely.

"Oh my gosh, is that homemade bread I smell? Yum! Look in this window, Schwarck. I could sure use a bowl of soup like that lady is enjoying."

"It is lunch time," Schwarck agreed. "Maybe soup and a sandwich will help us think."

Food is so conducive to clear thinking and the inviting smells and friendly atmosphere of the pint sized Dame Street Café were particularly pleasant. A hospitable young proprietor named Sean greeted everyone coming and going. A lively banter ensued and by the time we had finished big bowls of indescribably delicious Tomato Basil Soup, we had heard all about where the Irish go on their holidays. He encouraged us authors to visit a fishing village on the south coast called Kinsale. He also declared that we absolutely must take in the charms of Dingle, Doolin, and Killarney.

We wrote down everything Sean told us and reluctantly bid him farewell. He enthusiastically praised us for our "adventuresome spirit" and thought we were very "cool".

A few blocks up the dingy street from Sean's place was the Internet Café called "Wired"! A profoundly pimpled and pierced young man grunted as we entered the cockeyed doorway. The building reminded me of the Mystery Spot in the Upper Peninsula of Michigan. Pierced boy pointed a nicotine-stained finger to an open stairway leading to the basement where we would find our assigned computers.

"Dudes, go to room # One." He proclaimed.

"Schwarck, are we the dudes?" I whispered.

The creaky uneven staircase led to a maze of graffiti spattered walls, which defined the space of several tiny cubicles. I'm not usually squeamish, but our cubicle was reminiscent of Hollywood's view of where a hatchet murderer resides. The place smelled of mold and old smoke and there was a gummy layer of grime on every surface. I decided to keep wearing my gloves. We gingerly lifted two rusty metal folding chairs and scooted them along the sticky cement floor up to a kitchen countertop showcasing two ancient computer terminals and two filthy, worn and mismatched keyboards. Mine was missing several keys and most of the alphabet was worn off.

I worried aloud, "We should probably burn our shoes and clothes when we get back to the hotel, if we live to get back!"

"Okay, Crawford, this is how you get on the web!"

Within minutes, despite the grunge, I was on MSN Hotmail and my message was being relayed across the vast sea to Hugh who has no idea where I am.

TO: Friends and Relatives back home

SENT: Weds. April 7

SUBJECT: Wherever I go…..Here I am!

We are sort of in a fog from travel, time change, fried fish, and Guinness. We slept for 12 hours when we finally got to a bed after three days.

It's entirely possible that we were in the wrong line at London's Gatwick….so we just went with it….and continued flying to Dublin Ireland. The plane was chock full of obnoxious screaming red heads.

Things I've learned so far:

We spent half our money in the first 24 hours.

No one understands our accent.

Never eat black and white pudding again with a big Banger chaser.

The Irish breakfast with our hotel room features two eggs…that is, per room, not per person.

No smoking pubs mean all smoking drunks clutter the highways and streets so they can puff in the face of all non-smokers trying to navigate the sidewalks.

Enough for now.

Love you!

Kathleen…that's what Schwarck says I need to call myself over here

---

After paying pimple boy a few Euros for the use of the grungy computers, we traversed back to the Tourist Bureau and took a number, more confident knowing that the travel gods had been with us this day.

"They called our number, Crawford, let's go! Well, what d'ya think? Do you want to stay in Dublin for awhile or are you anxious to get outside of the city?" Schwarck asked excitedly.

"It doesn't feel like Ireland here to me. Sean said Kinsale is where he heads when he's on holiday, so why don't we just go there first?"

The Tourist Bureau clerk found us a Bed and Breakfast in Kinsale that she said was within easy walking distance of town. Many of Kinsale's hotels and rental cars were booked up because of the Easter holiday. She suggested that we take the bus and directed us back down the stairs to the bus booth.

There was a handsome young man perched on a stool in the Bus Eireann booth. He had sparkling, mischievous eyes. "Americans, aren't ya!"

It was a statement rather than question, and how did this guy know we were from the US, just by looking at us? I actually think I look like a healthy red-cheeked German, and Schwarck, well, she looks like a more mature and maybe Polish hippie.

He held up a colorful brochure entitled "The Open Road Pass" and said, "Ere's sumthin ye kin yoos, luvs. It's suh nnewww, nuh bodee reely knows how it wurks, so ye gurls mite git ah lot moorr out of it!" He professed that the Open Road pass is cheaper and we can go on any bus, anywhere, any time. This is such a new service, some of their drivers have not seen the pass yet and they might have questions. However, his charming sales technique had us hooked. We threw all caution aside and bought two shiny Open Road passes.

The bus booth also displayed flyers for optional Dublin activities and Schwarck was all quivery to see a flyer for her all time favorite show, "Shirley Valentine". The story is about an older British housewife who believes her life is boring and un lived. She wants to "drink a glass of wine where the grape was grown". It's a chick comedy with suffering. Tonight's British production is a live, one woman show. Years ago, Schwarck required me to see the Shirley Valentine movie because she was convinced I was kin to the main character.

My pal is a Hollywood disciple of such fanaticism that she is known to purchase and watch her favorite movies over and over and over again. A surprise ending is no longer unfathomable after I have seen it for the fifth time!

"Oh my God, Crawford. We are supposed to go this show. I feel it! The flyer wasn't even obvious. It was under a stack of papers. Something is telling us to go to the show tonight. Let's get tickets." Schwarck exclaimed.

"Really? Something is telling me that we should be sound asleep by 8 P.M. when the show starts. Besides, you've seen this so many times, you could recite every word along with Shirley. Aren't you tired of it yet?"

The live "Shirley Valentine" production was to be performed in a small theater only five blocks away from the Tourist Bureau and it was necessary to go there for the tickets so we went. If we grabbed a sandwich and some chips on the way back to the hotel, we'd have time for a little packing before the show. I was looking forward to tomorrow's departure from Dublin and decided to lighten my luggage contents in hopes of making my walking more fluid and lively. The giant bottles of shampoo, conditioner, a large mirror, and extra converter seemed expendable, so they became the subject of my very first digital photos. It seemed only proper to take a picture in respect for items that must be left behind.

Buddy Schwarck spent her time calling and being put "on hold" with New York in order to convince Ms. Smith to give us money. She was finally successful and Ms. Smith proclaimed that we could have some of our money every day. Schwarck also spent time developing a dynamic computerized spreadsheet of our expenses. "We started out with the $6800 on the card and we spent $700 on air fare to get here, that leaves $6100. If we can find accommodations for $40 US for 35 nights, that leaves $4700 that will be used for transportation, food and tours, or entertainment, like tonight. See, look on the spreadsheet."

I thought I should appear interested so I focused intently on her computer screen to get a good view of the glorious spreadsheet.

"Oh, wow!" I said non committed.

"Do you want me to show you how to do the spreadsheet on your computer, too? You could keep track of everything you buy." Schwarck offered.

"Uh, no. I don't want to keep track of everything I buy because then I might not buy it! Do you think I should leave the shampoo behind? I hate to leave the mirror here, too, but you can tell me if there's a hole in the back of my hair. Oh, my, gosh! It's almost time for the little ten block hike in the dark to the theater. We don't want to miss any of the show!"

The theater seating featured shabby plywood risers with twenty rows of metal folding chairs. This was a bit of a letdown because I expected the UK to be the Mecca of theater greatness. I always presumed the UK to be more artistically advanced than the US. Think of Andrew Lloyd Webber, Shakespeare, Benny Hill, and Monty Python. All the greats had performed on fabulous ornate stages over here, hadn't they? This theater was completely dilapidated.

As the audience of mostly women over the age of 40 took their seats, I noticed that we were the only ones in attendance wearing slacks and not carrying a black handbag over our arm like the Queen. This was an audience of Shirley Valentine replicas, who were more than likely in attendance to revisit the essence of their feisty girlhoods.

One of Ireland's most popular actresses, Mary McEvoy, was the lead, and I was caught up in her perpetual smoking and potato frying on stage. I had never seen those activities as a performance. She was very convincing and the fried food made me ravenous. Halfway through the performance, Schwarck came up missing. I decided she was nauseous, famished, or attending a bathroom festival.

I met her in the lobby after the show and she explained; "I had to get out of there before my headache got any worse. It might have been the smoke."

"Really? This was your number one favorite show of all time, if I recall, and the spirits told you we needed to come here tonight. I wanted to sleep instead, but I stuck it out to the bitter end, while you were in the lobby eating peanuts and drinking wine."

There was no chatter as we trudged the ten shadowy blocks back to the Drury Court, medication, and sleep to follow.

"Goodnight, Shirley!" I muttered.

CHAPTER 12

KINDRED SPIRITS IN KINSALE

Traveling for five weeks with a friend is somewhat like being married to her. After a week, a natural assumption of roles takes place. Our roles have evolved over time in a harmonious way with a clear perception of each other's strengths and weaknesses.

Schwarck's natural strengths include the following:

- Chief Financial Officer
- Transportation Authority
- Tour Accommodations Officer
- Spiritual/Mystic Advisor-non religious
- Naturalist and Horse/Cow Whisperer
- Palm, Aura and Tea Leaf Reader
- Technology Education
- Architectural and Façade Interpretation
- Artistic and Color Clarifier
- Physical Fitness And Trivia Game Coordinator
- TV programming & Remote Controller
- Coffee and Tea Procurer

My roles, though less impressive in length, are no less vital and include:

- Plumbing Inspector
- Handicapped Access Inspector
- Meteorologist
- Fashion Accessorizor
- Timekeeper (she claims her body is too magnetic for a watch)
- Nutrition Analyst
- Security Officer
- Current Events Announcer and Storyteller

I am also in charge of sarcasm, as well as all conversations that begin with "Really?" or "Are you serious?"

Our system of role acceptance works so well for us longtime sidekicks that neither of us lobbies for a specific duty. Everything just naturally falls into place.

This morning, after the hotel checkout, we took a taxi to the Bus Eireann Station. Schwarck needed the bathroom so I sauntered over to the bus counter to find out where we needed to be to catch our bus. The agent advised me to "get in the queue". What the hell is a queue? Is it a small closet? A place you go for a security check? He seemed quite emphatic, but did not point in the direction of "the queue". After some nervous looking about the terminal, I asked a friendly looking young woman standing by a curb with her luggage if she knew where the bus to Kinsale would meet. She said our bus would come to this curb and everyone would "queue up" here. Holy crap! A "queue" is "a line." Why didn't he just say that?

Schwarck returned and got in "the queue" with me. We observed passengers as they queued up in other lanes to wait for their buses. When the bus arrived, each took their cases over to the curb and put their own luggage on board. The driver never left the seat. A bus worker came along and closed the bay when it was time for the bus to depart. Schwarck devised a plan. I would get on the bus, show our tickets to the driver, and secure good seats while she took the luggage to the compartment and shoved it on board. This way we'd get seats together and I wouldn't have to do the heavy lifting. I liked this plan immensely.

The bus pulled up and "the queue" began to move. Schwarck grabbed the suitcases and jostled them toward the storage area while I stepped onboard. The fresh looking and cordial bus driver had never seen an Open Road Pass before and was perplexed as to what to do with it. After much discussion and notice of the winding queue behind me, he shrugged, gave it back, and I staggered over to a seat looking back apprehensively to see if the Open Road Pass Inspector was coming onboard to confiscate our tickets.

As soon as Schwarck got on, I explained the driver's reluctance to accept our Open Road Pass. I also expounded on my distrust of the Irish method of stowing your own luggage. "Did you put our bags right underneath us so we can see if someone takes ours off? What if they take ours off to get to theirs and don't put ours back in and the driver takes off?"

Schwarck did not seem the least bit concerned and just ignored my qualms.

The "Pod-Bay" doors were slammed shut and the four-hour ride through the countryside to our connection in Cork began. The city traffic eventually dwindled and the road became two lanes, which wound over rolling green hills and through small hamlets. This was the Ireland of my dreams. We passed colorful row house villages and lush, sheep-filled pastures with stone fences that looked like they had been there since the Dark Ages. There were also peculiar little glass entranceways to the homes. Inhabitants were sitting in straight back chairs, on display, as if in a tiny department store.

As I survey the green pastures, I find it odd that I have yet to see a trace of pigs, only sheep. More than likely they have made them all into Bangers, bacon, or black and white pudding. The Irish meals I have enjoyed thus far have all contained some form of pork…never lamb. There are also pastures with mismatched herds of cows but few offerings of steak on the menus I've seen.

"See how playful and frisky the cows are over here?" Schwarck delighted.

"Really? I don't see any difference between these and the ones we had on the farm. Our cows would pick up speed if they thought the bull was coming out of the barn, otherwise they pretty much just stood and stared all day." I explained patiently.

Undaunted, Schwarck said, "Look, Crawford, We are coming in to Cork."

Cork is a large antiquated city of massive blackened brickwork. There is a rugged coarseness here. The worn down bus station was busy and extremely crowded. Benches were jammed with people waiting for their bus. Entire families were traveling together on the bus. Most of the females in the station were pierced, tattooed, and were exposing blubbery, pasty midriffs. Their muffin tops were colossal and should have been kept under wraps.

We finally located our bus lane and the Kinsale bus was waiting. Schwarck wrestled the bags to the bay and I had to flat out run in order to beat two ninety-eight year olds on canes who were astoundingly speedy and probably disguised so they could get the "crippled" seats up front. I'm on to them.

The road to Kinsale was far beyond winding and there were frequent stops to pick up new passengers waiting in front of rural homesteads, or to let a passenger off in a field, probably to puke from motion sickness. Our entrance to the city was unannounced by the driver. All riders but us, seemed to be aware of where they were. Our only clue to get off was when all passengers got off and then the driver packed up his lunchbox and leaped off too. "Uh, I guess we're in Kinsale, Schwarck," I said looking around the empty bus.

Although the temperature was near freezing and the winds were whipping off the harbor, we were delighted by the view of the colorful row houses in this village by the sea. We passed an entrance sign proclaiming this city is known officially as "The Tidiest Town in Ireland"!

Our accommodations for the next four days was to be the The Hillside Bed and Breakfast. Since we had no idea where it was located, I suggested we step into Dino's restaurant on the next block, carbo load on spaghetti, enjoy some big glasses of red wine, and inquire about the location of The Hillside. Our friendly wait staff informed us that even though the restaurant sounded Italian, they didn't have spaghetti on the menu…just fish and chips with peas. She also suggested that we try Kinsale Lager instead of wine. She had not heard of our Bed and Breakfast but assured us that she would find out where it was located.

Instinct tells me that since we have arrived in a valley overlooking a harbor, the Hillside Bed and Breakfast is more than likely, most probably, perched precariously on top of a gigantic hill, and that would necessitate wrestling and tugging ponderous gear up a steep highland incline. Once we had consumed our daily ration of fried potatoes and slab of breaded cod, the manager of Dino's chatted with us and suggested that we should order a jitney because the Hillside "is out-of-town a bit".

Schwarck began an explanation of the subtle nuances of calling for your bill when eating in foreign country. She assured me that she has used this system all over Europe and it is what all waiters understand. "When you are ready for your bill, you merely catch the eye of the wait staff and use exaggerated hand motions pantomiming the signing of a check with a big curly flourish at the end." She caught our server's attention, Schwarck did the two-hand check-sign pantomime and the girl came over to see what was going on.

"I didn't really think that would work, Schwarck. We're in a small seaside Irish village, not Rome." I explained patiently.

The server brought back the bill and announced that our jitney was waiting for us. We weren't sure this was our cab because there weren't any signs on the old model car, but there was a guy inside who was waiting for something. He exited the vehicle when we rolled our luggage out the door and began to help load it into the cavernous trunk. Then up the hill we went and went and up and up some more. The uphill ride to the salmon pink Hillside Bed and Breakfast took fourteen minutes, so I'm confident that the "walking distance", toting luggage and backpacks, would have easily taken a chilling 60 minutes and there would have been a lot of puffing and perhaps a small stroke on my part. I may never leave the Hillside B & B.

The place looked nice though. The sunny entryway was enclosed with glass and led to another more formal entrance with a doorbell you turned like a key. We were "hallooed" by a high pitched voice much like Aunt Bea's from Mayberry. A neat, slender fiftyish redhead appeared, holding a paintbrush and wearing a large apron over a tailored knit suit. She was incredibly overdressed for a painting project. We explained that we were the Americans who reserved the room from the Tourist Bureau in Dublin.

"I'm Kah-rrhn and this is my friend KAH-thleen. We will be wrri-ting our book here and we'd luv to paaay yuu in ad-vahnce for ourr rruum."

What the hell? Schwarck was speaking with an accent of some sort. She's even rolling her r's. How weird!

We were ordered to wait for Innkeeper Margaret in the conservatory until she completed her door painting task, which was "a requirement of the International Bed and Breakfast Ordinance". After that, she would take us to our room and explain the rules of her home. We both already sense that Margaret is keenly obsessed with law and order.

The glassed-in conservatory was a delight and looked to be the perfect venue for us to begin writing THE BOOK. Margaret reappeared shortly and began a recitation of rules as she led us out of the conservatory. She told us that all rooms had doors, which were "to be kept closed at all times, for the comfort and privacy of all". When we walk into a room, we must be sure to close the door behind us. We followed close at her heels through several small, neat two-door rooms including a library, dining room, and living room. The emphasis on all "the doors" reminded me of how scary Alice In Wonderland had been.

Margaret continued to articulate the Hillside's regulations; rooms would only be tidied before noon, after that guests must do their own. Breakfast would only be served between 8 and 9:15 A.M., and she would take our order at the table. There was only one set of large ornate keys; one for the front door and the other was for our room. These keys are priceless and must be safely guarded at all times.

One glance at Schwarck told me that she had reached her limit with the rules recitation. Her eyes were beginning to twitch and blink excessively.

Our first floor room was wonderfully cheery looking with two plush beds covered in flowery quilts. The room was especially large with a lovely view of the neatly fenced and flowered yard. There was a small TV, our own hot pot with china cups and a hair dryer. Margaret curtly motioned for us to follow her into the bathroom, whereupon she began a complex pronouncement of the steps which would be necessary for a successful experience in the shower. In order to get water to come out of the nozzle, you would need to first pull the cord coming from the electrical box in the shower stall which turned on the light and the shower motor. There were knobs on the electrical box to turn for the desired degree of heat. Electricity and water together in a metal stall seemed perilous to my way of thinking. There was also a cork mat which we were to put a small towel over, then stand on. This would no doubt subdue the voltage which was going to course through our wet naked bodies. This mat must be replaced on the back of the stall as we see it standing now. Yeah, like we are really going to be in any condition for the positioning of cork after the electrocution. I'm going to rethink my need for taking a shower while in residence here.

Margaret finally left us and I had to contain my immediate desire to explode into laughter. Schwarck had sunk down on one of the beds, reeling from all the rules.

"Crawford, I know this woman. I'm not kidding. She is exactly like my Scottish grandma. We won't even get any heat while we are here no matter how cold it gets. We'll have to wear coats and socks to bed."

"Well, I think she is a riot! She's just a little uptight. Forget about Margaret and let's get unpacked and into the conservatory. You said you would give me my first computer lesson, right?" I asked.

I had not as yet opened my laptop nor did I have any idea how to open it or turn it on. This was going to be an important key element for literary success. After a muddled half hour of instruction, I begged off to go back to the room to make hot tea and eat crispy sugar cookies with currents.

When I returned, the conservatory was livelier with arriving guests who had been escorted here for the rules presentation. Schwarck was talking with a family from Australia and showing off her Apple laptop for their amazement. They were agog at our computers. I stepped up and offered my hand to greet the Aussies.

"Hal-looo. I'm KAH-theen and these ees Kah-Rrn. We ahrrr ahn a five week ad-ven-ture AHND are writing THE BOOK!"

CHAPTER 13

HEY COTTER. . . WELCOME BACK

As I gaze out the window from The Hillside B & B, I am struck by the profusion of white church steeples scattered throughout the tidy town below, and I remember that today is Good Friday. This really got me to thinking; if there's a lot of churches, most will be involved with Good Friday services today. I once was a chorus member presenting "The Seven Last Words of Christ" in Our Lady of Something gym for a predominantly Catholic crowd. That packed performance was on Good Friday between one and three o'clock in the afternoon; therefore, from the looks of things here, I predict all Kinsale commerce will come to a screeching halt between the hours of one and three at a minimum.

I report this morning's travel advisory to my unchurched friend, because that is precisely the time we planned to go downtown to email, shop, and eat lunch. She counts on me for all church and religion information as I was a singing member of the United Methodist Church Choir for 40 years and the enthusiastic chairman of the Save Our Sunday School Committee. Schwarck's religious affiliation consisted of singing a rousing first verse of "Onward Christian Soldiers" every Easter with her uniformed, Salvation Army grandma.

We entered the dining room at 9 A.M., for our Irish breakfast and immediately encountered a fluttery Margaret who was dressed in a white, loosely knit pantsuit embellished by a starched ruffled apron. She was poised with pad and pen and asked for our order, but never wrote anything down. She seemed totally distracted by the kitchen and kept nervously looking toward the door. She had the mannerisms of a nervous squirrel: penetrating eyes, quick, jumpy, flippy, brazen and alert for predators. She explained that Dennis, her husband, was "back in there, waiting for orders". She nodded her antsy head toward the kitchen door.

I predict he is a staggering freak of nature and must be chained to the floor but has an uncanny knack for food preparation.

When Margaret fluttered back with two slices of toast in a novel two-slice container, I observed that everything here was carefully portioned and positioned. There were no little jam jars or catsup bottles. She even brought a teaspoon to me, but only upon request. My friend's eyes narrowed and she leaned in to whisper through clenched teeth, "Margaret is just like Grandma Gurney and that's why I wore my flannels and socks to bed last night. The heat was turned off at 8 P.M. and all wall plugs have off and on switches. You can't even get water when you want it."

Eggs, tomato slices, sausage and Muesli arrived, none of which was close to the order either of us gave her. We didn't say anything for fear that a returned order might agitate a deranged Dennis.

Margaret appears to indulge her guests, but apparently just brings whatever Lurch slaps on a plate. She did inquire as to our plans for the day with a statement that many business people will observe Holy Days but we might find a few money minded folks with their shops open. The Easter holiday as celebrated in the UK, includes Maundy Thursday, Good Friday, Good Saturday, Easter Sunday and Easter Monday. Thank God, Tuesday isn't going to be Good, or we would never get to eat dinner downtown. I knew this many church steeples did not bode well for our touring activities. I rushed through breakfast in order to get an earlier start on the trek downhill. If we wanted lunch downtown, we needed to get ahead of the Irish worshipers.

Margaret cautioned us about the "saucy" neighbor dog and reported the temperature in Celsius. What do those numbers represent exactly because I don't seem to have a grip on it? I fall back on my hillbilly upbringing, if the rock is moving, it's windy; if it's wet, raining; and if there's snow on it, for God's sake wear a jacket and gloves.

We stepped outside and were greeted by blinding sunlight, but temperatures somewhere in the 40s. This was springtime, suitable for leather gloves, stocking caps, and Navy pea coats. There was an immovable fluffy little Pekinese stretched out directly in our path. Schwarck began her doggy speak, along with insistence that I take her picture with Margaret's pooch. It was evident to me that this canine was cranky because his lips curled way back over his teeth. She was mindless of his body language and thought he was smiling for the picture. Did she also think the growling was acid reflux? I backed away from "Saucy" and headed for the road.

The roadway was so steep, I found myself almost jogging downhill and way ahead of the ambling Schwarck who was inspecting roadside posies and talking to happy cows. As I wobbled past the pastures and entered the cobblestone streets of downtown, I began to notice a number of residents outdoors hanging up clothes or just leaning back in painted wooden chairs taking in the sun. As I passed one elderly lady in a sleeveless dress, she nodded and commented on the extreme heat. I'm quite sure she'll report to her congregation that she saw two old over coated and gloved Americans puffing downhill on this sultry Good Friday.

We Americans are so accustomed to having our personal needs and desires met 24/7, year round, that we find it beyond bothersome that we might be denied access to desired activities, goods, and supplies for any reason. It has always seemed curious that we want to travel in order to experience a different culture, yet we want the same conveniences we have at home. I once accompanied a group to Acapulco, Mexico, and they were incensed that the Catholic priest spoke Spanish during Mass. As they left the church he told them in English to have a nice day, therefore, there was no reason for him to speak a foreign language during the entire service. I attempted to explain that we were the foreigners, but this news fell on deaf ears. I'm talking seriously deaf here!

Schwarck caught up with me along the road. She was insistent that we look up Cotter, my maiden name, in town. We had picked up a brochure at Margaret's which said the Mayor of Kinsale was named Darren Cotter. We had even looked in the phone book and there were pages of Cotters. Surely I am related to someone here! So far, none of the people we have seen look anything like me or any of my Cotter relatives. These people have been short, dark, and almost gypsy-like.

My granddad, Robert (Pop) Cotter, was Tennessee Irish and known throughout the land as the most magnificent and entertaining swearer of all time. He lived with us on the farm and terrified me until I was about six years old. He always had an enormous jiggling drip on the very tip of his big hooked nose. All of his shirts looked like lace because of the live ashes falling on his chest from the hand rolled cigarette permanently affixed to his lower lip. There were only four fingers on one hand and the other arm was paralyzed, necessitating him to move it around with his good hand. He wore a squeaky brace on his paralyzed left leg, and he loved farming, practical jokes, and poker. He was raw and raucous. If you add his constant colorful swearing and tricks into the mix, it's a wonder we children weren't seriously psychologically scarred by his loud bellowing of things like "great steaming balls of monkey shit!" Our Cotters were fierce and funny, but I was desirous of meeting some genuine refined Irish Cotters; perhaps they were clan leaders and chieftains, not rowdy, crude comedians.

We soon found ourselves on a narrow lane of colorful storefronts in the middle of town. The largest sign facing us proclaimed: "Joe Cotter, Auctioneer/Estate Agent." The business was closed for the Easter holiday, but a small handwritten note on corner of the window directed all inquiries to Mary Cotter, Proprietor of Quayside Bed and Breakfast.

"This is awesome, Crawford! Let's go! We are going to meet some Irish Cotters!"

She was more geeked to meet the Cotters than I was, but her exuberance is infectious and we headed out to find Mary Cotter of the Quayside B & B.

We found a bookstore that was open, despite Good Friday. We went in to see if they had a map of town. Although tempted to buy an Irish book of ancestry, I controlled myself, because I can barely roll my luggage now. In the process of examining the various tables of Irish lore, Schwarck discovered a large hardcover, entitled Who's Who in Ireland. There, in the C's, for all to behold, was Patrick Cotter born 1761, Kinsale celebrity. He was a striking eight foot three giant who paraded himself around local villages as a sideshow until he died at age forty. How ironic that in all likelihood, my celebrated ancestor is an abnormally large, conceited human, who apparently died of hugeness at an early age.

We found an excellent city map and Schwarck grabbed my arm and we nearly ran to the Quayside.

"There it is, the Quayside! Hurry up and get over there in front of the sign so I can get your picture. Your relatives back home will be so excited when they see where you are."

My quirky relatives would be more fired up to see a picture of me standing next to Patrick Cotter's gargantuan shorts. She had already raced up the stairs and was turning the doorbell by the time I stepped away from the sign. A tall, balding, elderly man, who was neatly dressed, appeared in the doorway, looking as if he was just roused from his morning nap.

"Excuse me, is Mary Cotter in?" inquired my effervescent pal.

I moved her aside and stepped in front of her. After all, these were My Cotters.

"She's gone….won't be back for a two days."

"Oh, she's gone for two days? Is there a time, after that, when I can meet her? I am Kathy, I mean Kathleen Cotter Crawford and I am here from the states and trying to locate Irish Cotters. Are you her husband?"

"Yep."

Obviously a man of few words and Schwarck informed me at that point that he, not Mary, was probably my true relative.

"Mr. Cotter, do you know anything about your father's people?"

"Name's Joe. Don't know much, except my father came from a long line of bachelors."

I felt slightly bewildered for a moment. I've never been too quick on the pick-up of these things. Hugh frequently torments me with quizzes like "Who's buried in Grant's tomb?"

"Geeze, Crawford, this guy has got to be related to you. His father came from a long line of bachelors…that's hilarious!"

Joe invited us into his parlor because he said it was more civilized. It was also a fabulous photo op.

Joe knew very little about his people except that they were Danes who had probably blown off course and ended up in this harbor. He guessed they were tired of the plundering trade and just decided to stay. They even fought with the locals in the Battle of Kinsale. I expect that the giant Cotter's were in the front lines supporting the little people of Kinsale who probably fought with sticks and fairy dust.

The front doorbell rang and Joe excused himself to answer accommodation questions. The phone started ringing, too, so we knew our little visit had come to a halt. We left thanking him profusely, and I knew without a doubt that he was one of mine.

I really don't look anything like these Kinsalers, but Daddy looked like the son of Joe and I am pretty sure that the obnoxious giant circus bruiser, Patrick, was kinfolk.

I made a quick decision and announced to Schwarck, "Let's go back to the bookstore and get a book about the Danes. I bet they're the real Vikings. Then we'll go to the churchyard cemetery and look for Patrick."

The more I thought about it, the charismatic Patrick probably passed on his freak show genes to my Cotter relatives. Sideshow attractions must have been an inbred trait. Uncle Earnest Cotter, middle son of another Patrick Cotter in Michigan, had once purchased a petrified woman named Hazel from a sideshow at the State Fair. He would hose her off and haul her out of her special wagon at family reunions. He liked her a lot. Hazel's little bio said she was notorious in the early 1900s and had frequently been in trouble with the law. For some unknown reason, she had accidentally mummified herself by ingesting a deadly combination of alcohol and medications. Wonder what happened to Hazel when Uncle Earnest died?

I want to go to sleep at The Hillside tonight thinking of my people in this foreign place. The Norsemen were assuredly strong, muscular, and courageous. They were and still are the community leaders, chieftains, captains and mayors of cities. Oh, yeah and also gigantic circus freaks.

CHAPTER 14

KIN I PET YOUR DOGGIE?

Just because something is small and fluffy and tied up, does not mean it can't tear your face off. In this case, it was a hairy pooch tied to the legs of a bench in front of Kinsale's Grocery Store. A humorless matron wearing black from head to toe was sitting next to the pooch.

"Is it okay to pet the dog? Oooo, look how cute, Crawford. It's holding a little ball in its mouth, probably to keep it from barking. You should always ask for permission and then just hold your hand out like this, for it to sniff."

I am used to Schwarck's worship of creatures. I have been with her at a cottage where she set a trap for an annoying raccoon which was destroying everything in the cottage. When it was trapped, she talked to it for twenty minutes and then released it. I couldn't believe it. We had worked on that trap for two days. Later we saw a fresh carcass by the road, and I pointed out to her that she let it go so that it could be hit by a semi on the highway.

She was already bending over, reaching for the little wolverine-like face. Any moment she would begin some doting doggy-speak and scratch behind its ears. The woman on the bench didn't say anything. Suddenly, the ball dropped and there was some ferocious, pissed off snapping and lunging along with loud, infuriated, snarly barking. We both fell backwards on the sidewalk, nervously clutching our chest.

"Hhoouooo! Wow! Did you see that?" Schwarck angrily turned to the blasé' matron yelling; "Your dog tried to bite me!"

"H'es… naht….. ma ……dog!" stated the matron flatly.

"Well, vicious animals like that should not be out in public. They should be kept at home or in a cage!" she stated emphatically to the woman. The matron just looked off and totally ignored the situation.

I recall a similar scene in The Pink Panther and it was hilarious, but this is happening to us and it isn't all that amusing…..at the moment. What if we had been bitten or mauled by this vicious little canine? We would have to self-treat puncture wounds and all we have with us are tiny band-aids, antiseptic cream, and a plethora of extra long panty liners. None of the aforementioned could ward off killer bacteria from animals that have an affinity for endlessly licking their butt. I'm confident that later on, after two or three glasses of wine, we'll relive this event and it will be sidesplitting.

Even though she's usually fun loving and mild-mannered, Schwarck can become furious and unrelenting by what she views as injustice. I've stood in line with her at an airport when two elderly people stepped up to the front of the line and she verbally called them out. "Hey, you two. What do you think the rest of us are doing here?" Everyone else in line went mute, but I suspect were inwardly cheering her on.

I thought she might step into the store to make an announcement over the PA: "Would the owner of the wild biting dog out front, please report to the store entrance immediately!" Instead, she just gave a glaring look at the door and said, "Well….let's…..just get going. We've got to find the Tourist Bureau to book our next hotel and pick up brochures on touring. Wait till you see all the things these bureaus can do for you. I just love them. They are so helpful."

The Kinsale Tourist Bureau was housed in a large friendly looking log building with picture windows and a welcoming ramp in front; an earmark of accommodating services. The lights were on inside, but the door wouldn't open. A sign proclaimed; "Welcome - Open for Business" as well as the open hours, which were now. After much jiggling and peering inside, I determined that the door was not just stuck, but locked up tight. We sort of stood there on the little entranceway contemplating our next move, when down at the end of the block we noticed a uniformed female in heels heading very purposefully in our direction. Up the ramp she came, and we expressed our gratitude that she was not closed Good Friday. She informed us that she was going to be closed in a few minutes for the Good Friday Service. She had been shopping for Easter earlier and that is why the door was locked.

Okay…they say they are open but they're locked and pretty soon they are going to officially close and lock. Very accommodating, my ass!

"We're from the states and just met your mayor. My friend here has the same last name, Cotter, and we just met your mayor, Joe Cotter. My friend here has the same last name, Cotter, and her dad looks exactly like Joe Cotter, had her dad lived that long. We need to find some tours and also book a hotel."

It's painfully clear from where I stand, that this nimrod from the warm and friendly Tourist Bureau has zero interest in my relationship to the Cotter dynasty or our need to book tours and accommodations. She is uncommunicative and turning off lights. I wanted to spend quality time perusing all the souvenir shelves. I was in my zone smelling Irish soaps and punching all the Irish CD numbers to get song samples when she started shooing us toward the front door like she was herding ducks.

"Yu ladies shud jest gah outside an wait fur the Roadrunner. If ees' got enuf folks, ee'll take ya' on a tur taday. Turs start at 2 P.M. Ya' pay when ya' get onboard."

With that curt bit of information, she pointed to the front porch, then closed and locked the door behind us. We decided that since there was no indication of a van or Roadrunner sign, we might as well use this time to find a place to find the Internet place, then grab a sandwich, and come back to the bureau before 2 P.M.

Internet access appears to be a relatively new phenomenon in this town because the closest place for us to compute was in a small one-girl insurance office. A polite young woman greeted us and pointed to two computers in an adjoining room. In only a few short moments, I was receiving my very first messages from home. Hugh was sending a tragic "love-you-miss-you-miss-you-lots-kiss-kiss-kissy" messages and Don Schwarck was sending a very telling message that the Escapades Tour business takes up an exorbitant amount of time which he does not have. We sent back our replies and I broadened my email reader list to include some close friends as well as family.

TO: FRIENDS-at home and abroad AND FAMILY BACK HOME

FROM: KATHLEEN COTTER-CRAWFORD

SUBJECT: WILL EASTER NEVER END?

My legs are aching along with all my other parts. My fanny pack is now as big as my actual fanny because of all the extra stuff I must tote around all day. We are in southern Ireland in a very picturesque town called Kinsale. The entire countryside shuts down for Maundy Thursday, Good Friday, Easter Saturday, Easter Sunday and Good Monday. This interferes considerably with our eating schedule.

This town is full of Cotters…even the mayor is a Cotter. I'm going to the cemetery to take a picture of the grave of one of the town celebrities—Patrick Cotter—who died at an early age of hugeness. Prior to his death he was a circus freak, so I'm confident that he is one of our ancestors.

We are having a hard time understanding the language…. which we have discovered is actually English. People here pepper their sentences with things like "deadly" (which means brilliant or fabulous) and "red-arsed" (which means very drunk).

We are going on a "Tur" turday if we kin queue-up properly.

Things I have learned in the past two days:

- Look to the left before stepping into the street…no… look …really…. good!
- Make sure to review all shower instructions before stepping in to a watered down metal stall with electrical components.
- No one here seems to have the need for antiperspirant or to cover up their pasty lumpy midriff.
- The warm and friendly Tourist Bureau is never open fur business.
- Cute fluffy mutts gripping a ball in their teeth can still rip your face off if you get too close.
- Irish have heat in their homes and businesses but they don't like to turn it on.

Yurs, Kathleen

After a quick stop for hot soup, Irish bread, and lager, we headed back to the closed Tourist Bureau, and we saw a white minivan parked in front displaying a Roadrunner sign. The van door was closed and no one was inside. We surveyed the area for the responsible Roadrunner driver. There were two smokers loitering outdoors two buildings away, but no one else was in sight. After ten minutes, one of the smokers approached us and asked if we were looking for a tour. We nodded and Schwarck began searching in her wallet for Euros. I hurriedly whispered, “Wait! Schwarck! Don’t get out any money yet. We don’t even know if this guy is the Roadrunner. This one could be scammin’ us!”

“Ohhhh, yeah”; She replied thoughtfully.

“If ya ladies r’ lookin’ fer the tur, I canna take ya’. I need at least four people.”

I was really desperate for our first Irish tour, so thought I’d apply a little Yankee ingenuity; “Okay…..look……what if you thought you had four people in the van because you collected money for four. You really only have us two… but… you see…..you have the money for four!” Who wouldn’t buy this free extra money idea?

“Nah, I canna!”

End of discussion? How hard headed are these people? Even if more people show up, I figure this Roadrunner bonehead would just blow past all mystical sights going, “Beep-Beep-no time for photos-that’ll be two hundred Euros each! Ya’ ladees hav a nice daaaa’! BEEP-BEEP!”

Good fortune shined down on us, however; two wispy, willowy older women with the most towering bee hive hairdos ever displayed, stepped up to the bus and the driver escorted them up and into the front seat. He then sat down in the driver's seat. These two ladies were remarkably well dressed, wearing white gloves, raincoats, expensive knitwear, pearls, black handbag over one arm, and umbrella on the other. Their enormous hives were completely covered by oversized gauzy scarves.

We were still standing outside by the front of the minibus, so I stepped to the open door and inquired, "Do you have enough people now? There's those two, plus us two! Can we get on the bus?"

"Yep."

Huh? If I had not asked, would he have continued waiting for two more tourists to appear, and if they did, would he have just departed with those four? Maybe there's some supernatural Celtic power about the total of four over here and they have to be the right four! We got on the bus nodding to the quiet prissy women, paid our money and each took a seat. I got out my new blank notepad ready for book data and readied my camera for action.

Our guide, Neil, turned out to be one of the most engaging and informative guides ever encountered. His greatest desire was to show us the "real Gaelic Ireland" and the breathtaking Irish seaside. We were mesmerized.

Our first stop was to point out the exact location where the Lusitania sank on its voyage from New York to Liverpool on May 7 of 1915. It had been struck by a

German torpedo off the Old Head of Kinsale and sank in minutes with a total of 1,959 people on board; 1,195 perished. Locals were paid one pound sterling for each body they retrieved. Several of the victims are buried in Kinsale's churchyard.

We stopped at ancient Celtic sites known to have magnetic healing forces. One of these places featured a statue of the Virgin Mother in a little grotto, which Neil said used to vibrate every evening at dusk and adoring visitors would come to see her undulations. So many came, that bleachers, porta potties, and refreshment stands were installed to accommodate the hordes of worshipers. Unfortunately, vandals defaced the statue and since that day, the virgin had quit gyrating. I'm normally a skeptic, so I bet someone unplugged it.

We traveled through charming wee villages with lyrical names such as Ballinspittle, Lipatrick, Clonakilty, and Scilly (pronounced "silly"). There were craggy rock formations, Norman strongholds, castle ruins, vast ocean views and fields with mysterious Labyrinth patterns in stone. I'm sure these were the vistas that inspired my favorite smutty historical romance novelists.

Neil shared some personal history and political viewpoints regarding the difficulty for Irish residents to buy a home. Developers were purchasing all the available tracts of land and building condos and holiday time-shares. Homes in the new developments are sold for an exorbitant high price, mostly to wealthy foreigners. It was at that time that the two placid ladies in the front came to life and drawled, "We are he-ah from At-lan-ta cawse ou-r hus-bands won a con-do in a char-it-ty raf-fle. We don't lie-kit muu-ch, cawse it's sooo awe-ful co-old and win-dy he-ah and there's nuth-thin ta' dewww."

The slow drawn out cadence of the Georgia peach's speaking was hypnotizing but also exceptionally annoying. That's right! It's their fault that Neil and his neighbors can't buy a house in their homeland. These Georganians were taking up space on Irish real estate and they didn't even like it here! We were rankled by these two.

When the tour was finished, we bubbled over with praise for Neil and the fabulous excursion. We gave him a hefty tip and apologized for the shallow Georgia peaches. We disembarked and headed out, lost in chatter about the wonderful day. We were anxious to hunt up an Internet so we could tell family and friends what we had seen so far, then on to dinner. I'm already thinking about Irish stew.

The Curtain Electric Shop and Hardware displayed a tiny sign offering "High Speed Internet", so we stepped in to get on-line and our next accommodations. We were still following Dublin Sean's suggestions and wanted to find a Bed and Breakfast in Dingle. There were two nice clean Dell computers in the corner among fry pans, curling irons, Tampax, and charcoal grills. We paid the owners a few Euros and within a half-hour we had read our mail and Schwarck had made sleeping arrangements in Dingle.

We then found a quaint hotel across the street that had a lovely smelling dining room. The Irish bread was phenomenal, and we chose a fish feast which was chased down with our new favorite, Kinsale Lager, followed up by an exquisite Rhubarb/Apple Tartlet with English cream. There was no way I was capable of walking up to the

Hillside so we called the jitney again. We also asked him to pick us up tomorrow morning because we would be leaving town after breakfast.

When we arrived back at The Hillside, the conservatory was abuzz with new guests. Two separate groups of Americans had come by car, which was part of their package. I inquired as to the ease of driving over here and all indicated they had a few unnerving close calls. One said she had a slight accident, not her fault because a tire came off when she hit the curb causing her to veer off the road into a stone fenced pasture. She was missing a front bumper and had some other dings, but she was pleased to report that no other car was involved. She said her son had been up in the room since they arrived feeling nauseous from the drive. Another's rental car had a giant dent and gash on the passenger side. They all highly recommended the driving experience. It did seem like something we should at least try for THE BOOK!

One of the new guests was an Irish lady who reminded me of an older plumper version of Princess Fergie. She prefers "traveling alone" and wants to know why Americans take so many vit-a-mins. None of us Americans had a good answer for the vit-a-min question, except to tell her that we suspect we're nutrition deprived which I suppose is hard to believe when you actually see us in person. I told her that most of my medications relate to arthritis and she proclaimed to have a "sure cure" for all arthritis suffering.

I am prone to medical experimentation; in fact, I had already been a willing participant in an arthritis cure prescribed by two 81-year-old twins. That cure involved soaking raisins in gin for months and keeping them in baby food jars in your refrigerator. "You must eat 13 raisins twice a day for the rest of your life," they instructed. Going through that many bottles of Beefeaters Gin was getting kind of expensive and I really didn't see much improvement. I mostly just sat around waiting till I could take my next dose. These were the same two people who wanted me to drink 1/2 cup of vinegar twice a day for prevention of something, but I can't remember what. I did not participate in that experiment because I'm still partial to the raisin/gin cure.

For what it's worth, this is the "sure cure" for arthritis as prescribed by the red haired Irish lady from Kinvarra. For God's sake, check with your doctor before doing anything or nothing at all. You might also want to pre dial 911 before you submerge yourself in a tub. It's a three-week regimen, during which time you cannot consume anything with caffeine or alcohol in it, which pretty much takes the fun out of everything for me.

Five times a day, you must drink the following mixed together:

1 tsp hot water 1 tsp black molasses 1 tsp lemon 1 tsp honey

You must also immerse yourself in a bath of hot water with a cupful of zinc every night before bed, then wrap your naked self in large bath towels and sleep that way all night.

I have not tried this cure yet, even though she was very convincing. I don't have any bath towels that large. I am contemplating a return to the gin-soaked raisins.

Another guest from Maryland was a twenty-year employee of the US Government and worked for the National Health Institute writing educational materials.

"Oh, wow!" I blurted. "I just returned from a conference in D.C. and your Surgeon General spoke. He was awesome. I loved that guy. He is so inspiring! Don't you think he's the best Surgeon General we have ever had?"

"I really don't know who he is," the Maryland guest admitted.

"What? You're kidding, right? You don't even know his name is Richard H. Carmona and you work for him?"

Schwarck could tell by my demeanor that this evening chatter could get dicey and should come to a close.

Schwarck started ushering me toward the door; "Well, nice meeting all of you. We're really tired—had a full day. And we have to pack for leaving tomorrow morning. I guess we'll see you all at breakfast."

Yes, I was tired, and I definitely did not want to chat any more with a federal government employee who was so out-of-it and oblivious, even in the midst of nationwide life threatening health issues. "If a lot of people outside of Washington know Surgeon General Carmona. Wouldn't you think that if you were in the same building and he was your boss, you'd at least know his name? He's the Surgeon General, for God's sake! I bet she even gets memos with his name at the top. I don't want my tax dollars to pay her salary I'm going to email the Surgeon General tomorrow and tell him his staff is lame."

"You know, Crawford, you should have wine with dinner instead of lager, I don't think beer agrees with you. Nighty, night!" Schwarck teasingly said.

"Hey, did you tell me we are going to Dingle next? That's funny! It sounds like something that hangs off the back of sheep. Are we staying in a Bed and Breakfast again?"

A sleepy Schwarck said, "Yeah…Dingle. We're at a new place. I asked for the first floor. It's called the Alpine House."

"Alpine? What are you thinking? We're on top of Mt. Everest here at The Hillside! Where the hell do you imagine the Alpine House will perch? Schwarck, did you hide my Salampas?"

All I heard was Schwarck's sleeping sounds, "Zzzzzzzzzz, Pffhhttt!"

CHAPTER 15

DARE TO DINGLE?

Our last breakfast with Margaret and guests of The Hillside was highly entertaining as our flustered, knit suited innkeeper was in constant motion shutting doors behind thoughtless guests who were entering the dining room. She stood before us with pencil and pad poised to take our orders while backing up to shut the door with her heel, then returning to our side. She was tapping her toes in agitation while we debated whether to opt for the Muesli with eggs and tomatoes or the pancakes. Once again, she did not write a thing on her pad but nodded impatiently when we finally told her and hurried off to prod her cooking serf into action.

Our hot orders arrived and Schwarck's pancakes turned out to be eggs and bacon with tomatoes and mushrooms and I got oatmeal instead of eggs. I don't know why she even asks for our order. Maybe Kitchen Dennis's leg chains were chafing this morning, causing him to be distracted when she turned in our request. We ate all that we could and departed the dining room, leaving the door ajar to see how long it would take for her to close it.

The jitney was punctual and we reluctantly departed the quirky Hillside but were excited to see what was in store for us in Dingle. We were dropped off downtown in front of a minute' sign that said "bus" next to a magnificent large yellow sign depicting a bent-over man and woman with canes, crossing a street. At least over here they let you know where old limpers should cross. That'd go over big in the states with all our levels of political correctness.

In less than an hour we arrived in Cork for the transfer to Dingle. The depot was so crowded; we chose to wait outside in the chilly spring air so that we could get a jump on other passengers. As we were poised for our bus strategy of me getting in line and Schwarck tossing the luggage in the bay, a plump mature woman dressed in a black wool coat, dress, handbag, and headscarf approached me with a very serious look on her face. She leaned in to request, "Two Euros for a bottle of black lemonade?" This seemed like some kind of alcohol derivative and I wanted no part of it, so I frowned at her and shook my head. She moved on, but I saw her heading for Schwarck who had just returned outside after checking the bus schedule. Once again the woman leaned in toward Schwarck and made her pitch. Thankfully, the woman received another frown and less emphatic shaking of the head. Shortly, Schwarck made her way back to me and said, "I didn't know anyone here would be collecting Euros for the Battle on Aides, maybe we should help."

"What? You mean that woman who came up to you asked for Euros for The Battle on Aids? She asked me for Euros for a bottle of black lemonade!"

It was at that moment, along with the sad sympathetic look on Schwarck's face, that I realized not only do I have arthritis in every joint and may be going blind with macular problems, NOW I am more than likely losing my hearing! In hindsight, The Battle on Aids sounds remarkably similar to a bottle of black lemonade. I wonder how many other inquiries I have misunderstood in the past few years. This entire trip could have been a horrible misunderstanding. Maybe Schwarck had never said, "Do you want to go on a five week sabbatical?" She might have actually said, "Do you want to take a peek at my new patio?" And I said, "Yes, buy the tickets!"

We watched as the matronly gypsy sidled up to a frail looking elderly couple and leaned in. Apparently because they, too, were hard of hearing, they yelled back her request for all to hear: "What?" they shouted. "You need two Euros for a phone call 'cause you lost your handbag?" Her handbag was hanging over her arm, but this was not apparent to the old folks who began to dig through their pockets for loose change. Fortunately, our bus arrived before Schwarck could put the gypsy in a headlock and wrestle her to the ground in an attempt to get back the old folk's cash.

I secured our seats and began to unpack the snacks and get out reading materials.

I was already on my second book of this trip, Lost Nation by Jeffrey Lent. I loved it because it was an exciting story about a young woman who was won in a poker game during the westward expansion of the US. Schwarck was on page ten of her first book, Outlander by Diana

Gabaldon, about a reluctant time-traveler sent back to 18th century Scotland.

"I bet you'd read faster if it wasn't science fiction," I informed Schwarck. "That stuff is too abstract. You should read historical novels. My stories really happened somewhere, even if they are fiction, they are based on truth…things that actually happened to real people."

We have had an ongoing reading rivalry for years. Both of us buy lots of books, but she seldom reads one. Often she gives them to me so that I will read them and tell her what they were about.

I don't know why she describes my books as "smutty and slutty". The last one she handed to me from her little library was entitled "My Horizontal Life" and describes a collection of spectacular and bizarre one-night stands. The cover touts the author as writing like Judy Blume, if Judy was into vodka, Ecstasy, and sleeping with midgets! That book was hardly thought provoking or profound.

The swaying motion of the bus around numerous curves made reading difficult, but Schwarck managed to get all the way to page 12 before giving up and starting to doze. For me it was snack time!

I am a product of my past when it comes to riding in any vehicle. As a child, there was always a southern picnic being unpacked before we were out of the driveway. My grandmother always traveled with us on any trip, and she sat in the back seat parceling out sandwiches and fried chicken with abandonment. No drinks were allowed because that would mean we would have to make a bathroom stop somewhere between Michigan and Tennessee. We even carried gas and oil with us, and I suspect the fumes were the main reason we kids slept all the way south.

If my mammy offered you bologna and you wanted tuna, she would tuck the bologna under her two hundred pound thigh and hand you the tuna. She once sat on a rejected bologna sandwich all the way through five states. That circular bologna stain stayed with the Pontiac until it was traded in four years later. Those were the good old days.

The rolling green Irish hillsides and the flocks of shaggy sheep seemed untouched by habitation. Most homes were gathered together in tiny colorful villages. People were rarely seen. I wondered what types lived within the walls of these diminutive cottages. They must strangle the weak here, because I haven't seen one wheelchair, walker, or handicapped person. Also, where are the morbidly obese? Maybe there is only one and she is sitting next to Schwarck on a bus going to Dingle.

Five hours later, we arrived in Dingle to low hanging clouds and piercing icy winds. There was no bus station, just a bus sign at the curb of a main street. Dingle was not a tidy looking seaside village like Kinsale. It had a no-frills toughness about it. The buildings were mostly dark colored and every other one was a pub. There were no people on the sidewalks at 4 P.M., and we began to look around for signs directing us to the Alpine House. Off in the distance and very far on a hill, we both saw it at the same time. There it was: Alpine House.

"This is not funny, Schwarck! I bet our B & B is a mile up that hill and not close to any restaurants or stores and I'm seriously getting shorter everyday from small fractures in my spine." I spouted.

"Quit, cher' bellyaching! I told you there'd be a lot of walking over here. I asked for a first floor room because of your knees. That'll be good, right?" She said apologetically.

When we finally attained the summit and entered Alpine House, our glasses steamed up at the contrast from the frigid outdoors. Alpine House was new and pine smelling. A young ruddy cheeked man handed us the keys and pointed to the stairs uttering the fateful words; "Yur ruum is at the top. Will ya' be needin' any help?"

I was stupefied as I stretched my neck to gaze up the multiple winding staircases.

"No, we've got it!" Schwarck cheerily reported.

After four flights of huffing and puffing, with Schwarck running back down to encourage me upward, I arrived at the top landing, hopelessly out of breath.

"Are you all right, Crawford? When I booked it, I told them you had a knee replacement and arthritis, but maybe the top floor is all they had left." Schwarck was again apologetic.

I was sure that my nose was bleeding, but I stumbled forward toward the door. When our metal key was inserted into the lock, we opened the door to behold pure Austria. It was a "Hills Are Alive" moment. All of the furniture was rustic heavy pine along with log walls and wood floors. It was large enough for the entire Von Trapp family to put on their puppet show. It smelled potently clean and woody. There were two beds; one fluffy looking queen size with a lovely bed lamp and a small twin tucked under an overhanging dormer.

"Uh, oh…which bed do you want, Crawford?"

I said I didn't care, but I knew my swollen arthritic torso should be reclining on the comfy looking queen.

"Well, we need to be fair about it," she said, "so, I'll hold this Bewleys Tea packet in one hand behind my back and the other hand will have a coffee packet. I'll mix' em up and then you pick. Bewleys gets the little bed."

"Okay, left hand."

"Oops! Geeze! You get the little bed! Let's get unpacked and get down to the Tourist Office, then find some dinner. We better look for a laundromat, too!" Schwarck was enthusiastic.

"Maybe I shouldn't eat anything tonight cuz I think my stout Viking body might not fit on that baby bed. I'm sure I'll knock myself out on the low ceiling. And look at that lamp. Why should you get a light for nighttime reading? What a waste!"

I entered the bathroom and unpacked my significant number of toiletries, placing them on a wide shelf in front of her few aromatic creams, brushes, and containers of vitamins. That handy shelf was in front of a push out window, which I predict, will be opened, if I eat fried fish with Guinness again tonight. Maybe I should just spend a little quality time in here right now before we go to town.

I opened the window anticipating a need for ventilation. Unfortunately, as the window swung out, Schwarck simultaneously opened the door of the room. That action created a wind tunnel of such magnitude that all of Schwarck's cosmetics and vitamins were sucked off the shelf before I could grab them. They floated momentarily, and then plopped on a parking lot four stories below.

"Um, Schwarck!" I yelled out at her. "I just opened the window in here and all your stuff got sucked out…sorry! You better get down to the parking lot right away cause I think I see a dog heading for your vitamin C. Hurry! Some of it is blowing away!"

I heard her thundering down four stories and observed her running all over the parking lot retrieving her precious supplements, creams, and hairbrush. I helped by yelling and pointing out where they all went. Ten minutes later a red faced and short-winded Schwarck reappeared clutching all of her sullied and wet possessions.

"Isn't that weird? None of my stuff got sucked out…just yours. I think we're going to have to be more careful with the window."

She looked at me suspiciously, but returned all of her stuff to the shelf.

After some additional unpacking, we decided to leave the room and head downtown in search of the Tourist Bureau. Walking downtown was nippy but pleasant for no other reason except that we were going downhill. Also, it is so heartening to be unhampered by luggage and backpacks. As usual, I was plodding along but ahead of her.

"Well, here's a surprise for you, Schwarck. The friendly Tourist Office is closed and it's not even 5 P.M. yet."

"What's going on? These places were always open last time I was in Ireland." She paused a moment to ponder the dilemma. "Well, why don't we just go over to that purple pub and get an early dinner. We can come back here tomorrow morning. We need to write tonight anyway, and I want to show you how to put pictures on your computer. Wait till you see how we can put music with the pictures and make a slide show. You're going to love that! I think a saw a sign in that gas station next to our hotel that said they do laundry, so we should stop on the way back to see about it."

The pub food was remarkably like our last five dinners: lager, fish, chips, and huge round peas. Signs on the pub walls indicated that this town was famous for its Irish music and I suppose, if we could ever stay up late enough, we would get to hear some. As we left the pub, Schwarck noticed a sign on a lawn that said "Hostel".

"Oh, my, gosh! Look at that! Let's go in there and see if they have any rooms. I bet it would be a lot cheaper than where we're staying."

"Well, my sister Barbara told me that we would not like staying in a hostel over here. We're too old for it. You have to be willing to share your bedroom and bathroom with complete strangers. Plus, there wouldn't be a way to lock our stuff up. Remember, we have to be careful."

As we entered the door, a ruggedly handsome young man, probably in his twenties, greeted us warmly and invited us into the living room. He said his name was Chad and he was from Colorado. He led us past a rack of mismatched throws and army blankets next to the door. My guess is that you just pick out your blanket and go roll up somewhere. There were approximately five guitars leaning against a ragged living room couch and plaid chair.

Schwarck was drooling over Colorado Chad and chatting him up like a teenager, acting all interested in the energizing world of hostelling. While she prattled on, I scrutinized the place. There was a middle-aged woman sitting at the kitchen table, hunkered protectively over a cracked cereal bowl. The kitchen was tiny and Chad explained that everyone provides their own food and puts it in the fridge or cupboard with their name on it. Like that's gonna work. Staff lunches at our office were pilfered all the time by people we knew, so guess what total strangers passing through town, are gonna do?

"Schwarck, we have to go now to check out the laundry before it closes."

"Don't you want to reserve a night or two here? There'll be singing. You love to sing."

"Uh, no! We gotta go! Thanks, Chad. Maybe we'll catch ya' on the slopes in Colorado someday."

We exited with Schwarck sighing and offering little words of appreciation all the way out the door, with a promise that we might return.

"Did you see all those guitars in there, Schwarck? There were five of them and probably five people who play all night long. That vacant bedroom has bunk beds and one bathroom for the entire upper floor. I'd have to sleep with my computer and camera between my legs. That is, if I could ever get to sleep with all the racket. Also, how do you think you'd feel hauling out your Muesli, pastries, fruits, and coffees while starving backpackers are staring across the table chewing on their shoe leather? Did you look at the blankets? Our old horse blankets on the farm were cleaner and we never washed them!"

"So….you don't want to stay there at all then?" she inquired sadly.

"Are you serious? Ah… no!"

Next on our agenda was to hunt for an Internet Café, so we could tell people where we are. The wind and dampness was paralyzing. Spring in Dingle is about as delightful as it was in Kinsale. We popped into a hardware store to see if they sold any warm clothing. Schwarck said she needed a new pair of flannel-lined jeans or maybe snow pants. She had been wearing her old ones for over four days. They did have regular jeans in her size for forty dollars US. I thought that price was astronomical, but she would have gladly paid four hundred for anything that could keep her warmer. She got her jeans and directions to a little Internet place on the next block.

TO: Friends and Relative back home

SENT: Tuesday, April 13

SUBJECT: Don't Dawdle in Dingle

Here we are in Dingle, Ireland, and we are freezing! The trip over from Kinsale through the countryside was beautiful, but I was counting sheep most of the way when I wasn't snacking!

Things I have learned so far:

- I should have packed more warm clothes and lots of gloves. We must eat more to stay warm. I have worn my raincoat everyday and Schwarck has worn her flannel lined jeans everyday since we left home. We might have to cut them off her!

- We have ingested so much Muesli and grainy Irish bread that our intestines keep us awake at night trying to process it all. The innards noises are loud and scary.

- The Alpine House (our new B & B) is on the highest peak in all of Ireland, and the owner wanted us to have the best view, so he gave us a room at the very top of the fourth floor. I hate this guy. He probably hates me too because he was holding this adorable five-year-old and I asked him how old she was. He informed me the kid was a boy named Willem.

- There must be a shortage of washcloths in Ireland, because we got only one for the two of us. I plan to use it first!

- If we take a nap tomorrow, we might be able to stay awake until nine to hear some Irish music at a local pub.

- The gas station has a laundromat inside and you can only buy jeans at the hardware store. Things are utterly strange here. Schwarck tried to get me to stay at a hostel where you pick out your blanket and guitar when you enter. I said no! Most of the current residents looked like they had appeared in Deliverance, except for the handsome host Chad, who really wanted us to bunk in upstairs with four other hatchet murderers.

- We are here for three nights and hope to see the Dingle Peninsula before we go, if the weather is clear enough. Maybe it never clears.

- Dingle's friendly Tourist Bureau is closed just like the Kinsale one. They don't expect tourists at the bureau.

- Saw a great sign on the road today: "Large Plant Crossing".

Gotta go now!

Kathleen

On the way back to Alpine House, we made a stop at the gas station that had a small sign indicating they do laundry. We were met at the counter by an amazing apparition. I presume this thing is a laundry attendant. He or she was outfitted in a spectacularly smudged lab coat that strained around a considerable girth. He was also wearing big goggles and long rubber gloves. One fist held a thick stick, which I imagine is used for stirring dirty duds or maybe for lifting hot nylon underwear out of the dryer. In the station garage area, there were two gigantic rumbling turbine front loaders. This setup reminded me of the huge free dryer Hugh once brought home for me. It dried the clothes like a blow torch. You needed a stick to lift out your nylon underwear or it would cling to you like hot glue. Some of my underwear just melted away and all you had left was a rubber band for your waist. I do, however, believe the flames killed all bacteria in the process.

I have never seen anyone so shielded from pollution. Could there be some epidemic over here? We inquired as to how we submit our laundry for the disinfection treatment. He told us that dungarees brought in today before five will be ready by 1 P.M. tomorrow. No need to separate whites from darks as everything goes in the same vat. Our dirty American wardrobe will no doubt be somersaulting with the local's clothing most of who are fishermen who have been at sea wearing the same garb for months at a time.

"I don't like this, Schwarck. I bet our pants will be appearing at the Dingle fish market or on eBay. We'll have to wear old fishy stained knickers that they give us back instead of our own. Everything is going to meld into the same color, too! I've also got a weird feeling that the Oompa Loompas are out back sorting socks and trying on people's undies," I countered.

"I think it's just the way they do laundry over here. Our stuff will be fine. We can drop off all of our dirties on the way to the Tourist Bureau tomorrow morning."

"If we drop off all of our dirties, then we'll have to go to the Tourist Bureau naked! Of course it shouldn't matter if I'm naked there because no other people ever go to that office but us!"

CRAWFORD READY TO LEAVE KINSALE

SCHWARCK FREEZIN FOR FERGIE, DINGLE

CRAWFORD—ONE OF MANY CLIMBS, DINGLE

CARRICK-A-REDE, NORTH IRELAND

MUSIC TONIGHT, DOOLIN

BELFAST BUDDIES IN THE FERRY TERMINAL

LUNCH IN THE PARK, EDINBURGH

KEIGHLEY STATION, SUTTON DAY TRIP

VIRGIN CRAWFORD, EDINBURGH

SCHWARCK'S ROOM FRESHENER REACTION, BARROW

CRAWFORD & SCHWARCK AT BEAUTY SHOP, STAMFORD

THE BOYS WELCOME THE BABES HOME, DETROIT METRO AIRPORT

CHAPTER 16

LET'S NOT DAWDLE IN DINGLE

Breakfast in the sunny Alpine House dining room was a serve yourself buffet and quite tasty, but we missed the personal attention of the uptight Margaret and her kitchen serf. We had a good view of the street from the dining room and walkers were bundled up to their eyeballs. It looked like today's weather would not be cooperative with our plans to walk around town.

After breakfast we dressed in as many layers as we could to combat the day's dampness and frigid temperature. Our first stop would be the laundromat, then the Tourist Bureau for a tour reservation. On our way downhill, we dropped the dirties off with goggle guy. I really don't know how he figures out whose stuff belongs to whom. It might be kind of fun to see what we get back from the laundry.

Well, here's a bit of surprising news: We made the frosty twelve block hike down to the Tourist Office and it is closed this morning, even though the sign says it is open today between 10-5. Another door sign indicated that if we wished to have a tour of the famous Dingle Peninsula, we should proceed up the hill to the gas station/ laundromat.

Our eyes locked in utter disbelief. We came all the way down here again to this irksome office of tourism and it is once again closed, but even worse, it directs us back up the hill to get a tour from the laundromat we just left.

We grumped, but agreed that we had no choice but to march back up again. Our walk back up to the gas station/ laundromat/tour office through sleet and wind shears was not sprightly in the least. There was a person at the end of the laundry counter, not wearing goggles, so we approached him regarding tours. He nodded his assent and began to recite all that he would not do for us. He would not take us unless there are four passengers, but in the event there are not four people, he will take us, if we pay for four. Also, the roads are so dangerous that he will not talk to us, and we cannot go unless the sleet lets up.

"Can we pay now?" questioned an eager Schwarck already getting our credit card out of her hip pocket.

Has she totally lost her mind? She wants to hastily offer up our money to a tour guy operating in the gas station/ laundromat for a spine-tingling two-hour van excursion on icy roads so treacherous, no one in the vehicle is allowed to speak or even cough unexpectedly. And it will be a mute tour at that! We will not be told what we saw just before we careen off the cliff.

It is my opinion that warnings are usually issued after some poor sap has already experienced a serious problem. We've all seen those warnings on things, like the warning on an iron that says: "Do not iron the clothing on your body." Someone has actually done this before and sued the company with the result being the company posting this obvious warning. Therefore, I believe people have plunged off a Dingle cliff because they interrupted the tour guide's driving with a question and he turned around to answer. Boom! This ride today might be a little too edgy for me. With any luck at all, the sleet will not let up and we won't be able to go. I'll sincerely pray for that. We stepped across the street into a couple of wool shops and bought warm scarves and wool mittens. We really bought them to take home as gifts, but thought we should test them ourselves first.

"Crawford, look! It stopped raining and I think it's clearing up a bit."

"Great." I halfheartedly agreed.

Well, this trip is all about the adventure and will be the real essence of THE BOOK. I'll be dead soon anyway, and I suppose our ravaged remains could be shipped home or buried at sea. Real serious prayer could become imperative today.

There was a flash of memory of when friend Diana and I lied excessively about our weight before we got into an Alaskan floatplane that was to fly over mountains and glaciers. Once airborne, came the stunning moment when the pilot explained the importance of knowing of our exact weight at those incredible heights in a small plane. "Our Father's" became critical during that excursion and, I believe, will be crucial again today.

The sleet let up enough that the tour manager gave us

the okay. We entered the van in hushed silence and our speechless tour began. The scenery, even under wet, cold, and windy conditions, was dramatic. The landscape was completely deprived of trees and habitation. The occasional sheep herd was grazing right up to the cliff's edge. This was a harsh unforgiving landscape. Our first stop was at a farm site where we were instructed to go up the hill past the little stone barn, and we should pay the farmer's son one Euro each to walk through the field up to the stone huts dotting their property.

The ancient Celts had scant resources at their disposal in order to survive in this merciless region. There were the sea, rocks and a little grass. The beehive huts were constructed by placing hundreds of stones the size of grapefruits in such precise order that no light was apparent between them. These people also made stone fences and fire pits which burned using sheep dung. Just walking over the steep rocky pasture was challenging, and you had to be astonished by the fortitude of the early Celts.

We passed by the picturesque on-location movie sites of "Ryan's Daughter" and "Far and Away". We also made a quick stop at the Gallarus Oratory which was a church made entirely of stones chiseled and set so tightly that they have held perfectly without mortar for over four hundred years.

Our arrival back in Dingle was synchronized with the sight of the Tourist Bureau staff closing up the office. We went up to the door anyway, to see if they left us any notes. A man on the next block started shouting at us and was waving. He was standing next to a statue of a giant dolphin.

"Ya ladies want ta see a real dolphin? E's out in da harbor, dere. Da boat is takin folks out now. It's unly an hour and ten Euros each. You gurls'll get to see Fungie ta-day! He ran off course a few years back."

"Oh, wow! Let's go, Crawford. After the cruise we can get some hot soup and shepherd's pie, then head back to the Alpine House." Schwarck was persuasive.

"Schwarck! Do you see what the Captain's matey is handing out to people as they get onboard? Army blankets! We sit outside as we go to sea looking for Fergie the dolphin," I said firmly.

"His name is Fungie and he must be the town's mascot or something. Get your camera out so we can get an up close picture of him," Shc summarized.

Unfortunately, the Captain was feeling particularly big-hearted today and decided to stay out an hour and a half longer. Our frigid little tour turned out to be two and a half hours of persistent spotting a fin off in the distance while perched on narrow, icy wooden benches. The German tourists weren't even wearing coats, but Schwarck and I were huddled together trying to kindle some warmth. She had found a garbage bag which she tied over her head. My fingers seized up and refused to bend as the icy blasts hit us head on. I hated that igit Fungie. The energetic Krauts were leaping from starboard to port trying to catch another glimpse of a frolicking Fungie. I took so many pictures of waves in hopes that the dodging dolphin would at least show more than a fin. I think we were conned. That little fin could have been any kind of fish or maybe some mechanical gizmo.

When the seahunt was over, we staggered numbly off the gangplank and headed for the warmth of the nearby Internet Café. I wanted to communicate with the family in case I had contracted pneumonia and would never make it back home.

TO: FRIENDS AND FAMILY BACK HOME

SENT: FRIDAY, APRIL 14

Well, we are trying to stay awhile in the Internet Cafe in order to thaw out after our 2 ½ hour boat cruise into the headwaters of an icy Atlantic to see some dolphin named Fungie who had blown off course twenty years ago. When we got on the boat, it became apparent that there would never be enough blankets, gloves, or layers which could keep us warm on that open tub with icy blasting winds right through our heads. There were about twenty-five people besides us onboard…mostly Germans in black, but no gloves, coats, or hats. We were so totally covered up that Flipper could have jumped onboard with us, and we wouldn't have seen him.

I must have at least 50 pictures of that Igit Fergie - Schwarck says it's Fungie. Not one picture shows his head or any part above water. The good Captain just kept shouting port or starboard, and the Germans would rush over to point. We didn't do that!

The Tourist Bureaus in these towns have it out for us. When they see us tourists coming toward the office, they quickly close up.

Enough for now…I think I hear music across the street and I smell something, but I don't think its cabbage. No one seems to serve corn beef and cabbage over here. Why the hell have we been serving that for years on St. Patrick's in the states?

Love to all!

Kathleen

We managed to totter across the street to eat and enjoy two Irish songs before we fell into our hot toddies. The music was okay but not our anticipated rousing songfest with tourists joining hands with the Celts and belting out "I'll Take You Home Again, Kathleen". There was no singing at all just two old fiddlers fiddlin' around and a seventy-year-old lady on an old tambourine. Schwarck and this "Kathleen" left the pub.

We awakened the next day to pelting rain and wind shears.

"I've got an idea, Crawford. Why don't we go down to eat breakfast as late as we can? Then I'll go down the hill to get us a nutritious lunch and pick up our laundry and bring it back here. You can just stay in the room and read or hopefully write a lot on the computer. We've got to keep writing everything down so we won't forget anything. How's that sound to you? Tomorrow we leave for Killarney, and it's kind of a long ride. You can catch up the writing here as well as rest up."

"That sounds fabulous to me!" I replied gratefully.

I watched as Schwarck leaned into the wind and rain heading down the hill. I suspect our cleaner dirties will be wet by the time she gets them back up the hill, but maybe they won't be our dirties anyway.

Wonder what mountaintop she has us perched on in Killarney. It'll be my turn for the big bed there.

CHAPTER 17

THE GREAT FLOOD OF KILLARNEY AND AN INTERNATIONAL INCIDENT

As we bounced along on the all day ride to Killarney, I probed Schwarck for the lowdown on our upcoming Bed and Breakfast, how long we'd stay, as well as what we could expect to see in the area. Schwarck had trouble getting accommodations because the Tourist Bureau is never open so she had to find a Bed and Breakfast by searching the Web.

"You're going to love this place because our B & B is right across the street from the bus station and the picture on the Internet looked really nice. It was a lot cheaper than what we have been spending," Schwarck explained.

"Really? A lot cheaper? Don't you wonder why it's cheaper? You better not tell me you booked us into a Hari Krishna commune. You know, I no longer trust the Irish interpretation of what's nearby and across from. So far they have shown a gross misunderstanding about distance and convenience. Oh, my God, look at that…it's sleeting!"

By late afternoon we pulled into the Killarney Bus Station. Sure enough, right across the street was our lodging. It was perched high on a bluff, but it was definitely across the street from the bus. We exited the station and gingerly made our way onto a sidewalk of little hail pellets. I looked over calmly and stated, "I'm going to kill you, Schwarck."

"Well it looks real nice though, doesn't it?"

"I'm not sure how it looks because I can't get the ice off my glasses nor can I crane my stiff neck that high!"

We rumbled along the sidewalk and up three flights of cement stairs to the front of the house where we found a sign that stated: "Please Use the Back Entrance." This could only be accomplished by going back down the three cracked cement flights and up the road to a steep and slick asphalt drive. Once we schlepped up the drive and around the back of the house, we found a doorbell, but it was broken. So we both knocked and yelled loudly, "Hellll-ooo! Anybody here?" Just as we were ready to give up, the door opened and a smiling, slightly disheveled woman, probably in her thirties, came to the door. Her blouse and well worn jeans had an abundance of stains and she was wearing matted hairy slippers on her feet.

"Hi, I'm Liz. Ya lookin' fer a ruum?"

"I'm Karen Schwarck and this is my friend Kathleen Crawford. Did you get our booking from the Internet Agency? I paid them on-line."

"Nah, I dinna get it. I told them we weren't gonna be take'n reservations this spring, cuz the husband needed ta do some wurk on da place, but they musta taken your reservation by mistake. I have room fur ya though, and we kin use the munny. Ya kin have the pick of the three bedrooms upstairs. My family kin jest stay in the other two. I kin book ya on any turs ya like, too."

We followed her into the well worn living/dining room area, and Liz explained a little about breakfast. We could come down and eat whenever we wanted, just help ourselves to coffee on the stove, or the electric pot was available to brew whenever we desired. She led us to the stairs and said all three rooms were at the top of the landing and we should just make ourselves at home. We thanked her and yanked and tugged our weighty bags up the stairs and peeked into each of the three bedrooms, selecting the largest one overlooking the street. The unadorned room was painted a dull orange with gold trim. The furniture was sparse and featured two beds; one worn looking double with a frayed bedspread and a saggy little twin under a dormer that looked weary, but was neatly made. Only the double bed had a nightstand with a lamp. The bathroom appeared to be freshly painted and the undersized shower stall looked modern but more like a camper in size. There was a very petite sink, one towel bar, and no shelf or medicine cabinet.

I whispered to Schwarck, "Do ya think we're sleeping in her room? This is probably the bed her babies were born in. When she said her family will just take the rooms we don't choose…what do ya think that means? She might have a thundering herd of kids under the age of five! This doesn't look so good to me."

"It'll be fine. I'm still kind of confused about our reservation. If she didn't get our reservation and she is closed for the season, how does she get the money? We can't afford to pay her too and then try to collect from the Internet. Oh, well. Which bed do you want?" Schwarck concluded.

"What do you think? I'm the oldest and the heaviest and have been sleeping on a baby bed every night since we left home. The law of averages tells me I am going to get the big bed tonight. Where are the Bewleys and the sugar packet? This time I'm going to hold them behind my back and you have to guess. Bewleys gets the little bed!"

I grabbed the packets and put them behind my back, switching them three times so that I didn't even remember which was for the little bed. She started this weird circling with both hands, then rubbed and clapped them together and started circling again over my closed hands.

"Oh for God's sake, Schwarck, just pick a hand!"

"Well, I'm trying to feel the energy of the Bewleys. Okay! There it is! I'll take the one on the right."

I reluctantly brought my right hand out and it was the sugar. I was still holding the Bewleys and therefore would enjoy another restless night on a twin under a dormer with no way to have light for reading. How is it possible that she can win the big bed every single time?

"Ha! I can't believe it. I got the big one again!"

A beaming Liz appeared at our door and said she thought we'd pick this room. She also informed us that if we wanted to tour the famous Ring of Kerry, we needed to be mindful of the weather. Tomorrow was supposed to be clear so we should plan on going then. The rest of the week looked iffy. That's an understatement. I wonder if she thinks today's weather is fabulous. She said a tour driver would pick us up right across the street, and she would prepare our breakfast early so we could get going. She also shared her favorite restaurants downtown and told us about the brand new indoor mall that was on the next block. She was like a girlfriend you could be comfortable with.

"Okay, let's get going downtown to find the Internet and on to dinner. Liz, please book us on the Ring of Kerry Tour tomorrow."

"Have fun, gurls. Mind the toys on the steps, now. Kids are back frum school. I canna help ya with the Internet. Don't know where it tis."

It was a damp and piercing cold, but the sun was trying to peek through as we traversed the winding walk downtown in search of the Internet Café. Schwarck kept popping her head into stores asking for directions, and we finally arrived at a storefront with a big sign stating this was the home of "Ri-Ra", which is Irish for "talking". We entered the strange looking place to be met by a chalk-skinned, satanic pierced girl, outfitted from head to toe in black. She acknowledged us dully and pointed her ring-filled digits toward two cubicles in the corner. The room was pitch black and was not unlike a room in a haunted house. I was stepping on what could be peanut shells or possibly bones of small sacrificed animals. Schwarck and I reached our assigned stalls, removed our backpacks, and turned to each other with reassuring smiles. Our pearly whites were glowing in the dark under powerful black lights.

"Wow! This is awesome! Look how those stains on your sweatshirt glow, Schwarck. Hey, how about my plastic fingernails, they're glowing. This is amazing! Smile really big…whoa!!"

TO: FRIENDS AND RELATIVES BACK HOME

SENT: APRIL 15

SUBJECT: IT'S A LONG, LONG WAY TO TIPPERARY

We left the frozen Dingle peninsula today so that we could be frozen in Killarney. The little red-faced fairy man who owned our Dingle B & B told us he would "pop up" and help with our luggage. When he lifted mine, his face went from red to white instantly. I think I helped him find same muscles he hasn't used in awhile.

My rugged flight attendant suitcase that Hugh picked out for me is holding up well, but Schwarck's is starting to crack up and already must be duct taped.

Right now we are sitting on very high stools in a Killarney Internet Café called RI-RA. The outside of the building is totally black and the inside is too, with curious little cubbyholes and black lights in each computer space. It's like a haunted house in here. My nails are purple.

The climb up hill to our new Bed and Breakfast was exhausting. I almost didn't make it because in my infinite wisdom I decided to purchase snacks at the bus station - bottles of water, chips, tea, sugar cookies, and an entire lemon tart cake. The laptop, surge protectors, battery packs, adapters, digital camera, and all the snacks, not to mention my medications and extra long panty liners, are all in the backpack which caused me to lean over to such and extent that I almost touched the ground with my forehead. Oh yeah, and that climb was done on ice! I deserved to eat the entire lemon cake all by myself once I got up the hill.

We are still checking out phone book listings for Cotters. Haven't found any around here.

I'm having a little trouble with the measurements, temperatures, distances, and money. Other than that, I am doing fine. I don't trust the locals with directions or distances. "Five minutes from downtown" can only be accomplished if you are a seasoned Olympian runner.

We have left things behind at every stop to lighten our load, and we take pictures of them as a parting gesture. Last night we left some pants, chips, tomatoes, and two large cookies. I'm not going to leave food behind again.

We took our laundry to the gas station, which is also the tour office. Laundry man wore a surgical mask and goggles with his stained lab coat. Guess he heard about our underwear. We had put "Cotter" on the laundry slip and almost couldn't get our stuff back because we forgot and asked for our clothes under “Schwarck”. I am sure that they gave me the wrong clothes. These are considerably smaller.

Enough for now.

Hugs,

I’m calling myself Kathleen Cotter over here.

We exited the RI-RA and ambled down the street past intriguing little shops and eateries. Killarney was much larger than the past two towns. The streets and businesses were postcard perfect just like the pictures of Ireland in coffee table books. We chose the Squire’s Pub for dinner and picked a place near a tall iron fireplace. Every pub we have been in over here has a blazing fireplace. Thank God.

“I’m getting concerned about booking our rooms with the Internet Agency,” said a worried Schwarck. “Liz never got our reservation and our next stop is Doolin, and I only had a choice of three B & Bs. I couldn’t see pictures of what they were like, but I had to give them our credit card number. What if they take the money and we don’t get a room?”

“Well, I guess if worst comes to worst, we can always bunk in a hostel. I’m awake most of the night anyway. We could take turns standing guard. Right now, I’m starving and can’t wait to eat and get back to the room for a hot shower and warm up, followed by a big hunk of that lemon cake before reclining on my baby bear bed!”

Dinner was the usual fish and chips accompanied by lager and treacle pudding. Schwarck can't figure out why we're not losing tons of weight. We entered a few shops on the way back to buy more wool scarves. My family probably won't notice the stains from my wearing them here everyday.

On the walk back we noticed a few frosty tulips and hyacinths peeking out of little gardens along the sidewalk. This was a welcome and sure sign of warmer days ahead. By the time we got back to our room at the top of the stairs, it was dark and we plopped down on the bed to read some tour brochures.

"Well, Schwarck, I'm getting in the shower to thaw myself out. Are you going to write tonight?"

"I don't think so. I'm going to start my exercises called Pilates. See, this is called a pelvic thrust and it's very good for you. You should do some, too. You only have to do ten or twelve and you just do them in bed."

"Really? I would be particularly fond of exercise that can be done while lying down, but the gynecologist told me I have a tipped uterus and that doesn't seem like a good thing. One intense pelvic thrust could force my tipped part to shoot out or something. I should be careful. Besides, I never got my episiotomy sewed up after Amy was born 30 years ago, weighing in at a whopping 10 pounds 14 ounces. The doctor told me if I didn't get it sewed up, it could get hooked on something. What do you think that would be…a park bench? Besides, don't you think the fifteen miles we walk uphill everyday carrying sixty pounds on our backs and pulling our 200-pound carcasses is enough exercise?"

Schwarck looked as though she was seriously pondering the possibilities of my crotch getting hooked on something. Who would she call in the event of that grim emergency?

I did a couple of her "pelvic thrusts" just to show her I was up to it, then gathered up all my shower items along with a worn towel Liz had laid on the bed. The shower looked brand new and only had one big knob to turn. This simplicity was a welcome relief in view of the complicated bathrooms we had been dealing with recently. I wondered how expert Liz's husband is when I draped my towel over the little towel bar and the whole thing pulled out of the wall and fell to the floor. Nothing I can do about that except report it to the owner tomorrow. I pulled out the shower handle and adjusted the temperature. Wanting a little more warmth, I turned the handle again, but this time the entire fixture pulled out of the wall, fell into my hand, and water blasted out of the wall. Good God! I tried to put my hands over the geyser, but it was extremely forceful and the water was flooding over the shower ledge. I grabbed a glass from the sink and started bailing, but I knew this was an effort in futility. I yelled out, "Schwarck! We have a situation here! It's a flood! Do you know how to turn water off in a wall? I can't shut it off!"

I abandoned the flooding stall, grabbed the towel on the floor, made an effort to wrap the skimpy towel around at least part of my wet torso, then leaped into the bedroom holding the fixture in my hand. Water was shooting out every which way. This must have been a stunning sight for my pal because she froze in mid-pelvic thrust.

"Help me here before we have to start collecting sets of animals!"

She snapped to attention and leaped adroitly from the bed and accompanied me back into the little stall where we worked on the troublesome waterspout. Both of us were completely drenched, but she finally found a knob in the wall that stopped the deluge. We continued bailing for a while, and then I had to finish shampooing my hair in the sink.

"Good Lord! First the towel rack, then the shower fixture. We better not sit on the toilet because it might fall through the floor and land on the dining room table!"

The next morning a rumpled but cheerful Liz met us in the dining room with coffee and sat down with us, coffee cup in hand, telling us enthusiastically how much she loves the states. They had lived there for a year and she had obsessed about zip lock bags. She can't find them anywhere in Ireland. I related the flooded shower story, and she promised to have her husband take a "peek on it" today while we were on the Ring of Kerry Tour. Of course, it was her husband who had installed the towel bar and shower in the first place, so I didn't hold out much hope for improvement. She had packed us a little snack bag just like we were preschoolers and walked us outdoors to the bus stop waving as we got on. We love our new girlfriend!

A mini-bus stopped for us and our tour guide, Timothy, was very cheery. He said we would pick up some more people and then go to the office where we would get a larger tour bus. The bigger coach held about 50 people and it was nearly full. We had gotten on early and commandeered seats near the front. Timothy began our Ring of Kerry Tour with a recitation of the rules. We approve wholeheartedly of bus rules because we have led such tours in the states and rules keep things fair and tidy for all. He told us there would be "no eating" on the coach, that we would make a stop for lunch. Each side of the coach would take turns exiting at stops. We were to stay behind all fences and barriers because he didn't want to besmirch his reputation by losing a paying tourist over a high cliff.

As the coach drive progressed, two young women sitting in the very front seat, talked incessantly in what we presumed to be German. They persisted in conversing loudly during Timothy's tour guide speech. Schwarck's sense of justice was getting revved up, particularly at the first stop, the Peat Bog Village, where it was the "Driver's Side" off first, but the leggy Germans took cuts and leaped off the bus first. "Did you see that, Crawford? They are so rude!"

"I know. Maybe they don't understand English or maybe they just don't care, but we aren't in charge here. It's up to Timothy to straighten them out. Let's get off and see what this bog thing is all about."

We were greeted inside the main cabin with a warm delicious rum drink. The sun was shining brightly, and I actually am beginning to believe that spring is in the air.

Our next stop was at the Coomakista Viewing Point, seven hundred feet above an unruly sea of rocky outcroppings. This was a spectacular sight.

Timothy warned us once again about the barriers. The Germans illegally leaped off the bus first and immediately climbed over a fence on the highest precipice.

"Just look at that! Can you believe those two?" a peevish Schwarck declared.

"He told us all to be sure to stay behind the barriers. They don't think rules should apply to them."

We took lots of pictures at this scenic overview and then Timothy led us up to a little building called the Skellig Pub and Tea Room, perched on the side of a cliff where we were to enjoy a little lunch break. By the time I got through the bathroom line, it was almost time to leave so I had to guzzle my tea and polish off a big Shepherds Pie lickety-split because I knew we were not allowed to consume food on the bus.

We entered the bus to a vision of the two rule breakers slurping from a gigantic jug, lustily feasting on powerful smelly cheese, and noisily gnawing on enormous loaves of French bread. They were eating on the bus! To make matters even worse, they were laughing and talking out loud while our friendly guide was delivering his new commentary. This was one rule infraction too many for my sidekick. Her nostrils flared and there was growling as she arose from her seat, which was also a rule infraction. I was fascinated as she made her way forward up to the closest German and put a rigid hand on her shoulder. The twenty-something Kraut turned to see a pair of steely hazel eyes locked and loaded. Without a word, Schwarck pointed in the direction of the "No Eating On the Bus" sign, then with precision movement her index finger advanced to her mouth in deadly "Shush" action. She focused back on the target and squinted. Commander Schwarck returned to her seat, grabbed her backpack, and made her way back up to an empty seat nearer the enemy so that she could keep them in line for the remainder of the day. The entire episode was stupefying.

Very quickly I acquired a new seatmate who had been watching all this action, hoping for an opportunity to move forward on the bus. She was astoundingly pint-sized and couldn't see anything over the seat backs. This little old pixie had a mammoth-jutting chin which showcased two sizable moles. She wore a soft white sweater over a long black dress with a long flowing blue scarf wrapped around her neck. She made it her job to interpret Timothy's remarks, and I couldn't help but notice how her moles bobbed up and down as she emphasized a point.

Schwarck was staying the course with the hostiles through the village of Sneem and on to the exquisite Lakes of Killarney, silently willing them into submission. My personal tutor was explaining the differences between the leprechauns in green hats who were the authentic ones versus the others who had been anglicized.

The wonderful day of touring came to a close, and we gave Timothy a fat tip for his humor, perseverance, and knowledge. We decided to stay downtown and look for dinner.

"Hey, Schwarck, why don't we try something different tonight? I don't know why, but I feel like we should find a beer garden that serves Wiener Snitzel."

"Very funny! I'm exhausted from being on guard all day. Hey look, there's a nice looking Chinese restaurant. Wanna go there?"

I was already through the door hoping for a change of menu this evening. The eatery looked quite sophisticated and the Asian wait staff was dressed in crisp black pants, black tie, and starched tuxedo shirts. We were greeted by a young Asian woman who had been standing at attention by the door. She led us to a table in a large, well appointed room with a water feature and tables with linen napkins and tablecloths, but no other patrons. Other wait staff immediately greeted us, and I decided to use my two Chinese words on them, "Nee Hou" and "tsu tsu." I have no idea how either of these is spelled or how to pronounce them very well, but I can tell you that these two little words created quite a stir in the Killarney Chinese Restaurant. Once the staff overheard my utterances, they came running from every nook and cranny chattering away in Chinese and wanting their picture taken with me.

"Geeze, Crawford, what'd ya say?"

"Well, I think it was only hello and thank you, but I was told by some Chinese friends to be careful about voice inflections or it will have an entirely different meaning. For all I know I could have said, 'Lick me till I scream or spank me till I'm chapped!' At least whatever I said, they seem pretty happy about it, don't they?"

We enjoyed a delightful evening and assortment of foods. At the end of our dinner, we had a large group photo taken by the only other patron in the place. We headed back up the bluff to our B & B in hopes that the husband had worked on the plumbing. We only needed one more day out of it! The shower nozzle had been replaced, but I was leery. I opted to steer clear of the shower, perform five pelvic thrusts, and do a little reading if Schwarck would tilt her lampshade toward my dormer.

The next morning we chatted with Liz and another guest over a hot breakfast and lots of coffee. Finally we tore ourselves away from the socializing and headed down to the mini-mall with our computers, hoping to write for a few hours. This was the only mall we had seen in Ireland, and it only had about 11 stores with a deli court upstairs along with some offices. The bright sunlit space upstairs looked like a tranquil haven for authors so we pulled up some café chairs and opened the computers.

"Crawford, this place is perfect for creativity. The tables are round which is so good for the right side of your brain, and we'll have plenty of room to spread out all of our writing stuff. I'll go get us some coffee and sweet rolls which should also stimulate our brains."

The first gooey bite of cinnamon buttery-loaded pastry was accompanied by mysterious heavenly sounds coming from the floor below. I walked to the staircase and peered over into the lobby below. There were two astoundingly large stereo speakers and between them stood a small brightly costumed and barefoot native couple. He was playing a wood flute type instrument and she was pounding on a set of wood kettledrums.

I reported my discovery to Schwarck. "I can't believe it! This guy, or some of his Guatemalan kin, has been everywhere I go. I've seen' em at the Michigan State Fair, the Novi Fifties Fest, Hawaii, New Orleans, San Antonio, and now Ireland! Amazing. Don't you just love the way he plays Born Free?"

"No, I don't. Now we have to deal with that loud distraction. We've got to get more serious with writing or we'll forget everything. I'm almost caught up to Dingle with the writing and pictures to match. Where are you?"

"Well, I've got all the pictures in and some music. The writing is coming along. I think I'm going to go down and get his CD to put in the computer, too."

"What? Right now you're going to buy one?"

When I returned with my CD, her computer was put away and her arms were folded over her chest. What had really put her over the edge was the loud high-pitched chatter of five dozen middle schoolers who had descended on the food court.

"I can't take all this noise. We can't be creative in the midst of all this chaos."

"Well, I think it's the chaos that makes the story worth reading. But this is a bit much, so let's go shopping and get to the Internet."

We perused the shelves of the outlet stores. We also looked at Ireland's famous Waterford Crystal, but knew we'd never get any of that back home intact. Besides, it was too expensive for our meager budget.

The Internet Café was nearby so we popped in to let folks at home know we are heading out of here tomorrow and may not communicate for a few days. We also had to check on our Doolin reservations.

TO: FRIENDS AND RELATIVES BACK HOME

SENT: APRIL 16

SUBJECT: THERE ARE THINGS THE IRISH SHOULD KNOW

Hello, from Killarney again. We went on a fabulous all day tour on the Ring of Kerry. Our tour guide was the best I ever had, but I sure had to listen carefully because of his accent. A little Irish fairy lady sat next to me all the way and interpreted what he was saying. We even stopped at a Leprechaun Crossing at which point she turned to me and said very seriously that the ones in the red hats are anglicized but the ones in green hats are fine. I looked at her for a smile or some indication that she was pulling my leg…but none came. I asked her about the trolls and she said they are low-life and not to pay any attention to them.

Two German girls sitting in the front seat did everything they weren't supposed to do. When we had a photo op, the tour guide told us to stay behind the barriers because a tourist had fallen off the cliff the week before. I was very careful…like I could EVER get my thighs and fat ass over the fence! The loose ground gives way before you know it. The Germans climbed over the fence. He told us there was no eating on the bus, but they chomped away on the nastiest cheese you ever smelled and ate an entire loaf of French bread. Schwarck assumed the role of Commander-In-Chief of the bus and stationed herself behind the Germans to whip them into submission.

I love the Irish music so I bought two more CD's today, plus a CD of a Guatemalan flute player. That'll mean I have to leave behind two pair of underwear so I'll have room in my suitcase.

I'm seriously getting shin splints from all the walking up hill. Our B&B here is low budget, but we love our inn keeper. The sink faucet pulls out of the basin, the shower nozzle pulls out of the wall, and the towel bar won't hold a towel without falling down.

I have managed to lose the draw for the bed every time, so I always get the littlest, flimsiest bed. By the way, two live crows reside outside our window and "CAW" incessantly.

We have been so excited about our food and drinks over here that we have taken a picture of it every day.

Here's what I have learned so far:

- The Irish need to mix their water in one faucet…not two faucets with glacially cold in one and the other boiling hot.
- There should be washcloths - at least one for each tourist.
- Where is the Kleenex? Don't they have that over here?
- No one here says any "th" sounds. "Thing" becomes "ting" and "thought" becomes "tot".

- Mirrors are never anywhere close to where you can plug in a hairdryer.

- "Cheers" means thanks and "Spot on" is right on!

I'm taking some great pictures and would send them to you, but no one seems to know how to do it…something about pixels or pickles.

Rugby is so popular that loud cheering from men and women can be heard in the pubs every day of the week, and you can bet on the games and horse races in betting parlors.

Love to all,

Kathleen

"Crawford, I just booked our ferry passage over to Scotland and set up a B&B in Belfast. But our next stop, Doolin, is my most favorite place in all of Ireland. There are castle ruins and the Cliffs of Mohr. We're booked into the Daly House there."

"Great. Let's eat and get back soon because it's going to take awhile for me to pack up the new things I have to make room for. Maybe I'll just wear all my clothes tomorrow because it will no doubt be freezing," I murmured.

As we packed up, we decided to leave Liz a little gift bag of cookies, a smutty novel, new slippers, and a handful of precious zip lock bags. We placed them on the bed with a little note of thanks telling how much we enjoyed our stay with her. She had never asked us to pay for our stay. If she's not worried about it, why should we?

Our breakfast was hearty and we had a little chance to chat with Liz before we had to leave for the bus station. She had packed us each a little lunch for the long bus ride and escorted us out the front door and watched us thump down the three flights of cement stairs waving. Liz yelled out, "Och, I been meanin ta ask ya'….how's that shower wurkin now?" In unison we answered, "Oh, it's fine."

Neither of us had the courage to tell her we didn't try it again. We'll shower in the next town.

CHAPTER 18

DOOLIN IS GRUELIN'

As I sat on the bus waiting to pull away from Killarney, I realized some things that never concerned me before are starting to bug and worry me. This is enlightening because I come from a lengthy line of blasé non-worriers. For example, when I was seven our house caught fire and my granddad stood next to me watching the blaze and just uttered a quiet, "Da-mn." It wasn't a loud, excited or enraged "Damn", it was a damn of amazement, sort of like "wow, would you look at that!" This inherited detachment gene has served me well throughout my life, so I will strive to reactivate my indifference to trifling impositions.

One big pain in the ass for me is the incredible amount of toting and traipsing required over here. Schwarck's little, "You better build up your muscles before we go cause you're gonna have to walk a lot in the UK," was grossly understated. Arnold Swartzennegger would have trouble with all of this exertion, but do I complain? Absolutely!

The miserable arctic spring was a complete surprise and a messy nuisance, but do I gripe about it? Every day! My latest approach to these mind numbing weather issues is to silently chant, “My forefathers fought in the American Revolution with George Washington at Valley Forge — this is nothing!”

Another item plaguing my life at this moment is my expensive fanny pack of multitudinous zippered pockets. Each nook is filled to capacity with weighty items I have determined are necessary to exist in this vagabond lifestyle.

“I’m worried about my fanny pack, Schwarck. Most people’s butts aren’t this big. People are starting to point at it. It’s so heavy, I can’t adjust it and it’s swinging between my legs like the udders of those cows we saw yesterday. I haven’t seen any stores that carry packs like this or I’d buy a new one.”

“Why don’t you take it off? I bet we can staple or tape it so that it won’t keep drooping,” Schwarck suggested.

“Great, if you’ve got enough tape. I’ve got a lot of other stuff that’s hanging down you could tape up for me, too.”

Our ride to Doolin was going to be a long one and would involve changing buses. I loaded up my flowered shopping bag with comforting snacks and reading materials. This would be a non-walking leisure day of reading, munching, and enjoying green vistas of the hills and dales in a more remote Irish region. Our departure from the conveniently located bus station was gratefully uneventful. We stashed our gear in the usual fashion and took a seat three away from the driver. Our bus was approximately 2/3 full as we pulled away and began our journey. I have come to appreciate the energizing effect of moving on to a new place. It’s sort of like wiping your magic slate clean.

As we began climbing to higher elevations, it began to snow, then sleet. The driver appeared to be a little frazzled by the weather or something. He was unwrapping candies like crazy throwing the wrappers on the floor. I bet he's diabetic and trying to dodge a coma. Or maybe he was at the pub late last night and icy mountain roads won't even keep him alert. What if today is the day he made the decision to give up his three packs a day cigarette habit? He looks pretty rumpled and disheveled from the back. His hair is all sticky-uppy. Who knows if we are even on a road right now? I can't see one. Am I worried? Ah, definitely!

"Wow, Schwarck! Look at all the ice piling up on the road. Don't they have plows or salt here? Maybe that's why our professional driver is weaving and having a little trouble staying on the road."

"Oh, geeze! It does look like he's weaving. It could be lack of sleep. I've never seen anybody inhale candy like that. On our senior citizen trips I talk to the driver if I think he's getting tired. I'm gonna go up there and talk to him a bit. That'll change his pattern and keep him awake."

I watched as Schwarck jerkily made her way to the front of the bus and took the empty seat across from the candy-eating coachman. Yes, my buddy Schwarck is a bona fide "take charge" person. First, it was the Germans and today it's risk management with a bus driver.

She had taken her new water bottle up and lightly tapped the driver on the shoulder offering it to him. She also started to open candy for him in an effort to keep his body functioning and both hands firmly on the wheel. When the driver turned his head in her direction, I immediately noticed a stunned and startled expression on her face. She patted him on the shoulder and made her way back to our seat.

"Well, what did he say? Is he tired? Diabetic? Just quit smoking?" I asked.

"Crawford, he's only got one eye!"

"What? One eye? Oh, that's just great! You made this guy take his only eye off the icy road to see what you wanted. Do you think I'm going to be able to use your shoulders to climb up to that hatch in the roof? Hey, don't forget your seat cushion can be used as a flotation device!"

"How can a responsible bus company hire a guy with only one eye? Think of the liability," Schwarck explained.

Friends should always be on hand to distract and calm in times of stress. I chose to point out the plusses of having only one eye. "Well, maybe it's a special eye. You know I'm nearly blind in my left eye and I can drive well except for parking straight and running into curbs. Oh, yeah, and driving at night, but other than that I'm great! Maybe his hearing is especially good!"

I could tell she was starting to mull all of this over. Thankfully the bus began to descend the snowy mountain and was slowing down considerably. We entered a quaint village of small colorful stone cottages. The colored stones were the size of oranges and selected artistically to form patterns. The roofs were thickly thatched with long sticks or brush and little pebble paths led up to their doors. It was like a little fairy village. Abruptly the bus came to a screeching halt. The driver arose from his seat and pinned his one eye on Schwarck and sternly said, “Nah, ye kin git off.”

She got worried. “Who, me? You, you…want me to get off?”

“Yah! Ahm stoppin' heer fer yuu! Doan cha want a pichur ahv dis tatched roof cottage?” the driver asked.

“Uhm, oh…oh …okay, a picture! Yeah, yeah, sure. Thanks,” Schwarck said quickly.

She was making a weird face as she glanced in my direction, then grabbed her camera, and leaped off the bus. The cars trapped behind the bus started honking their horns in irritation. Schwarck hurriedly returned to the bus and her seat while mumbling gratitude to the driver and apologies to the other passengers for making the photo stop. She dropped into her seat and began rubbing her temples.

“I thought he was throwing me off the bus because I complained about his one eye. I have such a headache right now. Have you got any aspirin with you?”

“Are you kidding? What size do you want?” I exclaimed.

In a short while we pulled alongside the Limerick bus station. It looked like a small white post office building. Our one-eyed chauffer announced that we would have a fifteen-minute break and should get back on the same bus with a new driver. The bathroom break and the new driver announcement were both a welcome relief. We hurried off the bus to head for the restrooms because we had experienced nervous tinkle for the past two hours.

Drivers over here do not stand outside the bus door to assist passengers as they exit. I suppose it is presumed that if you are capable of walking two miles uphill on cobblestones to get to the bus stop, you surely can hold on to a grab bar and get off a bus without any assistance.

Our return to the coach found us face to face with a lively, wide awake looking, new driver who had picked up the candy wrappers and tidied up the driver area. He was neatly attired in Bus Eirean jacket and uniform pants. His spotless white shirt had an exacting starched crease. His brown hair had been combed and parted very precisely. Best of all, he had a huge toothy smile, big dimples and two working eyes.

"Ha-loow, luvs. Yer frum da staats, right, luvs?"

We smiled dumbly and nodded in acknowledgement. He was such a pleasant change from the grungy, candy sucking Cyclops. Quite a few people had left the bus in Limerick and now there were only five passengers with us traveling toward Doolin. Our new driver kept chattering enthusiastically to no one in particular, but every other word was "luvs". He remarked on the pleasant spring weather, the narrow lanes, the wind velocity, and the bus schedule. As we drew closer to Doolin, he asked where we were staying and said, "Daly's, ah, ya, I know da place, luvs. It's not near da bus stop, but I kin drop ya at the end of dat lane. Ya know, I ad a fella on de bus de udder dey. E stayed dere, too, and seemed ta tink Ms. Daly was a bit chaotic! Yu'll like it dere dough. It's a nice place, luvs."

He pointed out the famous Cliffs of Mohr jutting over 650 feet into a raging Atlantic Ocean. He pulled through the Mohr parking lot to see if any tourists were up there wanting the bus. He told us that the winds were usually too high to walk to the edge of the cliffs. According to him, we would probably see more of the cliffs from Doolin than we could here.

We bussed down a narrow blacktopped lane to Doolin. It can't really be described as a town or even a village. It was more of an arrangement of ancient stone fences enclosing an occasional cow, horse, or little pastel cottage. There were only about six buildings in the downtown village itself, sitting side-by-side, up the road from an arched stone bridge. In the distance we could see the surf pounding onto a rugged rocky shore beneath the Cliffs of Mohr. When he let us off the coach and pointed up a rocky stone incline, a freezing mix of side-ways rain and sleet pelted us. He yelled above the cacophonous hail that the Guest House was only about a half mile up the hill. We got off and opened the bay doors, hauling out our big bags and slamming the door shut again. With a little salute, he departed. We maneuvered and struggled to pull our cumbersome load over slippery little stones. There was no talking as the wheels of our heavy cases became lodged in crevasses and we painstakingly made our way uphill. I have never been so numbed by wind and rain. How do people live here?

"There it is, Crawford. Are you okay? It's just down this other lane, and we'll be there. See the sign: Daly's House-Bed and Breakfast-Rooms en Suite".

"No, I am definitely not okay! 'En-Suite' my frozen ass!"

We crossed a metal cowcatcher and followed a gravel drive up to the door of a cheerful looking yellow cement block ranch that was, marvelously, only one story high. As we approached the front door, two happy dogs of questionable lineage greeted us with wagging tails and smiles. We reached the door with all of our soaked belongings, and I resisted the urge to clutch Schwarck and happily dance in celebration for surviving the terrible trek. I was hesitant to knock on the door, fearing some frozen body part would break off and fall at my feet, but we both banged on the door anyway. A stocky middle-aged matron peeked her smiling curly red head out of the door.

"Kin ah help ya, ladees?"

"Yes. We just came on a bus from Killarney. Did you get the reservation we made two days ago through the Internet Agency?"

"Weel nah, I dinna git a reservation fur ye, or I wodda met cha at the buus wit my car. Ye kin stay inna-way though. I got one nice ruum left down at the end of the hall. Cum in, ladees. Let me show ya tah the ruum, then I kin warm ya up with sum cookies and a hot drink. Do ya' like tea or hot choclit? My name is Suu-zann Da-ly. Nah, ye gurls kin jest treet this place lak yur own home."

We slogged slope-shouldered down the hallway behind our new best friend. She was the epitome of Irish hospitality and the goddess of graciousness. Her immaculate home smelled of fresh made bread and lavender soap. She gave us a key and showed us into a beautiful golden buttercup painted room with a large window overlooking a grassy, bright green pasture and an honest-to-goodness ancient castle tower. There were cream colored bedspreads sprinkled with embroidered purple lilacs covering the twin and double bed. Each bed had a reading light above the headboard. The bathroom with stall shower was large and exceptionally clean. Susan explained there was a teacart in the hallway with coffee and tea and always available for guest use. She said she would bring the hot drinks and cookies into the living room when we were ready. When she closed the door behind her, we looked at each other and simultaneous exclaimed, "We love this place!"

Sizing up the big bed, Schwarck bolted from the room to grab a sugar packet and the Bewleys Tea and returned in anticipation of the gamble for the big bed.

"Okay, Schwarck. I'm gonna hold them again this time and the Bewleys packet is for the twin and the red sugar is for the big bed. I put them both behind my back and mixed them up. What do you want, left or right?"

She took a big breath, squared her body, and affixed her eyes on my arms. She then stretched out both arms and shook them rapidly like a competitive swimmer before a meet. She pushed up her sleeves and began to make tiny circular motions with her arms in front of me.

"Oh, for God's sake, Schwarck, knock off the voodoo. Right or left hand? The cookies and chocolate are waiting!"

"Well, I'm feeling for warmth… and vibration. Red gives off a vibration and that tells me which hand to pick!"

"For the love of God! Just pick a hand!"

"Left!"

I swung both hands around and opened them…there it was, the red packet in the left hand. She had done it again.

"Can you believe it? I got the big bed again! Why don't you just take it this time?"

"No way. What would be the point of the bed draw? We're just going to keep on drawing and I will get it eventually. Besides, I'm a mere shadow of my former self from all the walking, so I don't need that big huge oversized bed. Wanna pray with me tonight, Schwarck?

Now I lay me on this twin,

I pray the Lord next time I'll win

If I should die before I get home,

I bet that Schwarck will roam alone.

Amen."

CHAPTER 19

WALK A MILE IN MY ORTHOPEDICS

We enjoyed delicious cookies and hot chocolate in the living room. Susan introduced us to her daughter who was home from college for a couple of days. Susan was entertaining a number of visiting relatives this week and would be busy in the family quarters and kitchen. If we needed her, we were to knock on the kitchen door. We decided that unpacking was our first chore, and then we'd walk back down the hill to Gus O'Conner's Pub.

"My big bed is next to the glorious heat register. Yea! Hey! Wait a minute, feel this register. It's freezing cold! Do you see a thermostat anywhere? We aren't going to be allowed to regulate our own heat? This is ridiculous! I haven't been warm since we left Michigan," Schwarck complained.

"Well, me neither. In fact, I've worn that weird raincoat Hugh got me for fifteen days straight along with the umpteen wool scarves I keep buying for gifts."

My unpacking took more time than hers since she brought very few clothes and was wearing most of them.

My cool space age bags were sorted to contain underwear, another for tops, one for pants, and one for socks. I had rolled them up a special way to remove all of the air. Everything looked freeze dried and quite wrinkled. I can fit a lot more stuff in suitcase than Schwarck, but it's God-awful heavy.

We both spread out our toiletries and put them on the deep ledge of the cement block bathroom, mine in the front as usual. We suited up and headed down the hallway to find a fussing Susan setting the table in the daisy yellow dining room. The dishes were all Blue Willow and the tablecloth was delicate white lace over linen. Susan's table was the most pleasant looking and formal we had seen since leaving home.

"Hell-oooo, ladees. I'm settin' the table fur ya breakfast tahmarrah. Ya eat at nine. Are ya headin' to Gus O'Conner's, then? Maybe, y'all catch da music then," Susan suggested helpfully.

"Yep, we are heading to Gus's. The table looks beautiful. Can't wait for breakfast. See ya later," I replied.

We continued out the door and were met by our dog friends. Susan said the mixed collie was named Georgie. The rain had stopped, but the wind was fierce and cold. I was stunned by the incredible sight and sound of the Cliffs of Mohr. There were at least twenty-foot waves thundering and pounding against the base of the cliffs, as well as on the nearby shore. The wave pounding was so loud that talking was impossible. Georgie ran along the stone fence next to the lane and followed us down the hill right up to the door of Gus's.

Our eyeglasses steamed up as we entered Gus O'Conner's Pub and our nostrils were met with a potent whiff of stale beer, cabbage, and smoke absorbed wood. Even though Ireland now observed a no smoking rule, these old wooden beams had absorbed and thus emitted decades of pipe and cigarette smoke. There was a welcoming fire in the fireplace, and we headed for the table right next to it. Gus's Pub was made up of a number of little dark rooms with tables and bench seats. The ceiling was low so each room was delightfully cozy and featured its own ancient heavy wood bar. The only other patrons were three old rugged and rough looking types hunkered over bar stools.

A friendly young man wearing a Gus O'Conner shirt stepped around the ancient bar and greeted us. "What kin I get cha', girls?" His brogue was thick and enchanting.

I ordered a hot rum toddy and began to peruse the sparse and greasy plastic menu. We settled on the usual fish and chips with mushy peas. While we were lapping up our drinks, some rotund men with ponytails entered the pub, followed by teenage girls, and all began to tune up fiddle instruments. This place was bound to be fun! The young girls pulled up chairs facing the men and held their fiddles and flutes in their laps as the men began to play some lively tunes. It wasn't long before several boisterous families entered the pub and took bench seats at the deeply scratched tables near the musicians.

This Irish music wasn't at all what I expected. I thought there'd be lots of singing and lilting instrumental ballads, with a little step dance thrown into the mix. This was more of a music lesson or Irish jam session for the teenage protégées who were called upon in turn to play with a ponytailed guy.

We finished eating and headed back up the hill in the dark. The lane did have a few lights and we found the walk to be much easier this time without the sleet and luggage. Of course, the rum and ale didn't hurt our disposition either. It was quiet in the Daly House as we made our way down the hallway in anticipation of a restful night and tomorrow's delightful breakfast in the airy dining room.

After a little reading, we easily fell asleep after our long day of travel and fighting the elements. Sunlight greeted me the next morning along with a cup of coffee poured and delivered to my bedside table by my cheery travel girlfriend. What a life!

"Didn't you get cold last night, Crawford? I was freezing. I had to put on my socks! She never did turn on the heat," Schwarck complained.

"I'm telling ya', you need to take Tylenol PMs every night like me. You'll still be cold, but you won't know it! I'm going to warm up with a shower and then hurry down to the dining room. While I was reading last night, I heard other people come in late. Bet we'll have company at breakfast so that'll be interesting," I said.

When I exited the shower, I realized that I had stood so long letting the heat permeate my arthritic limbs that the entire room was steamed up. I tried to wipe the mirror off enough to apply makeup, but it was like a steam bath so I pushed out the window to unleash the steam.

"Your turn, Schwarck. I'm heading to breakfast. I'll save you a seat."

Delectable breakfast smells wafted down the hallway as I approached the dining room. Two other couples were already seated and enjoying their breakfast. I took a seat and introduced myself to the young couples. One very pregnant woman explained she is due next month so they decided on this little get-a-way. She and her husband have three other children under the age of five and he is a pilot in the US military stationed in Germany. I'm thinking she needs more than a little get-a-way. When she gets the fourth kid under the age of five, I'd say she needs for the husband to get a way! The woman and her kids live on the base so neighbors who have kids the same age are watching their kids. It's very brave to be traveling and touring so close to delivery, but it's a new age of pregnancy. I think I was in bed the last two months of my deliveries and not because the doctor ordered it.

We all enjoyed the intriguing tales of each couple's reasons for coming here. The Internet has introduced the public to expanded travel options. People are discovering little out-of-the-way places like Doolin, and we probably won't even recognize it if we come back in five years. What am I thinking? I have some concerns about future expeditions at my age. Maybe pretty soon I won't even buy green bananas!

Heaven help me, but I love introducing myself as an author on an adventurous book writing mission with my old girlfriend. These young people were thoroughly enthralled with our saviness, but especially the idea of writing a book. One young woman said she had always wanted to write and she would like to keep track of our progress so we exchanged email addresses. As Susan scurried back and forth bringing our orders, she also commented on our proposed literary achievement and no doubt anticipates being included in the exciting story. There's an unexpected feeling of power with book writing.

While we munched and prattled on, we were eyewitness to an extraordinary sight outside the floor-to-ceiling windows of the dining room. It was Schwarck in her flannel PJ's and slippers loping past the windows with Georgie springing along with her. Every curly hair on her head was standing on end and her face was all mottled red with the strenuous effort of running full throttle against a frosty wind. She was hurtling past the window attempting to retrieve flying zip locks, medications, and panty liners before Georgie or the wind got to them. It reminded me of Monty Python's "Running of the Twits". It was a truly spectacular and entertaining scene and quite surprising for us all. We heard a door slam and an embarrassed and breathless Schwarck skulked past us clutching her valuables to her braless chest. She mumbled something about running out the back door which locked behind her, necessitating this grand entrance through the dining room. Schwarck's morning lope-about was a vision I'll never forget. I advised all guests to be mindful of the wind tunnel created in the bathroom if you push the window out.

Schwarck reentered the dining room for breakfast and was properly dressed. Everyone else had left and I was the only one still eating. "That was quite a show, Schwarck! It was just like a Monty Python or Benny Hill skit! You must have hopped past these windows in your pajamas twenty times. I wish I had my camera. Did you get everything back?"

"No, I didn't. In fact, I never got it all back the last time it happened, and I can't believe the back door automatically locked when I went out. Didn't you notice that my stuff blew out again?" Schwarck asked.

"Well, I didn't see anything because my glasses were so steamed up. We are just going to have to be more careful because of the wind velocity in Ireland."

We asked Susan if we could stay in the dining room this morning to work on THE BOOK and she seemed a little put off by the request. She explained her sister would be here to clean, but that probably wouldn't cause a problem. The way she said this, though, it told me otherwise.

After the dining room table was cleared, we set up our little office and prepared to write, but the sister's vacuuming was so loud and her ramming into our chairs made writing impossible. I was amused by the ferocious cleaning antics of the sister, but Schwarck was pissed! Sorry to put it that way, but this is the perfect way to describe it.

"We might as well put all our stuff away and go for a walk. I know where there is a fabulous craft shop and I'll make you a deal. You won't have to walk both ways. We'll take a cab there and then walk back," Schwarck suggested.

I've visited big cities where there were no cab companies, so I find it mystifying that there is a cab in this miniscule burg. Turns out, Susan's brother is the cab company and he'll come to get us in his personal car. I actually don't care if he comes on a bike as long as I can get on it and ride instead of walk!

The craft store was a ride of approximately thirteen minutes over hill and dale. It was unimaginable that a place so isolated could draw enough customers to stay in business. The craft portion of the store was four rooms filled to overflowing with pricey wool products, jewelry, soaps, candles, and so much more. The owner quite proudly proclaimed that Hillary and Bill Clinton had come here a few years ago and purchased a number of wool items. Scant need for Secret Service out here.

There was an attached tearoom and bakery with a delightful sunroom for you to enjoy the heavenly food items. Tabletops were sparkling glass with each displaying a hand blown glass vase containing fresh flowers. The sunroom's shelves displayed local handmade pottery and blown glassware. Herb and flower gardens surrounded the property with all plantings identified in Latin and their more common titles. The owner stated horticulturists came from all over the UK to admire and learn about their superb gardens. This little business in the middle of nowhere was an unparalleled treat and as sophisticated as any shop you might find in a large city.

We girls have been bakery devotees our entire lives, and the breads from this little tearoom were out-of-this-world. Also, I have never tasted more delicious soup anywhere as their Tomato Basil. We loitered in the bright sunroom for over an hour. Reluctantly we departed and began a slow stroll down the endless lane.

I expect this green landscape has been unaltered for centuries. There are few trees or shrubs, just undulating grasses for as far as the eye can see. At the dirt lane crossroad was a stone-fenced cemetery of unusual headstones and graves. There weren't any trees or grass, just pebbles and larger stones to depict the outline of plots. Most had tall Celtic crosses at their head and there were volleyball size water filled glass domes with flowers inside sitting over the graves. Our quiet walk continued back toward Gus O'Conner's and past a Youth Hostel and up to a fortress-like property.

An Internet café was the last thing I thought we'd ever see in this little village, but surprise…the fortress complex had a couple of high-speed computers in their office for the public use. They also had a large gift store and restaurant as well as two buildings of hotel rooms. We had to share one computer as a Swedish hostel guest was using the other.

TO: FRIENDS AND FAMILY BACK HOME...PLUS A FEW BRITS

SENT: APRIL 19

SUBJECT: IT'S GRUELIN' AND I'M DROOLIN IN DOOLIN

Hi all,

I'm happy to report that we found a high-speed connection over here in a small hotel fortress not too far from our B & B…only fifteen walking miles away.

I'm perturbed about the way Irish lie to us about the weather and how far away something is. They seem to think forty-five degrees with hurricane wind forces enhanced by hail is lovely day. Our B & B owner was shocked by our weather complaints. "Are-nt ya ladees frum Mitch-ee-gin? Yah shud bee glad yur here instead of in yur freezing town." I can't say I have ever had to wear heavy sweatshirts under a hooded coat wrapped up in three wool scarves and donning wool mittens back home in April. We even have to wear this stuff indoors because no one here wants to turn on their heat.

I was so cold last night that when we got to the pub, I ordered a pint of lager plus some hot rum before dinner. NOTE: Eating a bowl of hot cabbage soup along with lager and hot rum will definitely make a trip uphill speedier no matter how much ice is on the lane.

Once again I lost the draw for the big bed. I don't get it. I think Schwarck is cheating, but I can't figure out how.

I've seen several great signs lately:

- Black Spot
- Traffic Calming Area
- Reverse Into Space
- Slow Down-Boys Know the Limits

After our visit in Doolin, we head to the dangerous Protestant North. Wish I had my Methodist membership pin with me. We are quite fearless though, and I'm so old and gimpy, no one should mess with us. All I'd have to do is slug someone with my snack bag and they'd think they had been pole-axed.

Our last bus driver told me that there is a town up the road called Lisdoonvarna, where all the local farmers go to get new wives. He said the road is so crowded in September that buses can't get by. He suggests that if we are having trouble with our mates, we should hit the town and give it a try. Why, oh why would I ever search for another when I have Hugh?

Lucky Kathleen

CHAPTER 20

DESTINATION. . . DEMILITARIZATION

Tomorrow we're heading to Belfast and the national news makes it look like we should be wearing flak jackets to go up there. I know tons of Protestant hymns and I am not beyond breaking out in mournful stanzas of "Abide With Me" at a checkpoint if necessary. Lucky for me, I have Irish Catholics and Protestants in my ancestry, so I will be whatever I need to be.

"Schwarck, do ya think armed guards will greet us at the border?"

"No, I don't think we'll have any problems. I've been there before and it was fine. We are going to have to get down to the bus stop early though. I think the bus leaves at 7 A.M. and there's only one a day. Let's ask if we can get a ride down in the morning. That'll save us a lot of walking and lugging time."

We attempted to write passages for THE BOOK in the dining room after breakfast, but it became clear that our writing activity was interfering with our hostess. We had removed the tablecloth, folded it neatly and commandeered the entire table for writing paraphernalia. The innkeeper kept emerging brusquely from the kitchen with little stacks of plates and utensils. She would set them down unnecessarily hard on the buffet and emit a little feigned surprised, "Oh, gee, sorry, I didna know ya lad-ees were still in here!" She is more than likely at war with herself, knowing she should not mind our writing on the table when it is not in use, but the crux of the situation is that she is a hopeless prisoner of routine and repetition. She has always set the table for the next breakfast right after finishing one, therefore, she cannot move on with her life until we are removed.

As lifelong observers of older adult behavior, both Schwarck and I can attest with assurance, that nothing will age you faster and make your life more stressed than refusal to "go with the flow". The pursuit of flexibility in both body and spirit should be the perpetual mission of people over the age of fifty. Rigid routines mess with your health in ways you cannot fathom! We believe, therefore, that we should help our innkeeper.

"Thanks so much for telling us to treat the dining room like we are at home. This is such an inspirational room to be creative in. We'll set the table for you when we are done this afternoon," Schwarck assured her.

That last statement of Schwarck's was the killer! Clearly, no one was ever allowed to set the table in the dining room. Now it looks as though we are in for it. I have seen a similar look on a ferret just before its ferocious chomping reduced an entire stucco wall to rubble. Our innkeeper departed briskly and there was some riled up cupboard slamming coming from the kitchen.

"Okay, Crawford, I think we've done enough here. Be real quiet so she'll think we are still in here. She can't see us from the kitchen door window. Let's just get ready and go out the back door to the Internet. She needs to get a grip and relax more!"

We enjoyed the remainder of our day leisure shopping in all three shops in the metropolis of Doolin. I purchased some postcards, wooly lamb magnets, a sweatshirt and more gloves. Schwarck found two snuggly cardigans to add to her insufficient wardrobe. We put on everything we bought because the temperature had dropped sharply and a blowing piercing dampness had commenced.

The best thing to do was to enter Gus O'Conner's for an early dinner and hot rum toddies before we trek back uphill to pack for tomorrow's early departure.

Irish Stew was on the menu and we were ecstatic about it. Peculiar how our usual complicated lives have been reduced to unparalled excitement over stew and hot rum toddies. One of the goals of our adventure was to determine if it is possible to live for five weeks unencumbered by duties and schedules. I will have to say a thundering, "Yes!! You can."

While waiting anxiously for our stew, we sort of got stewed ourselves on hot rum and Guinness. We were well on the way to our happy place when in walked two redheaded ladies, each named Pat who we had met yesterday at the Fortress Restaurant. They are both prison guards and having a little mental health week. We boisterously invited them to join us. There was a lengthy debate about travel with or without spouses. They had to divorce theirs in order to have a little girlfriend adventure. We honestly had considered those options at one time, but it was unnecessary. Happily, our spouses usually fluctuate between ardent support and total disregard for what we are up to.

Eventually, good-byes were said and all the husband talk prompted me to purchase an expensive Gus O'Conner's shirt for Hugh. We wound our way back up the lane pausing frequently to observe cloud formations and pet a horse that Schwarck insisted speaks to her.

We entered the front door rather noisily and Schwarck declared, "You should ask now for the ride downhill in the morning at 7 A.M. I don't think she likes me much. If it's raining and blowing, it would be an awful long soggy ride to Belfast. We'd catch pneumonia. Maybe she'll even call our Belfast B & B for us to tell them we are definitely coming."

"Okay. You expect me to ask her for a ride…then ask her to make a call to Belfast. Is that it?"

During our little discussion, our perfunctory unsmiling hostess smacked open the door from the kitchen. We were both startled and jumped.

"Hall-oo lad-ees! Whut kin I du fer ya?" She asked.

I plunged in and asked for the ride, the call and even about an earlier breakfast. The innkeeper seemed warm and reassuring and that all would be easily accomplished. She felt that a departure from here fifteen minutes prior to bus time would be sufficient and at 6:45 she would take us down in her car.

"Crawford, I can't believe how nice she was. You did it! I didn't think we could sweet talk old sourpuss into anything! She's even going to make an early breakfast for us! Wow!" Schwarck exclaimed.

We packed up our belongings and tried to get a good night's rest, but the wind and sleety rain rattled the windows. Schwarck was nervous about the terrible weather and had been awake most of the night. What if the bus didn't come at all today and we missed our connections and couldn't get to Belfast? We had already paid for our stay there! I always choose not to worry about these things until we know for sure it's time for action. Schwarck was dressed and went out the door to see what kind of breakfast was waiting. She swiftly returned to the room.

"Shit! I knew it, Crawford! The whole house is dark. I even knocked on the kitchen door and called her name. Now we've got to hurry to start walking down there. It's miserable outside, too! Help me put this garbage bag over my head so I can keep my computer dry!"

"Wow, I gotta have a picture of this! I never saw you look so stunning!" I said sarcastically.

As we rumbled down the hallway past the kitchen muttering complaints about people who say they will do things and then forget, a sleepy looking, robe adorned apparition appeared.

"Haa-loo, lad-ees. I toad ya I'd tak ya down. Just hav a seat der in the dining room and I'll bring ya some Muesli and here's some bread. Me husband is bringin the car round. You lad-ees shud lern tah re-laxx more. Ach….there he is himself, hurry up nah, ur yu'll miss da bus!"

We were forced to compress our load of baggage and ourselves into a compact car so tortuously tiny that we could not even see the driver.

Schwarck asked if he was her husband and he mumbled a serious, "E-yah, paurt time, it tis."

We would have locked eyes if we could have seen each other over the heap of bags. Our little car bumped down the stony lane to the bus stop where the part time husband didn't offer for us to sit in the warm dry car to wait. He hastily unloaded our baggage and held the door open until we could unfold our torsos and get out. I hurried to open my travel umbrella so that our computers and cameras could be protected a little from the icy blasts of a rain/sleet mix.

There we huddled with two young Russians from the hostel for twenty excruciating minutes in the horrible elements. They asked in painfully broken English if we were on a holiday.

"This is not a holiday!" I answered a bit too harshly. It would have been too difficult to explain that we are authors. I should have applied Schwarck's pantomime of writing a check. She says that people everywhere understand that. We never even got our coffee this morning. Things could get ugly.

CHAPTER 21

THERE COULD BE BEDLAM IN BELFAST

There was considerable trepidation on my part about crossing the border into Northern Ireland, but all was peaceful on the front. We were careful to follow all rules explained by our no-nonsense driver: "When arriving at the bus station on the border, do not go in the station, just transfer yourselves and all luggage from our green bus which will be at one end of the lot, to the big blue bus at the far end of the lot and then you will officially be across the border. Your money will no longer be Euros but will be Pound Sterling."

Schwarck and I are zealous disciples of rules, but these rules are especially critical to avoid incarceration or death, therefore, the transfer was made with efficient movements and no talking. I sincerely believed that there would be a wide yellow line on the pavement or maybe caution tape we would have to run through one at a time.

As we pulled away from the bus station in the blue bus, I remained uneasy but there were no signs of barbed wire or armed guards. In fact, the ride through the north was most agreeable; streets were all wide and paved, cars were newer, infrastructure more organized, yards were landscaped, and there was evidence of prosperity. Towns were modern with malls and big box stores. The countryside featured tall trees, shrubbery, lots of houses, and numerous schools.

Our ride took us through a town called Armaugh where Schwarck's family had some history. Some of her father's family, the Rayners, had been sent there as Orange Men when Irish land was given to Brits to settle, all part of Henry the VIII's answer to his scorn for the Catholic rule on "No Divorce". We had a little break at the station here and Schwarck took some pictures for the family album.

The ride to Belfast took all day, and we arrived downtown in the early evening where we were deposited at a monumental transportation station that accommodated hundreds of buses and trains. After securing a stack of pounds from the ATM, we made our way outside to hail a cab that would take us to our new abode in the suburbs. The 1940s style black cabs were surprising to see and exceptionally shiny and distinguished looking. I insisted that we secure one for our ride to our new B & B.

There was a vast difference between the remote southern Ireland of last night as compared to the thriving hustle and bustle of the busy capital of Northern Ireland. The tree-lined streets of the neighborhoods were cement paved and there were paved sidewalks on both sides of the street. Our new B & B was a three story, completely brick home. It was surrounded by tall, well-groomed hedges and there were lots of flowers in the back yard. The décor was pleasing and all the floors were a highly polished wood. Once again, the B & B proprietors had not received our reservation or our credit card, but they could accommodate us with a room. We were led to a spacious second floor room painted a bright cream and had a large double bed and twin bed both with reading lamps.

"Schwarck, what's the point of spending so much time on-line, trying to make reservations somewhere in advance. We should just show up and pay as we go and if they're full, just move on to somewhere else."

"I just don't get it. Internet reservations are supposed to work immediately."

"Well, forget about it for now. Let's leave the unpacking and bed draw for later, and get outside to find something to eat while restaurants are still open. I think I saw a food sign at the corner."

We found a quaint little Italian restaurant and discussed the plans for tomorrow over wine and spaghetti. Drinking alcohol in the UK is practiced with daily regularity. At home it's a socializing activity reserved primarily for weekends or special occasions. Since our adventure feels like a five-week special occasion, we have chosen to tipple daily with everyone else. We usually just have the house variety of red wine or a gin and tonic for fear that our alcohol naiveté will be noticed. Also, I feel responsible for the reputation of all Americans. Therefore, there will not be any displays of drunken debauchery, but there may be some stumbling and overly loud hilarity. We decide that tomorrow, we will catch a city bus downtown to a Tourist Bureau to see if there are any local tours available.

"Crawford, do you want to just take the big bed tonight?"

"No, let's just do the draw right here at the restaurant. Give me the tea and sugar packets. We'll try that. This time you hold them and the sugar gets the little bed."

I clapped my hands to warm them up and began using the same peculiar little circling tricks that Schwarck had applied days ago. I didn't feel any warmth or vibration at all. After some circling and chanting, I selected the sugar packet, thus drawing the twin again.

"Don't even say a thing, Schwarck. Let's just head back home so you can get in your big bloated bed and go to sleep."

Breakfast downstairs the next morning was jolly and enjoyable. Not only was the food tasty, but also it was quite different from the south. Now we get spoonfuls of cold canned pork and beans next to our fried eggs, plus slabs of bacon…no Bangers, no fresh tomatoes or mushrooms. There were about fifteen guests in the sunny dining room; all talking at once and we were the only women. The tables were filled with firemen attending a nearby First Responders Conference. I am an ardent supporter of First Responders, so we had some lively discussion. I feel safe and slightly titillated knowing that we are sleeping with brawny and muscular Irish firemen.

After breakfast the proprietor told us how and where to catch the city bus and it was a snap because the bus stop was right across the street. We had barely stood there a minute when the express bus arrived for a speedy trip downtown.

The Belfast Tourist Bureau was on the second floor in a downtown high rise on busy Main Street. The Tourist Bureau was not only open, but also bustling with tourists purchasing all manner of goods and booking tours, trains, hotels, and boats. I imagine all Irish Tourist Bureaus could be very busy, if they actually opened for the tourists!

"Oh, my God, Crawford, the lady there just said there are only two more seats for an all day tour tomorrow to the Giant's Causeway. Let's get 'em! That's my favorite place in the whole wide world. You will love it! I can't believe we can get on it so last minute. This is meant to be."

"Um, right! Okay with me. Look at these cute postcards. They'll be good to send to all our girlfriends. See, they can plant their own Shamrocks!"

We purchased the tour tickets and decided to shop around a bit, have an early dinner, then head back to our home hoping the virile firemen will lounge with us a little this evening.

Our B & B host greeted us in the entryway and asked about our day. We told him we expected to tour the Giants Causeway tomorrow and would be eating an early breakfast. He said the weather promised to be warm and sunny, but he would not see us at breakfast as he is officiating at a funeral. It seems he's a Mortician at a local funeral home as his side job. Tomorrow should be a long and lively day, at least for those still above the ground.

CHAPTER 22

A BROGUE BROUHAHA

We awoke to fluffy white clouds, blue skies, and bright sunshine. The warmer temperature and sun were providential. Perhaps we were finally going to get spring. We hurried through breakfast and called a cab because we had to arrive at the downtown Tourist Office by 9 A.M. in order to catch our tour bus.

We had been instructed to gather on the sidewalk out front where the bus would pull up. We should just display our paid invoice to the driver as we got on. This is a busy street, so he will stop only for a moment and then will proceed to the train station to pick up additional passengers off a cruise ship docked at the Port of Belfast. Everything is so efficient here and seems well planned.

As we got on the bus, our elfin like driver introduced himself as Stephen. He said he wasn't going to talk much until we had all of the passengers onboard and got out of the busy city traffic into the countryside.

Schwarck is revved up for me to experience the Giant's Causeway, "a geologist's dream!" I had no idea what she was talking about, so she gave me the version for dummies as we bused along city streets. We would see ancient basalt columns which are slow-cooled crystals from volcanic eruptions. There are tens of thousands of them. Many tower over twenty-feet high. She feels a strong magnetic force there. I consider that last bit of news and drift off during her enthusiastic presentation. The tour brochure also says we are going to visit the Bushmills Distillery and we can volunteer to be a whiskey judge, so I kinda lost interest in the stupefying magnetic geological site story.

We picked up approximately twenty cruise ship people at the train station and now that all were on board, our perky, red-headed driver started to go over today's itinerary. He was sprightly, round-faced, cheery, smiling from ear to ear and had a heavy Irish brogue. We leaned forward to listen more carefully as Stephen began his little touring speech, with, "Nah, hal-loo, fucks! I'm Stephen, and fucks…I weel be which-cha awl daaay."

Schwarck and I locked eyes and were instantly transformed into two four-year-olds who had just overheard a friend calling someone "Poopy Stinky Butt"! We could not contain ourselves and dropped our heads, covering our mouths with our hands. No one else seemed amused. Stephen innocently continued, "Ya fucks must mind da time ta-day. I canna wait fur yur fucks, fur the train, fucks, canna' be lait. Okay, fucks?"

We two could barely choke out a unison, "Ok-kaaee, Steeee-vehhhhn!"

Our first stop was to be at the Carrick-a-Rede Bridge. This was a rope bridge used for centuries to cross from the mainland over to a high rocky island out in the ocean. We would make a stop after that at the Fullerton Arms Pub for lunch, then on to Giant's Causeway and finish the tour at the oldest licensed distillery in the world, Bushmills. Stephen chuckled and said the ride home was usually quiet.

The 45-minute stop at the rope bridge would be wonderfully scenic, and I'm sure the walk would be very healthy, but I chose to stick around the parking lot, practice with my camera, and visit the little snack bar for hot cocoa. The day was warmer, but up on this steep bluff overlooking the raging ocean, the clean air was more than brisk. Schwarck said she wanted to go to the bridge and walk out to the island. She gaily bounced along with the bus crowd, and I watched until they became little dots off in the distance. I practiced with my camera magnification to see if I could find Schwarck on the Rope Bridge, but the distance was too great. It wasn't long before people were returning to the bus, but Schwarck was still missing and it was time to depart. Stephen was outside jubilantly assisting passengers up onto the bus steps.

"Yu fucks, watch cher step!"

"Stephen, my friend isn't here yet, but she doesn't wear a watch because she's too magnetic, so maybe she doesn't know the time. What should we do?"

"Waall, Ie'll wait as long as I kin, but ya know we got the train fucks."

I have to pinch my lips together every time he says that word. The bus was getting packed. Even the serious looking young Italian couple from the front seat just leaped in. They ran both ways on the rope bridge and were not even out of breath. A worried Stephen gave me an apologetic grimace as he fired up the diesel engine. I was on the lookout for my pal who would have to jog to get back in time.

"Wait, Stephen, I think I see her! There she is…she's coming! See the red shoes? She's kinda limping but she's heading this way!"

"Ok-kee, fucks, jest a min-ite, we gotta git' er!"

At last, a winded, red-faced, and wheezing Schwarck stumbled onto the first step and Stephen quickly closed the door behind her and took off. She banged her way down the aisle offering a breathy apology to all for her tardiness and gratefully sank into our seat.

"Crawford, I'm not kidding, I thought I was going to have a heart attack! It's miles to the bridge and when I could see that I was finally close, I felt like I had to go the rest of the way. I saw that Italian couple from the bus so I thought I had enough time. My legs are just shaking. I'm shaking all over! Gawd!"

"Well, guess what, Schwarck, Stephen said the Italians are honeymooning marathoners. They flat out ran all the way there and back and didn't even sweat! That's what you would have had to do to get back on time. You should wear a watch even if only for a day. Do the watch hands continually twirl around or something on your magnetic wrist? What did you see when you got there anyway?"

"I didn't see anything because the wind kept whipping my hair in my eyes and my eyes were all watery from the wind. I was so worried about the bus leaving! Gawd! It was horrible."

"I had two cups of hot chocolate and talked to some American ladies from the cruise ship that didn't wanna walk out there either. They want to have lunch with us. Well, maybe not you now!"

"Here we are! It's time fur yur lunch, fucks! Ye fucks jest git off da bus, nah. Da first fucks in da door, jest tell da pub fucks, yoooou fucks are with Stephen."

I love this guy, but the young male Italian honeymooner in the front seat is getting all riled, which makes the whole thing even better! Running honeymooner guy is being held down by his wife as he tries to leap to his feet. He vehemently implores in accented English, "Why-ah, dus-ah-hee-a- keep-a call-ling us-a fucks? Hees-a-all-a-ways-a -call-us-a fucks!"

Helpful, oblivious Stephen had already hopped outside to assist the passengers off and was totally unaware of the chaos he created. My kindly pal patted the Italian's shoulder as we passed and attempted to explain in a Kindergarten teacher style with her face all pinched and concerned, "Please don't be mad at Stephen. He is not really calling us 'fucks', he is calling us 'folks', but it sounds like 'fucks'. Stephen is really very nice." I gave

Schwarck the move along wave because I could tell that Romeo could only hear "fucks" even when she said "folks".

"Let it go, Schwarck. There are two American fucks in there saving us a seat."

"Well, I don't want them to be mad at Stephen because of his accent. They probably won't even give him a tip. I'm gonna try to collect the tip from everybody and give it to him in one lump sum."

"Let it GO! It's too much fun! Oh, there are our old girls and they've saved us seats!!"

The historic pub called the Fullerton Arms looked ancient and smelled of hops. There was a beautiful polished bar highlighted by a grand illuminated display of liquors. Some of the men from our group chose to stand at the bar with their feet on the foot rail like men surely have done for centuries.

Our new fortyish female acquaintances were on a holiday from important Washington, D.C. jobs. They never offered to say what their work was so I suspect they are either undercover or they make up beds at the Washington Mayflower. I doubt if it involves anything physical as they each are well past fluffy and one in particular is approaching morbidly obese. These two were nonplussed by our author status but wanted their picture taken with us in case we became celebrities. I was sitting closer to the larger of the two cruisers and became grossly aware that personal hygiene was not her highest priority. She was odoriferous now and promised to be reeking by midday. We all know people who are expensively dressed but somewhat slovenly. Such was the case here. I decided that I would strive to always be in front of these two and would avoid their half of the bus. No doubt Schwarck will feel that it is her duty to right this American's pungent wrong and will look for ways to tactfully tell her that she has a foul smell. I pass and choose avoidance at all costs for fear that someone will think that I'm the one reeking. Don't you think it's the most difficult thing in the world to tell people they smell bad? Why don't they know it? Besides, what can they do about it if they are out on tour all day?

"Oh-kee, yu fucks, time tah goo nah!"

I didn't have time to eat all of my lunch so I asked Stephen if it was okay to take a little carry-on box on board. I also asked if I could get a picture of him with me. He was thrilled to be asked.

Romeo's chair furiously scraped back and he strutted out the door alone. When we got back on the coach, the Italians had vacated their front seat and moved to the rear with the Reeker! A spunky little old Scottish lady wearing a long dress and shawl confiscated the front and became the commanding officer of the tour and Stephen whom she referred to as "Stee-vie".

It was a short ride to the Causeway and when we arrived, Stephen told us to hurry and get a ticket for the little shuttle bus that would take us down the steep hill so we could get up close to the columns. There is nothing that can prepare you for this odd sight. It's a mystical phenomenon. The shoreline looks like thousands of upright gray telephone poles were pounded side-by-side into the earth.

The columns are of varying heights and people were climbing all over them. Amazingly, there wasn't any caution tape or warnings, no "danger ahead" signs. You were on your own out here and responsible for your own accidents.

Schwarck climbed all over, and I took numerous pictures of her looking all pensive and serene. She was at her spiritual nirvana. We walked all over the beach and waited as long as we could before we had to go back to the bus. The D.C. dames caught up with us and wanted a photo with us. We told them okay, but we wanted to do it outdoors. If we had to stand next to them, we needed to have lots of air circulation.

"Ok-kee, yu fucks, time fur whiskey. We don't wanna be late fur that, fucks!"

We smiled warmly at Stephen as we got back on the coach. He was so splendidly cheerful.

"You know what, Crawford? When we get to the distillery and they ask for volunteers for whiskey tasting, let's both raise our hands so that at least one of us gets to do it. That'd be fantastic in THE BOOK!

"Schwarck, have you ever tasted whiskey?"

"No, but I'd drink it for THE BOOK!"

"Okay, we'll both volunteer, but if you're picked, I don't think you'll like it especially if you're required to drink more than one sip."

The Bushmills Distillery was first licensed in 1608 and back in the day was one of hundreds of Irish whiskey distilleries. Now only a handful are still in existence. A Bushmills guide met and led us through buildings that were gravely ancient, but well preserved. There was a lot more activity in the gift shop than in the buildings he led us through. Irish Whiskey is revered here. There is a whiskey-brewing heritage and recipe-stealing paranoia. We followed him in a line like cows heading for the barn. I paid careful attention to the location of the putrid D.C. crony, but an abstracted Schwarck chose to chat her up and follow closely behind her up a steep wrought iron staircase. Schwarck kept fanning her face with her tour book and was commenting about the odd smell of the hops in here. I did my best to give her a nonverbal signal to get out of line, but she was oblivious.

We reached a large reception area containing numerous tables and chairs as well as a big wooden bar and roaring fireplace. Our Irish Bushmills guide asked for tasting volunteers, and we both enthusiastically raised our hands along with about twenty other people. He only wanted six tasters. An exuberant Schwarck was chosen and so was the D.C. chick who said she is a whisky connoisseur. I couldn't believe it. The other selected testers seemed to be whiskey devotees, so pal Schwarck is going to be way out of her league.

"Oh my God, I hope you don't throw up. That stuff is strong and look, they're bringing out ten whiskies for you to test and those glasses are bigger than shots!"

This testing is serious business. Judges were to sit at a picnic table next to each other and Bushmills staff brought our paper placemats with 10 circles on them. Large shot glasses were put on each circle and the pouring began. They were to try each of the ten unnamed whiskies and then rate each for smoothness. He added that after the tasting was completed, everyone was invited to the bar for a drink of Bushmills or a hot toddy.

The judges began their jobs like scientists. Some sipped, some swilled it around in their mouth, and others just tossed the golden liquid back and swallowed. Schwarck watched carefully how other judges proceeded and began sipping the number one whiskey. She was careful to take a swig of water to clear her pallet in between each selection. This was going to be interesting. There was smacking, oo-ing and ah-ing from all but Schwarck as they knocked back each whiskey. Ten shots of whiskey is a lot to imbibe, but she did it! Her face was pretty red, though. The guide asked each for their favorite of all and one by one each gave their favorite choice. He explained that he had been doing this for over fifteen years and in all that time, no one had ever picked the whiskey that was Schwarck's favorite. He said it was the cheapest off-brand in existence. All the other judges picked one of Bushmills. He then thanked them and asked what each wanted to drink at the bar and Schwarck piped up very loudly, "I want a hot toddy!"

It was more of a demand than drink order, but the guy hurried off to get Schwarck's order filled first. The rest of us placed an order with the wait staff. We all enjoyed our socializing made more boisterous by the drinking of whiskey and toddies. Before we knew it, it was once more time to board our bus. Boarding the bus was only possible by us drunkards passing through the extensive gift shop. Everyone, being in such an expansive mood, made major purchases of Bushmills logo items, paintings, sweatshirts, and more. Bushmills had an incredible marketing strategy.

We returned to our bus and everyone struggled to find room overhead for all the new purchases. Schwarck was reduced to a puddle of giggles and kept trying to whisper something to me, but the whisper was so loud, half the bus could hear it. To get my attention, she kept tapping me on the head with her new gold embossed certificate, which was incased in a cardboard tube.

"Nah, I told you fucks that the ride home would be quiet. It's been reported tah me that someone might have their shoes off for there is powerful stench on da buss. So it maybee best ta put dem shoes back on, fucks!"

This "powerful stench" news put my festive pal into hysterical chortling. She just couldn't put a lid on it. I kept shushing her but it was no use. The whiskey had taken control. Stephen began to point out sights to us as we re-entered Belfast.

"Ok-ee, it's been nice day, but yu train fucks gotta git off nah."

The train passengers collected all their parcels and made their way down the aisle with Schwarck whispering and giggling goodbye as well reminding them all to tip Stephen. Our Washington acquaintances were the last ones off, lingering by our seats with their farewells.

Stephen hopped back in the driver seat and pointed outside through the open door to show us the large Belfast fish market and our little Irish Commander lady leaped to her feet. "Jay-sus, Mar-ree and Jo-seph, Holy Mother ah God, Stev-ve, close the bleedin door, it's a pa-rerful fishy stench in here!"

With that pronouncement, both Schwarck and I could no longer control our guffaws. We were reduced to howls of laughter and tears were running down our cheeks.

"Ok-kee, fucks. I've really had a time with ya, but cha awl gotta git off at the next stop. Watch cher steps, fucks!"

I made sure that Schwarck didn't give Ste-vie over a thousand dollars from us, but he was clearly worth it.

CHAPTER 23

ONE IF BY LAND. . . SICK IF BY SEA

Our plans for the evening, as usual, were to look for food first, then find an Internet Café. After that we would take a cab back to our B & B and pack for tomorrow's departure.

We are in love with the Marks and Spencer Store. Why don't we have them in the US? You can buy a designer bra, a lamp, a freshly made sandwich, and a decorated cake within ten minutes. They even offer as cute little place to sit and enjoy your sandwich. Everything is so beautifully displayed and convenient. The food choices are spectacular and especially fresh and delicious. We selected some "take away" items and thoroughly enjoyed our little dinners.

The Internet was close by and had computers available without a wait. We took seats in the smoky little store and started typing away. Everyone but us was seriously puffing away and I knew our time here would be limited based on how long we could hold our breath. There's something very revolting about smoke that reaches me which has just passed through the nostrils and innards of complete strangers. I never used to think about this, but now I do!

My musings were interrupted by Schwarck who was pointing to her computer screen. “Crawford, look at this! The Tourist Bureau booked us in some obscure Scottish B & B twenty miles out of town for tonight and tomorrow, and they’ve already charged it to our credit card. We can’t even get to Scotland until tomorrow night. Geeze, this is driving me crazy. They better refund us and re-book somewhere else, or I’m reporting them!”

“Yeah, well who you gonna call? The Queen? “

TO: FRIENDS AND RELATIVES BACK HOME

SENT: THURSDAY, APRIL 22

SUBJECT: WHERE ARE THE IRISH SETTERS?

Well, here we are in sunny Northern Ireland…Belfast… and it’s amazing but no one tried to kill us yet. No strip-searches either! I did see some rolled up barbed wire on top of a building.

Glad we left the frozen Cliffs of Mohr. Our hostess forgot we had to leave early for our longest travel day yet, so all we had to fortify us for the sleety pelting rain was a half bowl of dried Muesli and a little cold buttered brown bread wrapped in tinfoil. Her husband took us down the hill to the bus stop in a car that was smaller than the trunk of an American car. Schwarck got wedged in with her cockeyed backpack, which was covered with a garbage bag to keep the sleet off. I didn’t think we’d ever be able to get out of that midget stunt car. He dumped us onto the sidewalk in the howling wet wind alongside an intertwined, emaciated young Russian couple. What they were doing to stay warm didn't seem like it would work for Schwarck and me.

For those of you following the map of Ireland, we left Doolin for Ennis and on to Limerick where we changed buses That's where, when loading my suitcase, I whacked the back of my head excruciatingly hard on the luggage bay door. I must say, though, that my hair spikes up particularly high where the gigantic lump is located.

From Limerick we rode through the center of Ireland to Athlone where we changed again, then on to Monaghan where we changed again. We had a layover in Armagh, and since this was a place with history for Schwarck's family, we took quite a few pictures. Most of the drivers were really nice and seemed professional except for the one we had for the longest leg into the north. He actually looked a lot like the slapstick actor, Mr. Bean. He came to a complete stop every time an oncoming truck got even with us. I can assure you that there were tons of trucks on this highway, so the ride was much pretty stop and go.

Schwarck's ankles should be as big as her waist for all the ham she has consumed at breakfast and lunch everyday. Where are the little piggies, anyway? We still haven't seen a one.

Saw more signs yesterday:

"Get In Lane" (Okay…how do they know you are out of the lane?)

"Dangerous Bends Ahead"

Things are definitely more modern here in the north. They even use big Zamboni- like things to clean the sidewalks. We never even saw a sidewalk in the south, and I still have cow pies stuck in my shoes from the lanes in Doolin.

Our tour guide driver today was named Stephen and he called us fucks all day. I'm confident it was supposed to be interpreted as folks. Some Italian guy asked him, "Why-a- yu-a al-a-way- a call-a us-a fucks?" Stephen very innocently replied that he calls everybody fucks…black, white, whatever… "They're all fucks ta me!"

Romeo never got over it for the whole trip!

NEWSFLASH: We went to the historic Bushmills Distillery and Scwarck (of all people) got selected to be a whiskey taster. She can nurse a Marguerita all day and she was a terrible tester, but took her job very seriously. Every judge was supposed to pick the smoothest one out of ten whiskies. The Bushmills guide was astounded with her choice. He said in all the years he had been conducting tours; no one had ever selected her choice because it was the cheapest and most poorly fermented. She got a lovely gold embossed certificate, which was protected in a cardboard tube. She delighted in whacking me on my head lump with her beautiful award all the way home. What a ride that was.

We rode through a town today that had a population of 400 and 14 pubs. Wow!

Schwarck has been so smug rolling around in her big bed every night. My headboards are not even attached to my puny little bed, and I never get a reading lamp. She, who never reads, gets one. Life is so unfair!

Pray for calm seas, as tomorrow we set sail for Scotland at 11 A.M. I doubt if we'll get to an Internet in the next few days, but we'll try.

Love to all!

God Shave the Queen,

Kathleen Crawford…that'll work better in Scotland

We hailed a cab back to our last Irish accommodations and began packing up all of our gear for the day-long traveling tomorrow. The next morning our very obliging host called the Internet Booking Agency for us and solved our booking problem. He booked us in another place closer to Edinburgh. He also called a taxi that would take us to the Ferry Terminal.

The Ferry Terminal was deceiving from the outside, as it appeared to be an old warehouse but once inside, we were met with comfy overstuffed chairs, snack bar, and large clean restrooms. I enjoyed socializing with a mischievous, rotund, little old red-faced guy who introduced himself as Sammy. I'm sure that if you looked up "Scotsman" in the dictionary, Sammy's jolly picture would be there.

I was a little sad leaving Ireland, the home of my ancestors. Who knows if I will ever get back here? The way my joints are giving out, I should be grateful for the traveling I have already had. Don't you think that life is kind of backward? When you have less responsibility, more time and a little extra money to travel, you are usually dealing with two or more debilitating medical conditions and dependent relatives who prohibit you from enjoying the experience.

When it was our turn to board the ferry, we joined hundreds of people marching up the ramp. The brochure proclaims that our ferry can carry thousands of people. The ship design is ultra modern…bright colors and Jetson-style décor. There is something reassuring about a modern looking ferry. But then, wasn't the Titanic cutting edge? I don't think I'm going to like this much. We have all heard the tragic stories of some ferry that flipped over or some igit forgot to close the back door and the ferry took on water as they sailed off. The North Channel crossing is often rough, and I suspect that is why passengers are not allowed out on deck, which does not bode well for me on this two-hour cruise. I am a horrible sailor and despite trying the patch, pressure point bracelets, gingerroot, and hypnosis, I have still thrown-up on every one of the thirteen cruises I have sailed.

Seasickness typically overcomes me unexpectedly in populated places, such as the elaborate entrance of a gift shop with hundreds of passengers within easy viewing and spewing distance. On a wonderful Holland America Alaska cruise, I puked into their ornate antique bronzed ashtray, which was far too small for what I had to put in it. I should learn, though. When at dinner, if a dessert cart thunders by at 50 MPH or your wait staff takes your order wearing a life jacket, I should immediately go to my cabin. However, I usually choose to continue cramming myself with foods so rich that even if you were on land, they would be impossible to digest. Husband Hugh accuses me of thinking I'm going to throw up, therefore, I do. What kind of crap is that? Regurgitation has never been a goal of mine. He used to think I made our children have motion sickness because I gave them a plastic bag for the back seat. I call that preparedness and forward thinking, for I was the one they always barfed on.

We select some ferry seats with a table, hoping to spend some time on computers to catch up with THE BOOK writing. We set up our computers because Schwarck is very worried that if we don't write every day, we'll forget what happened. That could easily happen since I already forgot what happened this morning. Schwarck has made an amazing new scientific discovery today.

"Crawford, have you noticed that people here all have the same high foreheads and bushy eyebrows?"

Where does she get this stuff? Before I could give her a look befitting the inane statement, a rowdy parade of ten young women wearing matching sleazy t-shirts, head pieces, and raggedy jeans with high heels screamed by. They were singing some loud racy song. The leader kept blowing a shrill metal whistle.

"Yeah, Schwarck, now that you mention it, that group of bridesmaids over there look like they have high and seriously sloping foreheads. Their eyebrows look like they have been shaved, but I suppose they used to be bushy."

Schwarck went to the snack bar to get cheesy fries and me a Happy Meal while I stayed at the table trying to write a little but finding that I should just keep staring at the horizon line. Two hours later, we docked in Scotland. I was elated for the cruise to be over before I lost all of my Happy Meal. Buses were awaiting the ferry's arrival and we piled on the one heading for Glasgow.

The Scottish countryside is sparsely populated, even along the coast. Grasses here are brownish, tall, and willowy. We entered the bustling city of Glasgow and changed buses for our final destination, Edinburgh. It is our goal to spend at least four days in Edinburgh. According to Schwarck, there is a lot to see there, and she also wants to visit the part of town where her Grandma Gurney had lived as a young girl.

Edinburgh was humming with activity and exciting to see. Downtown is pedestrian crammed and the lush parks are filled with people eating their lunches outdoors in the spring warmth. There were a myriad of well planned flower gardens and the city has an abundance of statues and ancient buildings. This weather and city are a delightful change from what we have endured the last three and a half weeks.

Our new B & B is located in an Edinburgh suburb called Portobello. We hailed a cab to take us there, and departed the beautiful city going down the pavement through neighborhoods, which became increasingly seedy. We passed aging blocks of grand old homes that had fallen into disrepair and decline. The further we traveled, the business community became predominantly massage parlors, tattoo salons, Chinese laundry, pubs, tarot card readers and social service offices. Businesses displayed varying examples of entranceway protection such as pull down chain doors and heavy iron bars.

Our twenty-minute cab ride came to an end in front of an older three-story brick home that appeared to be a duplex. There was a wrought iron fence and elegant metal gate that contained a bright green yard with a sprinkling of flowers and concrete path leading to the large wooden door. It was fortunate that the home was located on the main avenue with a bus stop right across the street. Daily cab rides downtown would be far too expensive, so the city bus would be our best mode of transportation for the next few days. There aren't many large cities in the US where I would favor riding a city bus, but over here it seems safe and convenient.

We tugged our unwieldy luggage up the steep walkway to the front door of The Robert Burns Bed and Breakfast. I turned the carved knob and opened the wide antique door to discover an entranceway facing another door of smoked beveled glass. Schwarck knocked first and when no one came, we called, "Hall-loo". There was an envelope stuck in the door, and it instructed us to look in the little chest of drawers on our left. We began to cautiously open the tiny drawers to find another envelope with our names on it. There was a bit of mysterious treasure hunt feel to this reception. There was a note and four keys in the envelope. The two skeleton keys were for the front door and two other metal ones with the numbers 301 were for our room. The note welcomed us to The Robert Burns and explained the owners were away for the evening, but for us to make ourselves at home and they hoped we enjoyed our third floor room. As we entered the door a frustrated Schwarck explained, "Honest, Crawford, I did tell the B & B that you had a knee replacement and needed to be on the first floor. Sorry! I'll go up first and drop my stuff off, then come back down to help you."

"Well, I ought to be used to this by now. I'm feeling pretty muscular and it's a good thing because if we leave to go to dinner, I'll probably have to fight off the gang on the street that's going to jump us."

She headed up first and her voice sounded a mile off as I heard her exclaim over my grunting and groaning, "Oh, wow! You're gonna love this room. It's huge and you can see the ocean from here."

"I'm sure! You can probably see the United States from up there."

The closer I got to the top floor, the narrower and windier the carpeted steps became. We were definitely going to be sequestered in the attic. As I huffed and puffed my way up to the landing, I saw the door of another room open a small crack and then close. Schwarck came out of our room to grab my suitcase. I couldn't get inside the door quick enough. I whispered through clenched teeth, "Did you see that other door open a crack? There's somebody up here with us. It's creepy. Hope he picks you to take down to the cellar, like in the Phantom of the Opera. Anyway, we better keep this door locked all the time, starting now."

I put my ear up to the door for a few minutes to see if there was anyone moving out there. All was quiet.

She was right about the room. It was the biggest one yet with a desk, several chairs, two big windows and, yes, a small and large bed. What is it with these people? The bathroom was also roomy and had shelves for our equipment. There were two big chests of drawers and several lamps.

"Okay, Schwarck, here goes. Let's draw for the bed."

"You know what? Let's not draw this time. You just take the big bed while we're here. I've had it every time."

"Nope, come on. Sugar packet is the little bed."

This time there was no exclamation of shock and awe after the draw, just a look of disbelief on my face and a wince on hers. I stomped over to the little bed and hurled my cases up onto it and began to unpack. After the unpacking was done, I couldn't believe I was suggesting it, but I said, "Why don't we go out and find one of those grimy little restaurants we passed? I bet the food is really good no matter what the outside looks like. Maybe we can even get a glass of wine to celebrate our arrival in Scotland. Okay, when I open the door, let's run to get downstairs past scary attic guy."

We found a little café with homemade soups and sandwiches and everything was delicious. As we walked back to our room through the decaying neighborhood, Schwarck commented, "Look at all the people in the street up there. Maybe it's a sale of some sort."

"Uhm, from what I can see, if it's a sale, they're beating each other to a pulp to buy stuff. Have you ever seen people rolling around in the street at a sale? It's a big fight, and I think we should cross the street to get away from it. Nice neighborhood we live in here."

As we got closer to the fracas, we determined that the two guys pummeling each other had just rolled out of the pub and took it to the streets along with a bunch of patrons who were cheering them on. No sign of the authorities. They're probably too afraid of this region.

We hurried back to our B & B before the mob took sides and things got even uglier. I think I'm too old for a street rumble, especially if it is going to mean falling down and getting back up.

As we hurriedly approached our building, I noticed the curtains being pulled aside in the front window of our adjoining duplex. We quickly entered our side of the building, with me looking nervously back over my shoulder. We were being watched on all levels. When I thought about it, though, people here should be cautious, jumpy, and looking out their windows all the time. I would if I lived here. Hey, wait a minute…I do live here!

CHAPTER 24

OVER THE RIVER AND THROUGH THE HOOD

This trip is now beyond an adventure. I knew it would be life altering, but I never expected it would be life threatening. Our first day in Edinburgh and we have barely avoided combat in the street and being accosted by creepy attic guy. In addition, as previously mentioned, our B & B is a duplex, and we now suspect the other side is a group home as there are a number of adults in nightgowns who stand together at the window. These village people living in the same building could be hopelessly maniacal for all we know. Schwarck is totally unaffected by all this intrigue, but then, she is the one that selected this place out of hundreds, because she felt it had literary connotations: "The Robert Burns Bed and Breakfast."

We desperately needed to do some laundry. I washed out some things in the sink, hung the items at the window over the heat register, and attempted to write at the charming little desk but finally gave up on it. I chose instead to shower and get down to the ugly business of clipping my toenails, which are starting to work their way through the tops of my shoes. This would be a job for bolt cutters.

After all that, I planned to snuggle up in my baby bed with a fabulous tale of Henry VIII's lusty exploits.

Schwarck interrupted my nighttime reading wanting to discuss a plan for tomorrow. These evening strategy sessions of offering up a couple of stops we each want to make, are about as finite as our travel planning gets. We'll start out with breakfast, then search for a laundry, get the bus and go downtown for the Internet and some touring. Most of our activities evolve around food.

The next morning, I discovered my underwear and stretch pants were still damp, so I had to leave them hanging over the curtain rod and put on the least soiled duds. I do have one pair of clean underwear so other breakfast guests should not be gagging at breakfast. I'm not as sure about Schwarck's clothing situation.

There wasn't any action from the door across the hall as we tiptoed across the landing and hurried down the stairs. Our host served us coffee and his daughter took the breakfast orders. He explained that he is originally from the states and anxious to move his family to Florida as soon as his young son graduates from the prestigious middle school he's attending. His son is an award winning golfer and "on track" to becoming professional. There were photos of the father and son all over the dining room. Many of their pictures were with celebrities at golf outings. No photos of the wife and daughter were evident. One picture and trophy, in particular, caught my eye. It was a picture of the grinning owner with his golf team. They were surrounding a trophy as the proud winners of the Linda Lovelace Wide Open. He mumbled something about it being a charity function. Breakfast was wonderful and as we ate, calming classical music wafted throughout the lower level. Our host was chatty and offered several touring suggestions as well as laundry info. I was tempted to inquire about the attic dweller, but decided it might be better to know nothing about what we're dealing with here. Schwarck ran up and got our laundry, and we headed out to drop them at the laundromat, and then catch a bus downtown. She was limping today as we navigated the crumbling sidewalk.

"Well, the stairs and all this walking are finally getting to you, too, aren't they?"

"No! It's not the walking. I stepped on something in the room and it really hurts. I'm going to sit down here on this bench and take my socks off because maybe it's still in there. Whatever it is, it's sharp—it made a little hole. Oh my gosh, look! It's bleeding! I must have stepped on a steel shaving. Got any antiseptic wipes with you?"

"No…how about glasses' cleaner? That might work? How could there be steel shavings in the room? We're not staying in a tool and die shop!"

There she was, perched on the bench with her bare foot up in the air, trying to bring her foot up to her eye for inspection. Her sock was a little bloody. Then I got to thinking…..

"Um, Schwarck, whatever you stepped on, was it near my bed?"

"Yeah, did you step on something, too?"

"Um, no, not exactly, but I was sitting on the bed last night cutting my toenails and they were flipping all over the place. Maybe I missed getting a few to the trash. I doubt if that's what you stepped on though, but may…be."

I could tell by her face that she was pretty stunned and grossed out by this news. I hope there's no infection that takes root, or a bright red line that runs up her leg. That'll be a little hard to explain at the Universal Medicine Clinic: "My total lymph system is a raging fungus infection because I was lanced by my friend's razor sharp toenail clipping!"

She was dazed, but put her shoe back on and hobbled behind me to the laundromat. There was an attendant on duty, but it looked like most people did their own laundry here. The attendant agreed to throw ours in when a machine became available and we could come by tomorrow and get them.

"I think we'll be lucky to get our clothes back, Schwarck. Did you see how they were sizing us up to see if they could wear our big old American stuff?"

"Crawford, did you notice how deep set everyone's eyes are here?"

"Um, yeah, now that you mention it. I think the deep-set eyes are a direct result of the street beatings every night. Those big-fisted guys pound each other's eyes back into their heads making em' look very deep set."

The day was wonderfully warm and sunny and our city bus ride was quite pleasant. We got off right downtown Edinburgh in front of a large active Tourist Bureau that also had a computer room for its patrons. We reserved two computers and began immediately to communicate with friends and family.

TO: FRIENDS AND FAMILY BACK HOME

SENT: APRIL 23

SUBJECT: AYE, SCOTTY

Believe it or not…we are in Scotland now.

Saw a new sign: "TRUCK UNDER REPAIR". Why not just fix it instead of putting up a sign about it?

For you map followers: from Belfast we sailed across the North Channel to Scotland and took a couple of buses to Edinburgh.

Schwarck booked us way out of town in a rough neighborhood. Of course, our room is on the top floor of what I expect is a group home of some sort. She said she asked for the first floor…am I being punished? You would never believe how hard it was to tote all our stuff up these three flights to our room. The stairs kept winding more and getting narrower and darker the higher up we went. I think we're screwed into the attic. In any case, we are most definitely screwed! The oxygen is thinner and we can see the ocean out the front window. I actually think I can see the United States from up there.

Our room is really big but the bathroom is complicated. There are lots of gadgets and cords to pull and turn.

She won the bed draw again. I am obsessed with this bed thing. Someone creepy is staying on the same floor and keeps peeking out the door at us, but we've never seen him/her…only one piercing eye.

Tomorrow is Schwarck's 54th birthday, and I am giving her the entire day to do whatever she wants,within reason. She wants to visit the house where her Grannie lived and she has the address so we'll go there. The rest of the day will no doubt include piles of food and thick cake somewhere.

Scottish breakfast is a lot like the Irish, except it's served in Scotland.

Schwarck is starting to point out her observations about people. She thinks the people in Northern Ireland had high foreheads and bushy eyebrows, now in Scotland, it's deep-set eyes. I told her I counted how many deep set eyes I saw in southern Ireland and there were more there than here, so she is perplexed.

So far I haven't seen anyone who looks like they are related to Scottish husband Hugh, but that's probably because they are all indoors in front of a TV and a tray loaded up with macaroni and cheese.

Gotta go, for we are taking a little plaid tour bus around town.

Love to all.

Kathleen Crawford

We stepped outside the Internet office into the glorious sunshine. This weather was such a treat after weeks of sleet and dreary wet Irish days. I believe it's going to be a month before I get warm again.

There were several two story brightly colored tour buses waiting at the curb, and we purchased tickets from a sprightly attendant who was running up and down the curb soliciting customers. Our ticket allows us to ride for 24 hours, which is a bit too long of a tour for me. We can get off and on as much as we want. There is a docent/historian onboard each bus, and they provide the narration on all the historic districts.

Our bus guide was exceptional and very enthusiastic. She pointed out that we would see all the old and new parts of Edinburgh. The newest part of the city is still older than anything in America. That's amazing! As we passed an ancient churchyard, our guide explained that women suspected of being witches were once tied up and thrown into the lake next to the church. If the women drowned, they were found innocent, but if they bobbed to the surface, they were convicted and burned at the stake. I am positive that I know many obstinate, sometimes witchy, women who would have been tied up and thrown in, including Schwarck and me. It's highly doubtful, however, that we would have ever bobbed to the surface.

We were so captivated by our guided tour that we rode the entire route again with a different guide who offered even more historic anecdotes. We finally got off the bus at the foot of the Edinburgh Castle and gazed down the street which is known as the Royal Mile. At the bottom of the Mile sits the venerable Palace of Holyrood House. The Holyrood is the official residence of the Royals when they come to Scotland.

The Royal Mile is comprised of a multitude of interesting shops and eateries and as we proceeded down the steep hill, we stopped and made several purchases. It was fun to pick out plaid scarves for our girlfriends back home. We selected ones of the same colors and design so that we could start our old ladies clan. I was particularly enjoying the downhill aspect of the walk and was well in front of the still-limping Schwarck when I heard her call out, "Hey, Crawford! Come back! This place will take a picture of our aura. Come here!"

Walking back uphill with a sagging twenty pound fanny pack and big bag of twelve wool plaid scarves is not agreeable no matter what the enticement, so I waved her off and stood still. But, she entered the aura establishment, so I was resigned to the trek back uphill in order to hurry her along.

I entered the store completely out of breath and there she was, in the midst of gentle stone fountains, tinkling chimes, dangling crystal displays, magnetic bracelets, and aromatic candle pots, prattling with a young woman wearing a pastel tie-dye dress and leather headband with feathers hanging down by her ears.

"They can read our auras right now, Crawford. It'll be so cool! Let's do it! They just take a picture of the gas surrounding our body."

This situation sounded very similar to "Aromatherapy

Massage" at the airport. I double-checked with the feather hippie to make sure no electrical current was involved and nothing that would make my hair stand on end. She reassured me that it was just a photo of my gas and would cost a whopping Ten Pounds, which is the equivalent of about $20 US.

"Don't you think that's a lot of money to pay to see your gas, Schwarck? I bet there's going to be a profusion of purple around our butts because of all the greasy fish and chips we've been eating."

I went first and was told to sit in this overstuffed and well-used recliner. I was instructed to keep my arms bent and on the chair arms while I leaned forward for the picture. There were a couple of flashes but no electrocution. Schwarck followed me into the chair and then we waited for our Polaroid results. There were many aura pictures on the wall in the peculiar aura area. After ten minutes, our results were in and our hippie friend pointed to me and said; "Yyurrrr photo matches the one frrrrommm the ownerrrrr….e's frmmmmm the states, too. Eerrrr he comes now!"

She handed me my photo and explained to the owner that we were a match. He grabbed me in a big bear hug and went behind the counter. When he returned, he pinned a Scottish broach on me. The girl gave us envelopes with instructions on how to read our auras. My aura picture had to do with royalty and supreme leadership while Schwarck's indicated a life of servitude. I could tell by her slumping shoulders that she had anticipated a more positive interpretation of her gas.

As we left the store, I quizzed her. "Schwarck, seriously, how can a picture of your gas tell anything about your personality?"

"I'm not sure, but my spirit guides from my past lives have different color auras. I told you that in one of my past lives, I was a Viking man and my wife poisoned me, so maybe that's why my gas isn't as good as yours. I really trust my spirit guides to keep me safe."

"Yeah? Well, trust this! If you come up with any more expensive whacko ideas like aroma therapy massage or aura reading, I might poison you in this life."

CHAPTER 25

WE MIGHT BE IN PLAID FOREVER

We found a unique restaurant on the Royal Mile called the Filling Station and decided to top off our tanks with a gallon of light ale. Gas station paraphernalia including full size gas pumps surrounded our booth, and we enjoyed generous slabs of fried cod and a giant mixing bowl full of fries. We ate fast because we didn't want to miss the last double decker bus back to the Tourist Bureau and our transfer to the city bus, which would eventually take us back to The Robert Burns.

I have spotted a considerable number of things in Scotland named after Robert Burns, who is still a national celebrity even though he was born in 1757 and only lived 37 years. He was the composer of Auld Lang Syne and composed hundreds of other songs as well as authoring a plethora of well known poems. Hence, we are happy to be staying at The Robert Burns Bed and Breakfast, despite being creeped out by our neighbors.

The city bus was packed and the ride took a little longer because of the increased number of people heading home after work. Our stop was a block from The Robert Burns and we plodded along slowly, lugging all our packages. When I looked up from the street to our room, I was appalled to discover that my giant bra and underwear were clearly displayed in the big windows for all passersby and bus riders to enjoy. They looked absolutely gargantuan from down below.

"Wow, Crawford! Who knew you could see them so good from down here! Oh by the way, when we were in the Internet today, I heard from my friend Erik who is on the last leg of his six-month journey through Asia and Europe. He is going to arrive in Scotland and hopes to meet up with us. His traveling companion is a young girl named Karen that he met on-line. Remember, I told you I met him in Italy. He had recently graduated from college and wanted an adventure just like us. We had an instant connection. It was like I had known him forever."

"Oh, really? How long have you known this new best friend anyway…a week?"

"I met his parents first on the group trip and then he joined them, and we all had so much to talk about every night. It was just great! I think we were together for at least a week and a half, but we have been emailing a lot since then. I hope we can see him because you will just love him."

"Yeah, I'm sure."

We headed upstairs to our room praying there would be no startling encounters with creepy attic guy. No door creaking this time. He's probably out getting more whips and chains. I rushed to the window and took down my incredible display of massive white underwear. We were both really tired from our full day of fun in the sun and were looking forward to climbing into bed. We'll pray to the weather gods that tomorrow will be even warmer because it is Schwarck's fifty-fourth birthday and we will be on a mission to find Granny's house.

"Schwarck, watch out! Don't walk barefoot by my bed. I see a couple more toenails I missed. Did the bleeding stop yet?"

She applied ample amounts of antiseptic cream and bandaged her foot. I felt slightly guilty during the bandaging, but I seriously doubt it was my toenail clipping that made her lame. Besides, who could ever believe that a thick toenail sliver can permanently maim or kill?

We awoke to a fabulous bright day.

"Happy Birthday, girlfriend. Do you feel any older? Want me to bring you breakfast in bed?"

"You don't need to bring me anything. I just want to get down to breakfast and out the door to find Grandma Gurney's house. I'm going to call my Mom and Dad later to tell them what I find out and they'll sing Happy Birthday to me."

The ride downtown was uneventful and we were unloaded once again in front of the Tourism Bureau. We discovered that on Sundays the Internet was free, so we had a little wait but quickly began our Internet communications.

TO: FRIENDS AND RELATIVES BACK HOME

SENT: APRIL 24

SUBJECT: THE WEATHER'S GOOD BUT THERE'S A LOT OF UGLINESS HERE

We are lucky today because the Tourist Bureau is giving us free Internet access. It is fabulously warm, and we are thinking that we may never have to wear the gloves and wool scarves again.

I hope we can lose the gloves because Hugh bought me golfers' gloves, and they have a velcro closure that has picked up several items in stores, such as cashmere sweaters and scarves. There are bundles of things that attach themselves to me every time I wear them.

I think I have reached my limit with walking. Schwarck has nearly killed me with the sauntering all over Ireland and now Scotland. There is no ideal time for walking aimlessly. If it is cold and wet, you are miserable and if it is warm or hot, you are miserable. Schwarck is convinced that I am beginning to have a change of heart about the strolling. Today she said, "I believe you are moving a lot faster!" Well, yeah, I'm moving faster because then we can get on the bus stop quicker and I can get the suffering over with. I prefer riding for pleasure. I have more time to appreciate the out of doors while sitting in a motorized vehicle.

Edinburgh inhabitants are a feast for the eyes. There is an incredible lack of good taste, by my standards.

Women here pack their one hundred ninety pound pasty white torsos into radically tight jeans and shimmy them down to butt dimples. On top they wear a thin stretchy shirt two sizes smaller than needed that usually has a profound political statement on it like the one I just saw: "Masturbation Is Not a Crime". There will also be at least a foot wide gap between the jeans and the shirt to leave space for the display of kinky body piercing. Many here have face piercing with a lot of safety pins on the eyebrows. I presume the pins will keep the eyebrows attached to the face. Top off the ensemble with a pair of bright red six-inch heels with toes so pointy they look like a weapon and you can envision the captivating look.

We have to find a pharmacy today because Schwarck stepped on what she thought were steel shavings but it was my toenail clippings, and she has been lame ever since. We must go there also because we are both in desperate need of hair dye. A profusion of gray locks is not attractive on adventuresome old broads.

We are taking the train out of here in two days to head for Barrow-In-Furness where Schwarck's father was born. She plans to meet some of her relatives that no one in her family knows. She is beyond excited about this.

Spring has finally sprung on our adventure.

Love to all,

Two old ladies in the UK

After considerable walking, asking directions, and some whining on my part, we located "Convening Court" which Schwarck's mother told her is the street that Grandma Gurney was born on. We walked and walked some more and finally located "Convening". It wasn't a street at all, but a brick courtyard surrounded by three old multi-leveled brick buildings. While we were looking for addresses to see which building was hers, we met a man who was painting his part of the building. When we explained what we were trying to find, he invited us into the building. He was very interested in our quest because he has studied the history of the area and is dedicated to preserving its historical integrity. Unfortunately, he was quite sure that Granny's building had been torn down years ago. He told us that this area had housed a large number of poor families who had come to work in the tanning factory. The entire area would have been foul smelling and the factory waste was dumped into the nearby river called the Waters of Leith. That was the same water that everyone drank, so there was a lot of illness.

Schwarck gazed out the upstairs window trying to feel her Grandma Gurney's spirit. "Granny always said she could see Edinburgh Castle from her window." Seeing the castle from the window is impossible now because of the large trees in the courtyard. I took lots of pictures of her at this place, as she is the only one in her family to have come here. It was an ethereal experience for her.

Satisfied with our findings, we followed the meandering placid Water of Leith for over an hour. There was a profusion of colorful spring flowers and plantings along the peaceful river path, giving you an impression that the big city was miles away.

We walked quietly along the path which eventually brought us back onto a bustling city street full of shops and restaurants. I let Schwarck choose her birthday restaurant. After a celebratory glass of wine, dinner and birthday cake, we did a little shopping before catching a bus back to the laundromat.

Our laundry had been neatly folded and put into two wonderful clean smelling stacks. We were so pleased with the result that we didn't even look to see if it was our laundry. Schwarck talked me into walking the five blocks back to The Robert Burns even though we had to tote stacks of laundry. During the walk back, Schwarck announced that she had another email from best friend Erik and he said that they are definitely coming to Edinburgh tomorrow night.

"Crawford, isn't that great that we will have a chance to see them? I decided that since they don't have any money, that I'd just pay for them to stay at our place for the night, out of my own personal money. This will be a treat for them because they have had to sleep outdoors and in hostels for the past six months. They probably won't get to our place until about 11 P.M. and they'll be starving, but we can pick up some beer and snacks. Isn't this exciting?"

This was a staggering announcement and actually caused me to totally lose my voice. When it finally croaked out, I started my interrogation. "Exciting? Schwarck, I can't believe you actually paid over $200 for two strange hippies to come sleep with us. What are you thinking? You don't know these people. They probably haven't had a bath in six months, and they won't even get here till after 11 P.M. tomorrow night and after they arrive you wanna' feed them? In case you forgot, we are usually sound asleep by 10 P.M., and we have to be out of here the next morning really early to catch our train downtown. Man, this is bizarre, even for you!"

"No, it'll really be lots of fun! Well, at least I know he will be. I never met her. We'll hear all about the exotic places they have been. Erik said they have gotten to participate in a number of political rallies in some of the countries."

A chance meeting with someone from a group trip to Italy does not, in my estimation, equate to an enlightened affiliation or rapport. We must be extremely cautious now. I have consistently resisted sleeping with strangers, particularly unemployed, back packing, flaming liberals who participate in political rallies in foreign countries. Tomorrow promises to be freakish.

The next morning, we told our hosts that we needed to be out early tomorrow and they promised to have a breakfast ready for us. They gave Schwarck the key to the tiny room adjoining ours for Erik and his Internet babe. It had a little bed and washstand. Oh, my God.....they are supposed to use our toilet and sink.

Our plan for the day included the purchase of train tickets to our next destination as well as shopping for a carry-on bag because my suitcase can barely close now, and I still have to cram in all of those big wool clan scarves for the eight girlfriends. As usual, we will also plan things around lunch in the park and dinner.

We opted to go all out and eat dinner in a nice downtown establishment called the Abbotsford. This historic eatery was embellished with brass hardware and richly decorative woodwork. The solid square tables for four were set beautifully with crisp white linens, shiny ornate silverware, and tall goblets. We started out at the thick wood bar with Guinness and began conversing with a charming older couple that said they had met here long ago when he was in "the boy's brigade". They delighted in hearing about our five-week adventure and we all socialized well past dinner.

Much to my dissatisfaction, we had to stop on the way home to buy beer, chips, and cookies for our expected late night guests. Schwarck had wanted to go out about 9 P.M. to get beer so that it would be cold, but I reminded her about the brawling guys that hang out at the neighborhood pubs, not to mention all the other demented folks near us who probably come out at night.

It was well past midnight and I was dozing off when a taxi pulled up outside. There was talking in front of The Robert Burns, so Schwarck assumed it was our guests and she ran downstairs to open the door. I resented the intrusion of these two strange backpackers. I had been forced to stay dressed and made-up for the late night encounter, but after introductions, I planned to get in bed immediately.

As the hushed voices wound up the staircase, I eyeballed the door with dread. My mental picture of this pair included an oily ponytail for him and brush cut plus tattoos for her. They would more than likely be wearing filthy, smelly t-shirts and jeans with lots of holes and held together with safety pins. I expect each will be profoundly pierced and their backpacks will no doubt reek of pot or some other illegal substance.

The door opened and Schwarck swooped in all giddy like, dragging a handsome clean cut and smiling young man who looked like he just got finished bailing hay in Minnesota. He was tanned and had a scrubbed carrot look about him. His partner, Karen looked like an account exec dressed for a casual holiday in the Hamptons. Introductions were made all around, we cracked open the warm beer and snacks, and I readily forgot all about going to bed.

These young adventurers were thrilled and grateful for the opportunity they had to travel all over Europe and Asia. They both had journalled the entire trek and planned to write a book. She was in the travel business and felt this experience would enhance her profession. We swapped hilarious travel incidents for hours. They were rolling on the floor after hearing of our exploits, particularly Schwarck stepping on metal shavings and my adventure with aromatherapy massage at the airport. We showed our travel slideshow with music and before we knew it, it was 4 A.M. and we had to get up pretty soon. They said goodnight and thanked us profusely for providing them with the room and breakfast but, more importantly, for sharing our experiences. They expect us to keep in contact with them and want to know where they can buy THE BOOK.

I was stunned and guilty to be so judgmental and off target about Erik and Karen. There were no body piercings, tattoos, filthy lice infected bodies, or drug addictions.

In fact, I am the one using all the drugs. Also, I am the person with the abysmal incorrect bias about two young backpackers on an adventure of discovery, like us…not exactly like us, but a little. I have to say, I love my new best friends and I have learned a valuable lesson.

CHAPTER 26

PRIVACY MATTERS

The Edinburgh train station was a beehive of activity this early morning. Due to our late night guests, I was only about half awake when we staggered into the waiting area and plopped into two seats while awaiting our train. Announcements were piercing the air and no matter how intently I listened, I could not comprehend one word. Where do they get the people who make announcements at bus stations, airports, and train stations? If your only job is to deliver a short message into a microphone, why shouldn't you be capable of making yourself understood? I wish I could hire announcers. I would demand perfect elocution. Whoever does the hiring should fill the prospective candidate's mouth with pebbles and ask him or her to recite: "A skunk sat on a stump, the skunk thunk the stump stunk and the stump thunk the skunk stunk." The candidate who is most clearly understood should be hired on the spot; however, no one gets this speaking job because of perfect enunciation.

"Come on, Crawford, that's our train announcement. We're on this side of the tracks that are southbound."

“Wow, you understood it?”

It is marvelous and nothing short of a miracle the way Schwarck can enter a huge train or bus station, listen to some garbled announcement, make a quick assessment, and know precisely which lane we should get in and which side of the tracks we should stand on. It’s uncanny. I am clueless. In fact, aboard ships, I still haven’t got “port or starboard” down. I do know “aft” as long as someone shows me where “forward” is. At least I know that my disorientation is not a condition of aging because I have always been this confused.

“Oh, my God, Schwarck! Is that our train? The one that says “virgin”? I’ve heard of the airline, but I didn’t know there were Virgin trains. Geeze, the letters are gigantic! Well, it seems slightly naughty, but I feel like a re-cycled virgin, so I guess it’s okay to get onboard!”

We rolled our umpteen bags across the platform and onto the Virgin train. The ultra modern stream lined car had luggage bins in the front. We stowed everything but our backpacks and overflowing snack bag. I refuse to take a chance on someone making off with the snacks.

Our Virgin seats were thickly padded, and we both nestled in for a few hours of reading as well as planning the Barrow-In-Furness sojourn.

I’m sure there’s some significance for the curious name of our destination. According to Webster, a barrow is a heap of earth or rocks covering a grave. Sounds like a fun place.

"I feel bad, Crawford, that we are going to be spending so much time and money hunting down my family heritage, and we didn't spend much time with yours in Ireland. You have no idea how exciting it will be for me to see the street where my father was born in 1922 and hopefully the actual house he lived in. My mother researched forever to find out where it is and finally got the address: #4 Steel Street."

"Well, don't feel bad. It was my fault—I wasn't prepared like you. I am satisfied that we actually found an island with Cotters on it….uh that island would be Ireland!"

Our train ride was going to take approximately four hours with a change of trains in route. With each new stop, groups of students got onboard and were starting to pile up by the doors. They were sitting and standing in the aisles and communicating loudly with their friends. I wasn't excited about navigating my way through the teenage gangs to the bathroom, but when nature calls, I am forced to answer the call immediately.

"Crawford, you want me to go with you?"

"To the bathroom? I don't think that's necessary yet. It's right up there in the front, isn't it…by all those kids?"

"Yeah...but it's weird looking. You better read all the signs carefully."

I slowly bumped my way up front and when I arrived at what I presumed to be the bathroom, I comprehended Schwarck's toileting advisory. However, there weren't any signs that I could see, but there was a vertical row of four colored buttons next to a black curved glass door that looked like I'd get beamed up if I get in there. Not wanting to act the fool for the amusement of all the students, I selected the logical green button for "go" and pushed it; nothing happened. I pushed the red next, then the blue, and slowly the door rolled aside, and I quickly stepped into a no-frills stainless steel compartment. The door was still open and the students were peering in, so I found a row of buttons by the sink and pushed the top one, then the second. I didn't know which button did what. In any case, one button did shut the door, so one of the others must be the flusher. I hoped there wasn't a button for a bidet or something that would create a giant geyser in there. I hate to say it, but this was literally going to be a crap shoot! As I began to pull my pants back up, I pressed one of the remaining buttons anticipating flushing action, but much to my shock and astonishment, the door rolled open instead. I quickly initiated a rapid punching of buttons and the door made a swift open-close-open-close-open-close performance. I could tell by the muffled snickers that the students were taken aback by the panorama of my prodigious white winter thighs. Great God above! I completed yanking my pants up and leaped free of the compartment as it opened again. While readjusting my clothing I made a hasty departure from the area.

"Wow, Crawford! You created quite a stir up there with the kids. Were you telling them jokes or something?"

"No, I didn't tell them anything, but I did show them something." I sincerely hoped that Schwarck needed to use the facilities soon so that I could see how she handled it.

An hour later we changed trains for the final leg of our journey to Barrow-In-Furness, which is an industrial town on the northwest coast of England. At one time the town was well known as a major shipbuilding port. Schwarck explained a little of her family's history to me.

"Dad was a very young infant when his mother and grandparents decided to leave England and sail to America. While they were waiting on the dock, Dad's father changed his mind about leaving England, walked away, and was never heard from again. Dad has no memory of his own father."

"Geeze, that story would make a great movie, don't you think?"

"I guess it would. His father's sister is still alive and lives in Barrow-In-Furness. My Mom's detective work found her on the Internet and we are going to meet Aunt Gwennie and her two children. My Dad never knew any of these people. I'm getting nervous, Crawford. I feel like the official ambassador for my whole family."

We exited the train and walked into the dingy little Barrow station. It was obvious by the surrounding rag-tag buildings that this town had experienced hard times. We looked for someone to ask where or how we can get a cab, but seeing no one around, we just wandered outside to an empty parking lot. A trolley-like bus entered the lot and the driver got out to come in the station. We asked him how and where we could catch a cab.

"Ah, ladees, I'm headin up tah the place where ahll the busses come, so I'll just taake ya'. A cab might not come here fer quite a while."

The mini-bus driver was neatly uniformed and almost skeletal in appearance, but he owned a wonderful warm smile and was very accommodating. I suspect his driving job does not normally include taking people from here to another bus. In any case, we were very happy to see him and loaded our suitcases onboard while he checked in at the station. He returned quickly and told us that it was just a short ride to the visitor center. Someone at the Tourism Bureau could tell us which bus we needed for our B & B.

Schwarck rolled out the story of her father's life for the driver, and she asked if he knew where #4 Steel Street was located. He was touched by the heart-wrenching story of the baby boy whose father chose to stay on the dock, rather than accompany his family to America. He had no idea where #4 Steel Street was, but suggested that the staff at the Tourist Bureau might have heard of Steel Street. Despite our protests, he insisted upon carrying our luggage off the bus. We tried to pay him for the ride, but he refused to take any money.

"We dun't git meny visitors eerr, so ahm appy ta help ya."

As we got off the bus, several matrons hurried over to get in line for our little bus. The benevolent driver held his hand up to halt the oncoming passengers as he tugged my suitcase out of the bin and up to the door. In one invigorating swinging motion, he got enough momentum to fling my suitcase off the top step and out the door. Regrettably, he did not let go of the suitcase as he swung it out and my hefty bag transported him through the air and out the door, slamming his emaciated body onto the sidewalk below. We both ran forward to assist, but he had already arisen cavalierly and brushed himself off. He remained undaunted, but noticeably less enthusiastic as he lowered the rest of our bags. The driver's misfortune reduced Schwarck to nervous giggles that could not be contained. We reiterated our appreciation for his generosity and tried once again to pay him. He waved us off; no doubt glad to see the last of our monumental baggage and us.

The Tourist Bureau was a small room with glass counters displaying a variety of books and brochures about the area as well as a miniature collection of gift items. Most hotels have bigger gift shops than this. There were two ladies behind a counter and Schwarck addressed one with the story of her father and #4 Steel Street. Soon everyone in the place was involved and offering direction to Steel Street. Once again, no one was sure of where we could find it. They gave us maps and bus routes, and we left the building to get on one of the busses waiting out front.

We chose bus #1, from the three waiting because according to the map, it looked like it traveled the closest to the Browshead Bed and Breakfast. When we got on, Schwarck began to question the driver about our stop and immediately all of the other passengers chimed in on the discussion as to the whereabouts of the Browshead. The driver had never heard of it or the street address. A few passengers thought they had seen it, but believed we needed a different bus. We and our bags, got off #1, and headed back to the little glass enclosure to study the map again. So far, people in this town are relentless in wanting to give us assistance, or maybe they are all just nosey. A perky middle-aged redheaded woman approached us, said her name was Maggie and asked if she could help us find something. We told her what we were looking for and that the #1 bus driver said he had never heard of it.

"ACccchhhhhh….what is he, SSHtyoo...pid? That 'otel's only been dere twoo hoon-dred years! E' moosst be Irish."

Maggie marched us back up to the waiting bus we had just gotten off of and curtly explained to the driver where the Browshead was and how close his route comes to it every day. She stepped back off the bus, grabbed some of our bags and carried them onboard. We numbly followed her to a seat and all the time she admonished the passengers and driver regarding the location they should have given us. I loved this woman. She was the commander of the bus stop.

"IIII'lllllll ride with ya', ta' show awll the Irish where tis'."

We were somewhat ill at ease with all this attention along with Maggie's astounding goodwill. Schwarck began relating her story of her fatherless baby father and the magnitude of her quest to find #4 Steel Street. It was glaringly apparent from all of the passengers' enraptured faces that this tired town was desperate for drama.

Suddenly it dawned on me that Schwarck had booked us into a place called the Browshead. Get it? Brow's head…. features that appear at the very top of your head! These accommodations sound very similar to our previous cloud-kissing lodgings; The Alpine House and The Hillside.

"EErrr's our stop laaadees!" an enthused Maggie

stated. As Maggie accompanied us off the bus, all of the passengers enthusiastically bid us farewell and cheered for our success in finding Steel Street. We three hauled all the bags off the bus and my eyes glazed over as I looked up the enormous hill in the direction that Maggie was pointing. Sure enough, it was on top of a giant hill about three blocks up. Maggie left us and headed off on another uphill sidewalk just as it began a cold pelting rain.

We hurried as fast as we could to get up to the Browshead so that our backpacks would not get soaked. We didn't care about our clothes as much as our expensive equipment. It was a horrible hike but we finally arrived in front of a sprawling two story English Tudor style home. There were three doors in the front of the house with three steps leading directly up to each of the doors. We tried all three doors but all were locked. Then we knocked and yelled. Schwarck walked all the way around the sizeable building but found no other entrance. We scanned the area for signs of life and then decided we should cross the street and go up a block to the King Albert Pub and inquire about the Browshead owner.

"I had great communication back from the owners of this place, and they were excited about our coming. I told them the time I expected we'd arrive, and they said they were always here. Hope nothing happened because they have our money."

"I don't want to haul all this stuff over to the pub. Why don't you get out your plastic bag and cover our suitcases. Let's hide them here in the shrubs. We can get a table close to a window so we can watch our bags and if someone messes with our stuff, you can run over and clobber them,"

I instructed Schwarck.

It was necessary to navigate around two giant kegs that were laying in the yard of the Browshead in order to head across the street. The owner of the pub greeted us and said the Browshead Missus is usually only gone for a short time and would probably be back shortly. Thus, we decided we might as well order ale and dinner. It was a delicious fried fish of some type, and we ate and drank until we saw a car pull up across the street and presumed the Missus had returned home.

We uncovered our luggage and rolled it up to the door and knocked loudly several times. A guy, who looked to be about 80 years old and was seemingly blind, greeted us and said the Missus was busy but he would carry our luggage upstairs for us. Uh, oh! We tried to discourage him, particularly since he was already clutching his chest as he pulled mine onto the first step.

"Come-on, Schwarck. We better haul this stuff upstairs. My luggage almost killed one guy today already."

It was a relief to enter the high ceilinged room and discover that there were two fluffy looking beds the exact same size with reading lamps overhead. Yea! No Bewleys…no beds draw. The entire house and our room were furnished with antiques. The room looked clean and had lots of closet space as well as drawers. It also had a sink next to the window.

"That's weird. Why would they put the sink over there and not in the bathroom?"

"Uhm, Crawford…there weren't many choices of places to stay in Barrow and this one looked the best. The only drawback, if you could call it that…is that we don't have a bathroom. It's down the hall and we'll be sharing it with other guests. It should be fine though, cause the owner said it's mostly businessmen and they leave early and come back late."

"Well that's… just…. great! It's not bad enough that the air is thinner way up here on the Browshead, but now we don't even have a bathroom. How far down the hall is it anyway? Geeze, I'm gonna have to put clothes on to pee at 3 A.M."

"It's up to you how much you want to wear, but wasn't it you who exposed your privates to gangs of teens on the Virgin train? This oughta' be a piece of cake!"

"I'm not talking to you anymore, Schwarck!"

CHAPTER 27

IT'S ALL RELATIVE

"See, it wasn't so bad not having a bathroom in our room last night was it?"

"Really? It wasn't a problem for you, because you aren't the one who had to get up two or three times during the night and make the trek down the hall in the dark hoping no stranger is in there."

"Do you smell anything funny in here, like incense or room fresheners? My throat is kinda' tickly and doesn't feel right this morning. That's the way it gets when I'm around perfumes or room sprays."

Well, Schwarck, look at the ceiling light. There's some freshener thingys up there but they're up too high up for us to get them down. There's one stuck to the side of the sink too. Geeze, look at that, there's even one in the plant. We better do a little air freshener treasure hunt or you're gonna' pass out soon."

I made it my job to find all the room fresheners because my pal gets an acute allergic reaction to certain aromas, which might trigger a super migraine forcing her to be bedridden in the midst of her meeting the relatives and finding her dad's homestead. She needs to be in top shape this week in particular. Schwarck began to cough but croaked out her plans.

"After breakfast, I'll call to see when we can meet with all the Rayners. My dad's cousin, Malcolm Rayner is expecting a call. Oh my God, look! There's a cake deodorant on top of the dresser. That's number five in this room alone! I'll be dead by tomorrow morning!"

We easily rounded up seven deodorizers and decided to put them in a bag in the closet. When we opened the closet door we found two more in there. It wouldn't have been so bad if these were natural smelling odors like cedar or pleasant lavender. Noooo! These were heavy smells like the big white mints co-mingled with the foulness in a State Forest campground outhouse. As we left the room to go downstairs to the dining room, I identified no less than ten more fresheners. Most were impersonating sun catchers and were all over the windows and stuck to anything made of glass. These proprietors must anticipate hoards of evil smelling patrons. Or maybe, the Missus is the one who smells bad. No sign of her yet, but the Mister served us breakfast in the dazzling sunny dining room. The décor was all flowery, lacy and frilly. Classical music was playing on the radio and there was a delightful smell of cinnamon bread coming from the kitchen. Thank the good Lord the cinnamon was so potent; it overcame the oily mix of deodorizers. More than likely the Missus is absent because she is busy scouting up new locations for air fresheners or maybe helping to unload the semi bringing in more of them.

Our proprietor's husband was quite talkative and told us he was retired from the post office, so Schwarck immediately drilled him about the location of #4 Steel Street. He said that he would be happy to take us downtown after breakfast and point us in the direction of Steel Street, the post office as well as the Internet Café. Schwarck felt intervention from the Devine was evident here; connecting us to a retired postman who may have delivered mail to her father's house before the war.

We finished our breakfast quickly to get upstairs and grab the stuff we wanted to mail home and get back downstairs before he changed his mind about taking us downtown. We were able to wedge ourselves into his little car and he took off bouncing down the hill. He dropped us at the post office and pointed in the direction of the Internet Café and gave us more specific directions to Steel Street.

"This is so exciting, Crawford. These are the exact streets my grandparents walked on. I can't believe we're here. I wish my nose wasn't so filled up with those awful atomizers and my throat wasn't feeling like it's closing up. Let's hurry to get to Steel."

Each of us had one large cardboard box to mail home. Mine was quite heavy, as I had packed all the wool stuff I had purchased as well as some books, gloves sweatshirts, etc. It was a leap of faith to expect our weather to be warm from now on, but I took the chance rather than keep all the heavy stuff with me. I opted to send my box as fast as possible and that cost $100 and they said it could take a month. That's ridiculous. Schwarck chose the slow boat around China and hers was $40. No telling when hers will arrive, if ever. The post office was jammed with long lines of patrons who weren't too happy that we, at the front of the long line had so many questions about the service.

Our next task was to get to the Internet. While Schwarck called the Rayner's and set up our meeting, I went directly online.

TO: FRIENDS AND RELATIVES BACK HOME

SENT: APRIL 28

SUBJECT: WE ROLLED ON TO BARROW…SO WE'LL HAVE A BARROW OF FUN

There is something profoundly strange about this B&B… oh wait but hey, there has been something very strange at every one of them! This one, however, has a relentless need for oodles of stinky deodorizers…all sizes and styles in every nook and cranny. We've taken pictures of them because they are so unusual. Schwarck's throat is closing up and she thinks she may be getting hives. I'm swelling, but I think it has more to do with the thick bacon and slabs of cinnamon bread.

Guess what else……..there is no bathroom in our room. We have to share with six other guest rooms. Our room and the bathroom have pull cords coming from the ceiling that don't do anything that we can determine…but you can bet we have repeatedly yanked on them. People throw bread on the roof here for the doves…I know, because our room is up so high, I can look down on every roof in the city.

Barrow is the first place we have been where no one says "Oh, lovely!" People are very nice and really-really-really too helpful. They all have asked us why we would choose to come here, because no one ever comes here.

Gotta go…because we are heading for Mecca… Schwarck's father's birthplace- #4 Steel Street. It'll be a divine experience of epic proportions. More later.

K.S.C.

We set off in the direction the Mister had shown us, stopping several times to seek directions and at long last, four blocks ahead, we saw it, Steel Street. Karen felt her spirit guides were leading us or maybe it was angels or some form of otherworldly magnetism.

"There! Look …….the sign! This is it, Crawford!"

She was literally running to the sign and stood underneath it with her hand over her heart. No wonder it was so difficult to find. The street was only a block long!

"Where do you think number four is? I'm going to ask someone who lives here!"

She began a little skip down the street, which aroused all the neighborhood pooches. Every tiny yard had a small yipping dog. Down at the very end of the row houses was a gray-haired woman hanging laundry. Schwarck made a beeline in her direction and leaned over the short stone fence to make some inquiries.

The conversation looked very animated from where I was standing and I saw the woman point across the street, and then go into the house. I was yelling to Schwarck as I walked up to the fence;

"Does she know which one is #4 Steel?"

"This lady lives here, but doesn't know much about the old buildings. She says her husband has lived here all his life and will know, so she went to get him."

The woman didn't reappear for at least fifteen minutes, but at last emerged. She was laboring to push an old man in a wheelchair down a makeshift ramp and out onto the bumpy yard.

I leaned into Schwarck's ear, "Good Lord, Schwarck. She probably had to get him out of bed and dress him and now haul him over here. Oh, my God…look, he doesn't have any legs!"

The older couple finally struggled up to the fence and Schwarck began an immediate probing query of the old frail gentleman, despite the obvious havoc she had created for these two. He thought he remembered the family, and said this block and the buildings on it were obliterated during heavy bombing in WWII. He was sorry, but # 4 Steel Street was long gone. We thanked them profusely and I was witness to a more subdued Schwarck walking purposefully toward the place where #4 had once stood. This was the location her father was born on. There were tears in her eyes.

"Crawford, I can feel it. I can actually feel my Dad's presence here."

There were no cosmic vibrations for me but I respected this solemn moment for my buddy. She was picturing her Grandmother on this street holding her baby boy in her arms. I took a lot of pictures. Schwarck was standing in the middle of the street imagining what the house would have looked like. I know she was reluctant to leave the area, but I was particularly hungry from all the walking and emotion, so I suggested that we find a phone to call her Mom and Dad and then we could eat before heading back uphill. She hesitated with each step and kept looking back. I'm sure she was trying to memorize each blade of grass to describe to her folks.

"Crawford. You have no idea how awesome it is to be right here, where my dad was born. You're right. We need to find a phone now so I can call Mom and Dad. I just can't wait til' I tell them. They won't believe we actually found it, especially since the building got bombed in the war."

"Well, I gotta tell ya, I can't believe you made some poor old woman go get her old legless wheelchair-bound husband dressed, out of the house and shove him across the yard to tell you where #4 used to be. That was pretty incredible!"

"He was happy to show me, don't you think? And he knew the family! OOoo. There's a big store over there! Maybe they have a medicine aisle for drugs to combat this stupid allergy I'm getting. I do feel better while we're outside of the B&B, but we have to go back there.

I've got to be feeling 100% when I meet Aunt Gwennie and Malcolm!"

We crossed a busy street and were thrilled with this "big box" store. It was the first large store we had encountered since leaving home. It was called Tesco and looked very much like a K-Mart or Walmart. We were just like kids visiting an FAO Swartz for the first time. I found some washcloths in the linen department and was euphoric so, they do have them over here, but no one uses them.

"Just feel these, Schwarck. Don't you wish you could take some back to our shared bathroom tonight? I'm going to buy some!"

"Look at this, CD Crawford. Rod Stewart looks just like you in your spiked up hairdo! You two look exactly alike! Cool!"

We found the medication aisle and were astounded by the vast array of upper respiratory remedies. Schwarck read the backs of all the packages.

"Okay, this is it. I think I have Catarrh. Read these symptoms, Crawford. Every one of these medicines works on Catarrh and that sounds like what I have. I'm getting a bunch of these and taking them tonight."

"Catarrh is what, exactly? I have seen that word in some antique medicine catalogues. It's probably mostly alcohol or maybe even opium. They don't tell you everything they put in these drugs, like in the US. You'd better be careful!"

While she made her selection of medical supplies, I

looked around and noticed a big overhead sign near the front of the store.

"Hey, they even have a café in here. Why don't we eat here? Then, you can make the big phone call to your Mom and Dad."

We got some sandwiches and coffee, and ate them in silence. I knew Schwarck was anxious and excited contemplating her overseas phone call.

Before long, she got up, threw her trash away and approached the bank of pay phones. I repositioned myself to watch her, in case she fainted from emotion and I had to get the paramedics.

It is a real test of fortitude to call from the UK on a pay phone. Not only do you have to put a gazillion coins in; you also have to talk to fifteen different operators. In the beginning of our trip, we almost bought a disposable phone over here that would allow us to call the US, but when we thought about it, we really didn't want to talk to anyone at home that bad.

Schwarck was finally successful and gave me the thumbs up and a wide smile. After approximately twenty-five minutes, she hung up the phone and as she walked towards me, I scanned her expression. Instead of a wide-eyed happy look, she was sad and gloomy looking.

"Was everything okay in Florida? You look awful! What is it?"

"It's my Mom."

"Yeah, is she alright?"

Yeah....but she said it was a typo!"

"Typo? What was a typo?"

"Number 4 Steel Street was a typo! She said, 'Oh, did I write Steel? I should have written Settle Street. It was #4 Settle Street he was born on!'"

"You... have.....got...... to be...... kidding..... me! How could it be a typo, she wrote it longhand! We have spent well over two full days searching and inquiring about Steel Street. In fact, we've had the whole country looking for Steel Street, including a guy with no legs and he even remembered your family! You felt cosmic vibrations... remember? Holy crap, Schwarck!"

"I know, but she says we were in the wrong place!"

"What are the odds that in an old city the size of this, there would be a #4 Steel Street and a #4 Settle Street? I bet there isn't any Settle Street. You felt your Dad's spirit on Steel, right?"

"We gotta go. I need to get back to the Browshead and start taking the drugs. Let's call a cab."

"Okay. You know what? I think I'm gonna' take some of your drugs, too! Did she actually say she made a typo?"

The cab came very quickly and we asked the driver if he knew of a Settle Street. He said yes, but it was not on the way back to Browshead. We told him we wanted to go there anyway and stop for a moment to take a photo, even though it was getting dark.

Settle Street consisted of dismal little two-story brick row houses with little or no yards in front. There was a dim light in the window at #4 Settle. Schwarck stood in the street and I took her picture from the cab in front of the house. She started to knock on the door, but changed her mind. I refused to get out of the car because my heart was still on Steel Street.

"Crawford, this really is it! I feel it. Yep! #4 Settle. This is really it. I feel my Dad here."

"Really? Well, I feel like you ought to get back in the cab. We gotta go. It's time for your medication."

CHAPTER 28

RAYNER SHINE

I was gently awakened by Schwarck, offering me coffee in bed, and was delighted to look out the window to see clear and sunny skies.

"Wow, Schwarck. You must be feeling better. Did the medicine help?"

She croaked out a weak, "No, I'm losing my voice and I am so mad because I really want to be able to talk to the Rayner relatives tonight. I'm going to shower now, 'cause maybe the hot steam will help."

"Are you going down the hall like that....in your see-through underwear?"

"Yes, all the businessmen left very early."

Out the door she went and I sat up a little and began to read my lusty novel savoring the solitude and coffee. I soon heard feet pounding down the hall toward our room. The door burst open and a shaken Schwarck pasted her half-naked self against the closed door.

"Geeze, you scared me! What's going on?"

A breathless Schwarck began. "You won't believe it! The bathroom door was unlocked so I opened it and there was a tall naked man coming out of the shower! We both stood there for a minute. He looked just as surprised as me. Then I took off running! We can't go to the dining room this morning. What if he's down there?"

"Well, he didn't see my pasty thighs, so I'm going down. I told you not to leave the room like that. Come on, forget the shower incident. We've got to catch the train to Keighley to see if we can find another house your dad didn't live in. What time are your relatives picking you up tonight?"

"What do you mean picking me up? You're going too, aren't you? I need the support. We also have to get to the Marks and Spencer so I can buy a really beautiful blouse to wear and pick up a big bouquet for Aunt Gwennie."

"Well, they're your relatives. Why would they need to see me? Did you tell them I was coming with you?"

"They are expecting you and you might have to help me talk. My voice is getting worse! You gotta' come with me."

We got dressed and I cajoled her into going to the dining room, explaining how different she looked wearing clothes, therefore the naked guy probably wouldn't recognize her. We enjoyed a quick breakfast alone in the dining room and caught a cab to the train station.

The train ride to Keighley was soothing and short. We hired a cab to take us to Sutton, the little village where Karen's grandmother and father had stayed during WWII.

I had to wonder about Schwarck's family. Their history was really unusual. Her Dad's mother and extended family took her father as a baby to the US, while her Father's Dad stayed behind in Barrow In Furness. Then, when Schwarck's Dad was fourteen, his Mother and the extended family came back to England. Then, before WWII, her Dad's grandparents sailed back to the US, but her Grandmother and Dad stayed behind in Keighley, where her Dad worked in a textile mill until he joined the Navy in WWII. When he returned after the war, they both went back to the US. I don't know of anyone who went back and forth like that in the 30s and 40s, especially people who didn't have any money.

We found the house they had lived in, thanks to a relentless Pakistani cab driver, who really got involved in the story. He was determined not only to find the house, but also the factory where Schwarck's Dad had worked. Before returning to the train station, we asked our driver about a place for lunch, and he told us he would take us to a restaurant he knew was safe, whatever that meant.

I had never been in a restaurant that had its own big gravy wagon, with no less than eight different kinds of sauces and drippings. I hoped the sauces would coat Schwarck's increasingly raw throat. I didn't have the sore throat, but I did some serious throat coating myself too, with no less than four gravies. We pigged out on beef and Yorkshire pudding, before returning to the train station for the ride back to Barrow. We needed to make time for a quick shopping trip to the local Marks and Spencer for flowers and a blouse, and then beat it home to prepare for the evening at the relatives. The Rayners were picking us up at 7 P.M.

Our shopping expedition to find the perfect blouse was very successful with Schwarck finally selecting a seventy-dollar short-sleeved salmon colored top. For that much money, it should have had longer sleeves and maybe solid gold buttons. She must have held up over twenty blouses for my opinion. The luxuriant flower bouquet Schwarck selected was spectacular and sure to please Aunt Gwennie.

We had a little time to spare before Malcolm came to get us, so we decided to rest so that Schwarck could re-medicate and be at her best for the big event. She drank some hot tea and lay down for a while.

Later, Schwarck, who never took more than ten minutes to primp for any occasion, slipped on her frayed blue sweater to head to the bathroom to apply makeup and straighten her hair. Unfortunately, while in there, she pulled a cord activating a deodorizer next to the fan, which sprayed wet smelly stuff all over her. She returned to the room in disgust. Her voice eked out a croaking sound. "Can you believe that thing sprayed me all over? It's so late, I don't have time to re shower or wash my hair again."

"Forget it. It'll probably evaporate by the time we meet Malcolm downstairs. Just put on your nice new blouse. That'll make you feel better."

She went to the closet, lovingly pulled out the salmon-colored creation, carefully removed the tags, and stuck her arm in the sleeve. “Crawford, what am I caught on?”

She had one arm partially through one sleeve, but couldn’t pull the other one around. I hobbled over to help her.

“Uh, oh. You’re caught on something, all right and I think it’s you! What size is this thing?”

“Eighteen. Take a look at the tag, what size does it say?”

“I don’t think you’re gonna want to know this, but the tag says it’s a size twelve.”

“What? Are you sure? Let me see the tag. Oh, my God! I don’t wear a twelve! I haven’t worn a twelve since middle school! There was a big rack all filled with the same color. I know I picked up an 18, but I must have set it down to look at some others. I can‘t believe this! Let me try it again.”

She went through the same fruitless effort of trying it on and finally just sat down on the bed looking very disheartened.

“Okay, you need to find something else to wear quickly, because we have to be downstairs in less than ten minutes!”

As luck would have it, the only clean, non-t-shirt thing she had to wear with her jeans was the old blue sweater that had been saturated with sickly orchid stuff in the bathroom.

A dejected but determined Schwarck pulled the nasty sweater back on and downstairs we went. She was clutching the fresh floral bouquet up to her nose, trying to escape the heavy deodorizer smell permeating the ugly sweater. Malcolm and his wife were very punctual and we awkwardly shook hands and made formal introductions. Schwarck's voice was croaking and squeaking by the time we got to Aunt Gwennie's. I'll never forget that vision of Aunt Gwennie standing on the porch awaiting our arrival. There she was, the eighty something matriarch of the family, dressed to the nines. She was wearing a flowery dress, pearl necklace, earrings, sensible heels, and nylons. Both of her arms were open wide awaiting giant hugs.

I had a superb evening with all the Rayner relatives; looking at old photos and assisting Schwarck show photos of her Mom, Dad, brother and sister on her computer. Tears filled Aunt Gwennie's eyes as she saw her brother's son (Schwarck's Dad) for the first time. She told us how much he looked like her brother who had died years ago.

I was forced to do all of the talking for Schwarck, and we both enjoyed Aunt Gwennie's sherry way too much. I felt like these were my people, too. We took lots of photos, and Malcolm and his wife delivered us back to the Browshead by 11 P.M. The goodbyes were made with promises to keep in touch. We slowly plodded back up to our room and Schwarck tore off the smelly blue sweater.

"Well, Schwarck, I think the night was a big success, even though you couldn't talk. Your relatives are very nice and Aunt Gwennie loved the flowers."

"I couldn't even croak out the questions I wanted to ask them," she whispered sadly.

"Well, maybe you can come back again some day. I'll come with you if I can still walk."

"Thanks for being there for me. You're a good friend, Crawford. They loved you."

"Yeah, I know. I am really going to miss Barrow In Furness."

"You are?" Schwarck whined. "What will you miss the most?"

"Well, I'll miss the overly helpful people, the air fresheners, the Pakistani cab driver, the overpriced post office, and the English Rayners, but what'll I miss the most….hmmmm?"

"Yeah, what?"

"#4 Steel Street."

"Shut up, Crawford."

The next morning we entered the dining room of the odoriferous Browshead for the last time. Schwarck looked a little "down-in-the-mouth" this morning. It is probably a combination of the Catarrh and having to leave this special place in her family history. Or it could have something to do with the seventy-dollar size twelve blouse that she left in the closet for the Missus.

I ordered a heavy duty breakfast, knowing the day would be exhausting with the multiple transportation connections. The breakfast dining music this morning is Bach Chorales. I was eating my last bite of toast, oozing with orange marmalade, when Schwarck leaned over the table and gave me an eye-squinting stare. Her voice was hoarse, but she managed to croak out some words.

"You know what, Crawford? You would make a wonderful minister! The church would be packed every Sunday just to hear you. I think you should consider it."

"Re-ally? Tell me, is it the chorale music and all the stained glass air fresheners that are making you feel churchy this morning? Maybe you should let up a little on the cold medicine. I might actually be able to attract a small audience, though not with my Biblical prowess, which I am quite sure would be expected of a minister, but maybe if I served free refreshments and told bawdy jokes."

It was always mind-blowing to hear the latest thing Schwarck wants me to consider. Over the years, she has come up with a truckload of avocations she wants me to pursue. Why doesn't she ever come up with jobs she should have? I'm going to start laying some on her, like Crop Circle Spotter, Black Squirrel Counter, Aura Interpreter/Spirit Guide Counselor, Deer Herd Identifier, and Cow Whisperer. She would be excellent at any of those.

For myself, I would choose Weight Watcher lecturer over the ministry. Even though I have never been very successful at losing weight, I know first hand what chubby people should do. I have lost over nine hundred pounds in my lifetime. Unfortunately, it's been the same gnarly pound, nine hundred times over.

"I'm not going to be taking up the ministry, Schwarck. I'll be seeing Jesus soon enough. I also think I see the cab right now. Let's go."

CHAPTER 29

THE WRITE TIME

Today's exciting new destination is Stamford, England. As mentioned earlier, Sister Barbara has worked with Brits for years. She usually invites Brits to all of our family holidays, especially Thanksgiving because they are charmed and mystified by our historic celebration over corn on the cob and pumpkin pie. Most Brits think Indian uprisings were "brilliant!"

Barbara made arrangements for us to stay for a week at the new condo of one of her office associates, Nigel. He and his wife had lived in the States for a few years when they were newly married and I had met them on several occasions. Sadly, they are divorced now and he lives apart from her and their three girls. I felt a little weird about staying in his house, but Barbara informed me that he wouldn't be there. He is in Budapest playing rugby with "his mates" and would only come home long enough to grab some clothes and head to the States for business. Barbara had given him my email and in his last correspondence, he told me to treat his house like it was our own. I don't think he's going to appreciate that kind of neglect. Isn't it astounding that this guy would entrust his new condo to complete strangers for a week and even arrange for us to be picked up at the train station by his girlfriend? Barbara assured me that this would be no inconvenience. She gave me pages of numbers of employees over here who are dying to show us around. Really now, who would want to squire around two old ladies from the US every day?

We anticipated getting a tremendous amount of writing done while we were at Nigel's. We needed to get it all down while it was relatively fresh in our feeble minds. That way, we wouldn't forget anything that we wanted to include in THE BOOK.

Our Stamford destination required that we take the train from Barrow to Manchester, get off and take another train from Manchester to Leicester, get off and then go from Leicester to Stamford. I dreaded all the getting in and out while carting our weighty gear. We had to be very punctual, too, or we'd miss a connection. Trains in England keep a very accurate schedule.

The weather as we left Barrow was bleak, but as we made our way to Manchester, the sun came out and the landscape changed to rolling hills, small farms, and cottages. The countryside was brilliant with green grass and lots of flowers. The closer we got to the city, the more people got on the train. Before too many stops, there were no seats left, and people were standing up in the aisle.

We shared facing seats with two rambunctious elementary aged boys, and Schwarck's schoolteacher methodology kicked in. She had them doing tic-tac-toe, hangman, and "finish the doodle." Their mother chose to sit quite a distance away from them and was sublimely engrossed in a Harlequin Romance novel. She was wearing a leather mini skirt and a tank top, which barely covered half of her more than ample bosom. Her make-up was thick and her hair had been teased. She was a vision of the sixties and I imagined these boys cramp her style. At some point, between the games with the boys and the passenger noise from the overloaded train, we missed some of the announcements. The train was slowing to a stop, and a startled Schwarck grabbed my wrist to look at my watch and yelled, "This is our stop! Oh my, God! Quick! Get up…we've got to get off at the next stop…hurry!"

The panic in her voice propelled me into action. We said a hasty goodbye to the boys and mauled our way to the luggage rack, yanking our stuff into the aisle over people's toes and bumping shoulders in an effort to reach the door before it opened. Schwarck tried to squeeze her way past a lump of standing passengers, but couldn't make it through. The train stopped and the crowd closest to the door got off, giving us more room to press forward, but as soon as they cleared, a huge crowd got on, mashing us back down the aisle. There was no way we could make it to the door in time!

The door closed and the mighty train rolled forward. I was aghast as my compadre' continued to strong-arm her way through to the closed door and began frantically pounding on it with both fists screaming, "Stop the train! Stop the train!" She then turned a tear-stained face in my direction and shouted, "We'll never make our connection! We're doomed!"

Whoa! I have never known her to get so unglued and frantic. Must be the Catarrh! Geeze, can't we just get off at the next stop and take a cab if we have to?

Then, miracle of miracles, the train was slowing again to stop at another platform. We were near the door when it came to a screechy halt. The doors slid open, and we adroitly leaped free of the car, landing on a crowded platform. People were scurrying every which way and announcements were blaring.

"Did you hear that, Crawford? The overhead announcement just said this is the Piccadilly Station! It's the pic-a-dil-ly!"

"O-kayyyy, Schwarck."

"Get it? We missed the last stop, which I thought was Piccadilly! That's where we were supposed to get off to make our connection to Manchester. But, this is Piccadilly! Can you believe it? We're on the Pic-ca-dilly Platform!"

She was shouting this in a kind of halting-crying jag along with doing a little happy dance. We found our Manchester train and the next leg of our journey was gloriously uneventful. Schwarck's nose was starting to act up just before we got to Stamford, and she had me digging through my belongings for small items of clothing or anything that could be used as tissue. She was so desperate; she didn't even care if it was used as long as it had at least one clean corner.

Finally, the train slowed into the quaint Stamford Station and it was a vision of Victorian loveliness. The station was built of stone and had lots of crisp white Gingerbread trim, and looked very much like Walt Disney had designed it. I could feel my entire body begin to relax. Everything looked so perfectly peaceful here. We followed a winding cement path lined with delicate spring flowers and "Way Out" signs, all the time searching for someone who might be Nigel's girlfriend, Hannah. Bet she was over-excited to get this pick-up duty.

There weren't many people outside the station, but there was one very attractive young woman wearing perfectly fitted blue jeans, trendy top, and impossibly high heels, who seemed to be watching for someone. Not seeing any other likely candidates, I approached her.

"Excuse me, is your name Hannah, by any chance?"

"Yes!" The exquisite petite and pert brunette nodded her head. We exchanged awkward little hugs and followed girlfriend Hannah, to the diminutive parking lot and her impossibly small car. We literally had to fold ourselves in and drag the baggage in on top of us. She told us the condo was close, but Nigel thought we might be tired from our journey, so she was urged to pick us up. Sister Barbara probably warned him that I was painfully decrepit.

Hannah started the car and we got as comfortable as we could for the ride, which turned out to be two blocks long!

"Here we are, #15 Wothorpe Mews."

"You're kidding! We're already there?"

It took us longer to get into the car than to drive around the corner to the house. You could see the station parking lot right through the condo's shrubs. Even I wouldn't have minded walking there!

Number 15 Wothorpe Mews was part of a new condo development that looked like it had existed for centuries, just like all of the nearby medieval village structures. The condo facade was golden limestone surrounded by a beautifully landscaped little yard. The complex was adjacent to an enormous grassy park cut in two by a river winding lazily through the ancient city. It was going to be like living at the Renaissance Festival. I felt like I should buy a long skirt and peasant top to wear for a joust in the tiltyard.

As we stepped across the entranceway, Hannah began to report all of the things that Nigel wanted her to show us. She had picked up a few groceries, not really knowing what we like to eat. She unpacked a bag containing coffee, orange juice, croissants, and other pastries. She apologized for not having enough time to tidy up the place before our arrival. We quickly pointed out that it looked fabulous to us, and we were ever so grateful for the opportunity to be here.

She took us on a home tour, explaining the operation of the TV, stereo, and the washing machine. We went upstairs and she indicated that I was to have Nigel's king size bedroom and king bed with adjoining bath and Schwarck would have the little girl's room, featuring a ceiling and wall completely covered with glow-in-the dark angels and stars, and a hundred and twenty stuffed animals in the bed. I figured Barbara had emailed Nigel about the "big bed, little bed" business and this was her way of showing sisterly love. She led us back downstairs for the demonstration of door alarms and the locks. I was counting on Schwarck to remember all of the critical details. I drifted off after learning there were more than two steps to setting the alarm.

We followed Hannah outside and she asked if we would like to take a little walk with her. Nigel had given instructions to show us some of the best restaurants and hangouts, as well as the location of the Tourist Bureau and the Chemist (drug store). He suspected that people our age needed to know where the drugs are. We meandered down the walk, over the bridge, through the park, noting the graceful swans and beautiful flowers. The path delivered us onto a cobblestone shop-lined street where we paused as Hannah pointed in the direction of the various landmarks. She asked if we had any questions or needed anything because she would be leaving us here, but not before giving us telephone numbers of Brits who were poised by their phone awaiting our every need. She cautioned us that May Day was approaching and some businesses might not be open. We gave her cheery little waves and watched her depart over the bridge, and then we became giddy with our good fortune.

"Crawford, can you believe this place? The house is fabulous. Two bedrooms, TV, three bathrooms, and a washing machine! This beautiful town is within easy walking distance. The train is next door. I had no idea it would be even half this great! We are going to be able to write so much. This is a gift!"

Our first purchase in Stamford was a glass of wine and some pizza, and we headed home, hoping to watch a movie or something exciting. We had really missed TV. We also must have missed some important instructions about the three hundred channel satellite TV, because we couldn't get more than a couple of fuzzy channels. That was okay. Schwarck would figure it out tomorrow. Right now, we were ready to crash. The big bed was divine and I relished in the thought that Schwarck was nestled into a smaller, lower bed surrounded by bears, kitties, ballerinas and glow-in-the-dark stars.

The next morning, Schwarck was already in the shower and had made the second pot of coffee by the time I got downstairs. She was wearing a big fluffy white robe.

"You didn't bring that with you on the trip, did you?"

"No, it's our husband, Nigel's. Isn't it beautiful and cuddly?"

"Where did you get it?"

"In his bathroom."

Okay, I have known this person for over thirty years, and we have pretty much been inseparable for the last four weeks. I probably know her better than anyone, but her putting on someone else's robe was a surprising and a major violation. It was too personal! That bathrobe had probably covered Nigel's naked body and now it was covering hers!

As she poured herself a cup of coffee and lounged in her comfy borrowed robe, she began to relate her observations.

"You know, our new husband Nigel, is an intriguing man. He's very intelligent, extremely athletic, a good father, and has a healthy interest in the ladies."

"Really? How do you know all that?"

"Just look around. His choice of books and music is very highbrow and diverse. Notice all the photos and notes from his daughters taped all over the house. Also, did you see the nude art prints in the downstairs bathroom and the pin-up thonged girl on the bulletin board?"

"No, I missed all of that. Speaking of thongs…I need to wash my underwear. You want me to throw yours in, too? I may as well wash all your clothes since, apparently, you are going to wear his robe all the time."

I sorted our stuff and put a massive load in the washer. This machine was supposed to both wash and dry, but when the clothes were done, they were still wet, so I started hanging big mama underwear all over the place; on the banister, over the kitchen chairs, curtain rods or wherever I could find an empty space.

While I was doing that, Schwarck dressed and was busying herself in the kitchen, wiping counters, killing ants, and cleaning out a gunky fish bowl that actually had a little goldfish swimming in the stinky, murky water. She gently fished him out and put him in a glass with clean water, then scrubbed and cleaned the bowl. After letting it aerate for a while, she put the little guy back and gave him a smidge of fish food.

"Doesn't he look happy, Crawford? I bet Nigel will be grateful. He probably forgot about little Goldie."

We were trying to figure out why the washer didn't dry when we heard a car door slam.

"Uh, oh, I bet our husband is home!"

"Geeze, Schwarck, help me get all the underwear off the chairs and staircase."

It was too late! He was already coming in the doorway. Nigel was very tall, tanned, and muscular, with a kind-of ruddy handsomeness. He had a huge mischievous smile and he gathered us both in big huge hugs. We acted like schoolgirls and gushed profusely about his letting us stay in his home.

I looked at my big mamas drying on the nearby banister and felt slightly naughty. I could tell him they were all Schwarck's, but there was an obvious difference in size and style. Before I could think of a way to explain all the wet clothes hanging around, Schwarck took Nigel's hand and led him to the kitchen and the sparkling clean fishbowl. She had the look of a puppy that had learned to use the paper. She pointed in the direction of the shiny fish bowl.

"Oh, blast! I thought bloody Nemo was dead. My daughter won him at the street fair and we brought him home in a little plastic bag a few months ago. I never thought the little knob would live through the night, and here ees'…still alive!"

Schwarck's face showed signs of shock. Nigel turned to me then and asked if we'd had any trouble working anything.

"Well, we could use a refresher course on the washer-dryer concept and how to use the TV clicker."

He showed us the switch we needed to set the washing machine to "dryer mode", and then led us to the living room where he demonstrated how to tune in to SkyTV. Then he flew upstairs to shower and grab clean clothes and was back downstairs in less than twenty minutes resplendent in business suit and carrying a leather "man" bag. Our househusband was extremely cosmopolitan. We said our goodbyes and assured him that we would take very good care of things and kill the fish if he wanted. With that, he was off to the airport.

After Nigel left, we got our first phone call and it was from one of the office Brits, Ginger, wondering if she could pick us up and take us anywhere. We declined but thanked her and said we might meet up with her on another day.

Our plan was to head to the Stamford Public Library to use their Internet, pick up some groceries, and head back for a writing marathon followed by movie night!

TO: FRIENDS AND RELATIVES BACK HOME

SENT: MAY 5

SUBJECT: ALL THE NEWS THAT'S FIT TO PRINT

Hi all,

Thank goodness we have arrived at Nigel's wonderful condo in Stamford, one of the oldest villages in all of Britain. Nigel stopped in for a moment to make sure we were making ourselves at home, then left for Peoria.

We have definitely made ourselves at home. Schwarck is wearing his robe, I'm in his bed, we have moved furniture around, killed the ants, cleaned the goldfish bowl, and washed our clothes in a washer that is about as big as a salad bowl.

People here eat their lunches outside on benches in the cemetery. They have been dying here since 1086AD. The whole city is a burial ground. They have so many headstones that they affix the oldest to the sides of buildings. I imagine they wait for a century or so, till the body is gone to dust, and then they dig a new hole and put someone else in.

We enjoyed listening to Nigel's radio while writing THE BOOK. The announcer was describing an aggravated robbery in Stamford. It was not clear if the thief got aggravated or the victim.

We have decided to make one more stop before heading

back home. We will spend our last few days in Bath, which has a 2000-year history. The brochure says it is "beguiling".

I can tell you that right now my hips and legs feel over 2000 years old. We have booked a B&B in the heart of Bath. Schwarck said either we are going to Bath on Friday or we need a bath by Friday. I think my hearing is going, too!

Love to all,

Kathleen of Stamford

After the Internet, I popped into a hair salon to see if they took walk-ins. A very punk and pierced young plumpish red head wearing a bright, horizontal striped top and faded jeans, met me at the door and said she could take me. I don't doubt that for a minute. I stuck my head back outside and called to Schwarck, whom I caught heading for the bakery.

"Schwarck, she can take me now. Why don't you come in, too? We can both get cut and punked for THE BOOK!"

She nodded enthusiastically and followed me back into the salon. Reddish purple hair is very popular over here for some reason. I told the operator I was willing to get punked, but purple hair was out. Schwarck was sure that no one would be able to tame her natural curly locks that frizzed up with the least amount of humidity, but asked if there was anything that would make her look "punkish," too. She has been hankering for straight hair her entire life, and I have been envious of curly locks my whole life. Isn't that just the way things go? Our salon technician giggled most of the time during our treatments. She probably never imagined she'd be punking old American ladies today. When Schwarck looked in the mirror, she primped and posed.

"Aren't we the daring young things?" she said.

We were so proud of the way she made us look that we took her picture and tipped her well.

We thought our new hair made us look surprisingly sophisticated or maybe just surprised. In any case, we were so good looking that even though we were wearing t-shirts instead of dresses and pearls, we decided to head to the King George for High Tea.

The place had been recommended by Barbara's office Brits. Unfortunately, our short walk to the King George was fraught with an untimely downpour that totally flattened my doo and did a "Bozo" on Schwarck's.

We found the most secluded table at the King George, so as not to make the regular, sophisticated customers gag when glancing in our direction. At least Schwarck didn't have to deal with soggy makeup. My mascara looked a lot like Tammy Faye Baker's when her preacher husband was led off to prison in handcuffs.

I was surprised that the King George staff didn't suggest that we leave and come back when we could look better, but maybe they didn't think that was possible.

After the superb tea experience complete with fancy sandwiches, scones and clotted cream, we headed back home to get in a few intense hours of writing. Schwarck had made her little office in the living room on the giant rectangular coffee table. I had all my computer equipment set up on the kitchen table. Every once in awhile she would laugh out loud as she came upon some picture of me in distress or doing something weird.

For the next few days, we hunkered down at the computers, not wasting a minute of precious time. Schwarck went out for "take away" meals and short walks, but I was a writing prisoner at my little kitchen desk. There was a lot to catch up on. Each day, Schwarck would update me on her progress and ask me about mine.

"Crawford, how's your writing coming? I'm almost up to Stamford with all the notes and pictures. I don't think you realize how important it is for us to get this down now, while we are here. You know when we get home we won't be able to start the official writing until well into the summer. So if we don't have all of our notes on the computer, we'll forget the best parts."

"I know we're going to get very busy when we get back. Aren't we leaving for Mazatlan with Rita in August? I still can't believe we agreed to go with her to Mexico so quick after we've been gone for five weeks. It's so freakin' hot there, I'll just be a giant wet spot the whole time. You won't believe how hot it's gonna' be!"

"I know, but Rita asked me where I wanted to go and I said I love the Canadian Rockies. Maybe the idea of snow topped Canadian Rockies caused Rita to have brain freeze and she decided we should go Hell-hot instead. When she called me back, she was so excited about how fabulous the suites are in Mazatlan, I didn't have the heart to remind her about Canada. She said it would be cool by the water. Anyway, how is your writing doing? Are you catching up on the trip? Be sure to include all your thoughts and feelings."

"My writing is coming along pretty good. I just love all the pictures I took."

"Good. Keep writing, Crawford. We've spent all this time, as well as money, and told hundreds of people about THE BOOK, so we need to be very serious about it."

We wrote for a few hours, watched at little late night TV, and headed for bed. Tomorrow was May Day, and we didn't know what restaurants would be open. We had probably been on our computers a total of thirty hours each here in Stamford and were ready for a day out before one more good writing session and on to our last destination. The pagan celebration of May Day would be a good diversion.

The next morning, we had coffee and pastries and attempted to punk up our hair before heading downtown. When we arrived at the town square, there were already several hundred people gathered. Some brought their own chairs and snacks. Everyone also brought a big dog. Young girls in filmy pantaloons were waiting for their chance to capture a ribbon and dance around the pole.

When I was in elementary school, we had a May pole dance and all we did was just walk around it each way.

No one ever told us why we did it. I believe the Brits have perfected May Pole romping. It was more like a three hour Elizabethan dance recital. There was a Queen of the May and she was attired in a Renaissance costume. The pantalooned King of the May was at her side throughout the festivities.

Since it was an official holiday, none of the downtown stores were open so that all employees could pole dance if they wanted. I congratulated the Queen of the May and we took a number of pictures of the happy couple and the sprightly pole-dancing nymphs.

Tea and scones seemed the perfect way to celebrate May Day, or any other day for that matter, and we happily discovered the bakery was open despite the holiday. A half-hour in there fortified us with carbs, and we were exhilarated and ready to return to Nigel's Mews and tackle writing with vigor.

We returned to the condo and went straight to work. By early evening, Schwarck announced that she was going for a walk (she no longer asked if I wanted to go along) and set out to discover a nearby parkland. Before leaving she took a look at me working over my computer.

"I can't believe it, Crawford. Staying here in Stamford has been such a blessing for us. I have actually completed the writing up to today. All the notes are in order and everything we have done and money we have spent is recorded. How far along are you?"

"I'm at the airport, now."

"You mean you already wrote about going home?"

"No, I'm at the airport in Detroit, waiting to go to London."

"Very funny, Crawford."

"No, I've finally gotten the airport chapter finished; it's all done. Yay!"

"You mean to tell me all this writing you have been doing here in Stamford only got you to the part when we left Detroit? I saw you taking notes all the time at other places we went."

"Yeah, I was taking a few notes, but the most important part of a book is the beginning. Ya gotta hook em, and I've been busy with the hook part."

Schwarck looked a little testy. Maybe we'd been together too long.

She pulled on a light sweater and closed the door. I myself thought she shut it a bit hard.

An hour and a half later, a restored buddy burst through the door, grinning from ear to ear. Her face had a healthy pink glow and her curly hair looped off in every direction.

"It is so beautiful out there. I took tons of pictures of cows and deer and walked to a castle and saw a fabulous sunset!"

"Great! Sounds like miles and miles of fun!"

"How are you doing? Did you write from all your notes you took in the other cities we visited?"

"Well, kinda."

"Whaddya mean?"

"Well, I'm happy to report that I just finished with the day we arrived in Dublin. This book writing is really hard, but I guess if it was easy, everybody would write a book."

CHAPTER 30

THE BEGINNING OF THE END

The cab drivers we have seen and spoken to in Stamford all have the same look: shaved heads, earrings, and leather jackets. None seem to be capable of writing a receipt and one loudly raved about his favorite US TV show Jerry Springer. We tried to convince him that if he wanted to know about real Americans, he should watch Oprah, and then he would learn how sensitive and generous we are. He said Oprah is so much "blather…the best action on TV is Jerry!"

We walked to the Stamford Public Library to use their Internet, and I picked up a brochure promoting the city's museum. Their historic collection includes items belonging to a Stamford guy buried in the churchyard. They have his pants in the museum. The poor sap weighed 40 stone and that seems to be the only reason he is famous. How pitiful is that? Surely he had other attributes. Actually 40 stone is the equivalent of 560 pounds which I don't think is all that large. I am going to pray tonight that in my remaining lifetime I will lose enough weight so that my gargantuan pants will not be under glass at the Detroit Historical Museum or the Science Center.

This library here has a glut of commotion. Whatever happened to the "Sshhhush" system? There used to be a painfully thin, hunchbacked woman in a black dress, hair severely pulled back and knotted on top of her head, who would pop out of nowhere at the library and lock beady eyes on loud offenders. She would jerk an elongated pointer finger up to her nose and "Shush"! To be "shushed" at the library was mortifying and so abominable that you remembered the repugnant offense for the rest of your rule-breaking life. I know this.

Despite loud babbling, I attempted to compose an impressive email to the states that is more likened to a journal or a chronicle and addressed to forty anxious recipients. This may be my last commentary from the UK. I needed quiet to compose this novella, and my concentration was severely challenged by loud unattended children running all over as well as aggressive foreign speaking people seated three and four abreast at nearby computers. They argued loudly about what the mouse holder should do next. The quibblers' and squabblers' racket emanated from each of the library's twelve computer stations. These little clamorous computer gangs surround Schwarck and me. No one else is concerned about the racket…no "shushing"! Even the Stamford librarians don't have governors on their voice boxes. The librarians here give verbal directions at decibels far above acceptable standards. The chatter volume exceeds normal conversation for any business; in fact, the local pub is quieter.

Schwarck reached her limit with the noise and usurped a set of earphones, which she put on with great exaggeration so that the loud people could easily observe her extreme measures to tune them out. Buddy Schwarck is a certified expert in silent expressions of abhorrence and loathing. I am never good at this because I'm not normally bothered much about anything. Her confrontations with injustice are oftimes surprising and can be very entertaining. She will be further annoyed and repulsed when I point out the unhygienic aspects of those foul earphones that may have been worn by street people for years. Slimy germs now have direct access to her brain.

"Schwarck, get those earphones off. Don't you know they are probably never disinfected?" She pulled them off and took a good look at the earpieces.

"Oh, EUWwww! Look at them… these are disgusting!"

TO: FRIENDS AND RELATIVES BACK HOME IN THE US

FROM: ME…KATHY CRAWFORD

DATE: MAY 4

RE: WE'RE PUNKED!

Hi all,

We're still here in Stamford and we got punked at the beauty salon. We looked fabulous for about seven minutes, and then the monsoons came and wrecked our dos. I had never seen Schwarck's hair so straight. She was thrilled. She thinks that my look was sort of like a blond Liz Taylor after she went down hill.

Yesterday was a big pagan holiday here…May Day. Lots of young women were pole dancing. We have pictures to prove it. Everything was closed down, and we were forced to raid Nigel's cupboard for food. He had two cans of beans and four bottles of beer. We drank the beer first so we'd forget how hungry we were.

Handicapped signs here are a stitch. There's one with the silhouette of a hunched over man and woman with canes crossing the street. Today we saw people getting picked up in front of the grocery store by a white van with a big sign on the side saying "Tuesday Handicapped Club". Who wants to be a member of that club? I guess it would be okay if you were only handicapped one day a week, but what are the chances of that?

I can't write anymore here at the library because it is so loud and chaotic. We are heading to the pub for a little peace and quiet.

Tomorrow we leave Stamford and take the train to Bath and then home. I can't believe we have been gone almost five weeks. My bank account sure believes it. We both had to beg the husbands to put more money in our accounts so that we wouldn't have to sleep in the cemetery our last few days. We already have our flights, so they can't stop us from coming home.

See you all soon!

Did anyone shave the queen yet?

Kathleen of Stamford

We decided to enjoy our last Stamford dinner at the haunted "Candlesticks" restaurant. I threw caution to the wind and ordered black spaghetti with squid and mussels. Food does not normally frighten me, but this came close. We are all accustomed to our food appearing in the proper color. Butter should be yellow, chocolate ice cream should be brown, cauliflower and spaghetti should be white. Black food should taste like licorice or, at a minimum, be scorched or burned. Schwarck was too much of a chicken to try anything as peculiar as black spaghetti. I liked it, but then I like all food that will lie still on my plate long enough for me to stab it.

The Candlesticks owner was exceedingly hospitable and led us on a little tour of the basement, which he declared was haunted frequently, and looks exactly like the catacombs in Rome, only brighter and airier. He said a female ghost lives in the bathroom. I went in the bathroom and there was barely room for me, so I think toilet ghost woman has moved on. Schwarck wouldn't go in. The walk back to Nigel's at night was a little spooky, reminiscent of a "Jack the Ripper" movie. The night air was misty. The buildings and the narrow cobblestone streets are ancient and the oil lamps at each corner provide a dim light, which cast lots of scary shadows.

When we arrived back at Nigel's we needed to pack as well as tidy up the place. Earlier in the day we had selected little gifts for our host and girlfriend, Hannah as well as a gift to share with the office folks who kept trying to give us rides and take us on tours. We were so fortunate to have this Stamford respite. It was a glorious gift. Before departing the next morning, we gave one last look around, waved to Nemo, the half-dead fish, and off we rolled to the train station next door.

It took us three trains and close to eight hours to get to Bath, and I was in no mood to haul our luggage in the rain over damp cobblestones for six-plus blocks. I lobbied for a cab, but Schwarck was firm about saving money and she was confident that our B & B was within easy walking distance. My suitcase wheels kept getting stuck in the crevasses and Schwarck's case looked like the wheels were starting to fall off. After a miserable rainy fifteen minutes of tugging and hauling, we saw it; Abbey Green, which was a beautiful courtyard, encircled by attached historic looking brick homes and a few small shops. I stepped up to the door, turned the bell, and immediately was greeted enthusiastically by a deeply dimpled white haired matron who was smiling broadly.

"We're expecting you. My name is Pat and I'll take you to your room. We have just opened our B & B and you'll be among our first guests. You'd probably rather have the first floor on the fourth story, but it was already booked when I got your reservation, so I have a lovely room for you on the street level."

Her statement was a revelation. For the past five weeks Schwarck has been asking for the first floor of every B & B and apparently now we hear that the first floor is at the top of the building. All of this time, we should have been asking for street level or ground level! Excuse me, but holy shit!

Pat escorted us to a heavenly periwinkle blue room with Scandinavian style twin beds, covered with fluffy white duvets. The bathroom towel racks were loaded with fluffy pristine towels and washcloths. Proprietor Pat stated the rack heated the towels and washcloth, which was a supreme treat of orgasmic proportions. Our room was the largest and most magnificent one we had ever had and it was on the ground floor! I sincerely wanted to punish someone for the excessive painful effort I have exerted in order to haul my suitcases as well as my over age sixty-two fat ass up to top floors the past thirty two days. Guess it was our fault for not knowing the system over here. It still didn't stop me from wanting to slap Schwarck around a little.

We have decided to enjoy Bath in style, relishing in our good fortune to find a room in this spectacular historic place. We unpacked a little then stepped into the courtyard in search of dinner. We happened upon a narrow building with a sandwich sign and a rickshaw type contraption out front. The business proclaimed to be the oldest house in Bath (c1482) and was the actual home of Sally Lunn and the original home of Sally Lunn's gigantic buns.

"Schwarck, we have got to eat here. If these people revere big buns, wait until they get a load of ours!"

We entered the Lilliputian size building and took seats in two chairs which were snuggled up to a table the size of a TV tray. The building was only wide enough for two such tables across from each other, but fortunately was long enough to accommodate approximately sixty diners. No matter what you order, it is accompanied by a gigantic bun that is made from scratch and was introduced to her menu in 1680. I ordered the famous "Beef Trencher" which sounded colossal enough to pair with a bun that is four inches high and as wide as a dinner plate. I loved this place. After dinner we went on a little tour of the basement museum at Sally's, which was the site of her ancient kitchen and displayed some of her baking implements as well as her apron. The rickshaw out front of Sally's establishment was a replica of the ones used to pick people up at their homes and transport them to the Roman Baths. People came to Bath from all over England to be healed by the natural hot spring waters of the Roman Baths. I sincerely wished I could climb in that rickshaw now and have someone haul my battered body to The Baths for the healing.

The rains had subsided and the early evening was pleasantly warm for a meander. We strolled leisurely along the wide timeworn cobblestone path toward our Abbey Green Guest House. We are beginning to prepare ourselves for reentry into the topsy turvy lives we left behind five weeks ago. We discussed how magnificent this journey has been and reminisced about all the funny parts. As we neared our B & B, I looked forward to lounging in the fluffy bed with my nighttime reading The Queen's Fool by Philippa Gregory, and Schwarck just wanted to get to bed after this very full day.

"Crawford, how do you think we should autograph THE BOOK? There's an art to book signings, you know. Also, what should the title be? We've got to have all of this figured out soon. I think we should do a guest appearance on Good Morning America, too. What do you think?"

"Really? Well, I can't think about it right now because Jane Boleyn is returning to Henry VIII's Court and the silly Katherine Howard is trying to seduce the King by bowing very low and making a slight pause at his crotch as she arises. Who knew that would work?"

Our hosts Pat and John served a beautiful breakfast to us in their sunny little dining room. John explained that this home was on the square that had at once been part of the Abbey's Monastery. They were both interested in what we wanted to see in Bath and made several suggestions including encouraging us to visit the Roman Baths and to take the Double Decker Tour bus. In as much as we only have two days, we must maximize our time here. We decided to just meet for lunch and dinner someplace but would split up to scout for last minute gifts. Schwarck had been to the Roman Baths on a prior visit, so she opted to shop and meet me for lunch at Bath's famous Grand Pump Room.

The Roman Baths are intriguing and ingenious. I walked on the same stones next to the baths that the Romans trod over 2000 years ago. The Romans believed that Gods presided here and they erected a Temple to Minerva, the goddess of the thermal spring. What was so remarkable is the immensity of the Roman bathing structure and the plumbing they invented to supply the regular baths, tepid bath rooms, hot baths, and the cold plunge rooms. Life size Roman statues were underwater so that the deities could protect bathers as they submerged. I wanted to run my fingers through the waters of the tepid pool and really considered taking a medicinal dip.

There were some smaller pools that bathers used to make wishes by throwing a coin into the sacred waters so the Gods would listen to their pleas. Often, tradesmen would be hired to engrave the wish onto the coin. Coins have been discovered with inscriptions hoping that death and pestilence would visit some problem personage. Schwarck caught up with me and we proceeded to the Pump Room for lunch and a glass of "the waters".

A brochure stated that there has always been a charge for "taking the waters" in the Pump Room since it opened in 1706. In the early days, waters were taken in the morning and usually a pint or two was sufficient, but as much as a gallon a day might be prescribed by a physician. When the "new" Pump Room opened in 1795, it was criticized for lacking facilities for when "the waters begin to operate on the system." We opted to try "the waters" which were served from a pump by a goofy looking page.

Neither of us could believe we paid $1.50 each to drink six ounces of stinky warm sulfur water. After we gagged the water down, we noted a sign advising patrons to be near a toilet when the intestinal healing starts to take place. Yikes!

Over a delicious salad lunch with a plentiful bread assortment, Schwarck told of her experience at the charming little Faerie Store that was hosting a Faerie Party for five little girls wearing gauzy wings and outfitted in colorful tutus and wands. The Faerie Store party festivities included tea and fairy dustings. Schwarck had purchased a three-foot lawn Fairy to take back home and a bag of Faerie Store dust came with it. Hope she packs her dust in her suitcase so that we aren't held up at security because of suspected drug running.

I can't believe you bought that big angel thing to take home. You can get those at Home Depot. How are you going to pack that?"

"I've never seen these at home. I'll just carry it onboard rather than taking a carryon bag. I think it will look so wonderful in the yard of our new house on Mackinac Island."

"Yeah, it'll look real cute the three months out of the year when she's not up to her wings in snow. Hey, guess what I found out at the Baths? Romans were so ingenious that they developed a way to drain all the baths each night for cleaning. Also, when Victorian ladies came to the bath, they were carried in litters by brawny Irishmen who sometimes had to go up three stories to get them from their bedrooms. Those lazy ladies wanted to be the first to bathe because if you were at the end of the day all manner of crap would be floating in the water…literally. Probably anyone bathing after 3 P.M. was doomed to die from the sludge in the healing waters."

Schwarck's outing included entering a mystical crystal shop and she bought some magical crystals that would protect her from all manner of predicaments. While in the shop she overheard a fascinating conversation, which she, of course, had to share with me.

"Crawford, did you know that last Saturday was the Beltane …the Vernal Equinox? Two ladies in the shop said that their systems were way off kilter. Everything that has gone weird this past week is probably a result of the Beltane. You see, our brains float in liquid…our blood is liquid and our bodies are mostly liquid. So if the moons make the tide of the earth move, why wouldn't the same tidal effect occur in our bodies?"

"I...don't...know...but now that you mention it, I did have a lot of gas last week. You should just forget about magic crystals and the Beltane and take two nighttime Tylenol every night and your brain will still slosh around but you won't know it."

We took the Double Decker tour bus around twice, and we thoroughly enjoyed a hilarious nighttime walking tour called "Bizarre Bath" that included ghost encounters and a major police arrest right in the middle of our "Bizarre" guide's speech in the Abbey courtyard. We loved the way our guide made fun of all the people on the tour. He even put the Germans in irons and spoke slower for Americans from the South.

Our last evening in the Abbey Green was spent repacking all of our gear to include the newest purchases in the burgeoning load, and we set our bags by the door for the 6 A.M. departure from Bath.

All too soon we awoke to our last day in the UK and as an added benefit, it was pouring down rain. Our wonderful hosts, Pat and John had graciously packed breakfast bags for us. Our 6 A.M. departure was too early for the regular breakfast. I suggested that a cab would be the best option this rainy morning, but Schwarck insisted that we were too close to the station. I'm sure we looked like pack mules as we yanked our considerable loads out the door and onto the slippery wet cobblestones. I put my head down for added leverage and marched along as fast as I could, trying to keep the pelting rain off my glasses. Thankfully, the pouring rain was washing all the vomit off the sidewalks in front of the pubs we passed. Schwarck was having trouble hauling this time. I could barely see her behind me, but I caught a glimpse of a cockeyed Angel Girl lashed to her bag.

"Schwarck, where are ya? Are you coming?"

"Keep going! I'm coming, but…geeze… this thing is so hard to pull!"

I grinned smugly at this news. As we neared the station, we had to use the long winding handicapped access hill to get up to the platform or else we would have had to navigate up three steep flights of stairs. I arrived at the top gasping for air, but Schwarck was worse off. It seemed her wheels had cracked and frozen up, so she was forced to pull with added resistance. Yes! I loved this news.

The train manager on the platform explained that the sitting train was ours, but was experiencing engine trouble. It had unexpectedly stopped three times before it got here. The train manager said we might have to cross to the other side of the tracks and catch a different train. That would involve traversing three steep flights of stairs to get over the tracks and three steep ones down just to get to the other side. My knee replacement trembled at the thought of all that maneuvering. Finally the broken train left the station and another one pulled up. The manager told us to get on this and we could still make it to London in time. He also added that he loved our Canadian accents.

Once seated, we broke out our breakfast bags to discover that we had a BLT on a giant, potent onion roll. There was also a banana, oatmeal bar, and a can of tomato juice that was more like tomato sauce than juice. I've never eaten an onion roll for breakfast, but it did contain a slab of bacon, my personal favorite.

"Schwarck, I've decided that I can never be cremated because I have eaten so much bacon my whole life that the fire would probably burn like a blow torch or the Eternal Flame and never go out."

"We've got to get in position to get off this train so we can catch the next. Think you can still jump?"

"No!"

We did manage to leap free of this train and get to the next one quickly and without incident. This would be our last train and would deposit us directly into the Gatwick Terminal where we started out five weeks ago. It seemed like decades ago that we had arrived here Easter Week. The Gatwick Terminal appeared much less hectic, but perhaps we have become more accepting of chaos. Since we had some time left, I wanted to shop in the extensive Duty Free store before we had to get to the gate. I commandeered a shopping cart and put the back-pack, snack bag, and fanny-pack in it. What a welcome relief! I suggested that Schwarck put the three-foot angel inside the cart, and I would meet her at the gate in awhile.

I fell madly in love with a gregarious, darkly handsome, perfume salesman extraordinaire. He called me "Luv" and I lu-ved him so much I bought perfume for everyone in my family, including the men. I also bought two big bottles of gin, a case of Cadbury Chocolate bars, and I received free gifts as a thank you for all that I purchased. My cart was filled to overflowing as I headed down the corridor leading to all the gates. Imagine my astonishment as I was met by a giant sign that declared: "No Carts Beyond This Sign". What? How in hell am I gonna' get all this crap down to the gate? There's an over-flowing backpack, fanny pack, giant snack bag, two bottles of gin, case of chocolate, eight bottles of perfume, free gifts and a three-foot angel! No one else was around to ask for help, so I began to stuff as much as I could in the bags and repositioned everything into my arms for the long excruciating walk to the gate, stopping every few feet to breathe and shift stuff around. I must say, the angel was fairly light but particularly awkward to carry. I arrived at the gate in time to see Schwarck blithely meandering holding a cappuccino. That was the extent of what she was carrying…coffee.

"Hi, Crawford! Want me to get you a coffee?"

"No, what I really want right now is an orthopedic surgeon!"

I unloaded all the stuff off my shoulders and waist and very deliberately delivered the angel over to Schwarck. What relief! I'm going to give Schwarck something extra heavy to carry onboard along with that insipid Angel Girl.

Once again we were treated like Queens as we entered the lovely first class compartment up front with the Captain. We plopped down on comfy leather recliners, ordered USA Today, and champagne. The flight attendant took our picture as we celebrated the end of five weeks of research for THE BOOK. Hors'd oeuvres were served immediately after takeoff, then more drinks, and we settled in for the long night of TV plus sleep. We were in heaven until a ruckus erupted in the rear and flight attendants were hustling fore and aft carrying big black bags. I assumed that someone had a medical emergency, but Schwarck was concerned about a heist. She had to get to the bottom of it and started asking lots of questions of the staff. It seemed that some guy in the riff-raff section was yelling that he was a Rock Star and expected better treatment and attention. They gave it to him. Staff said he finally went to sleep…probably with the help of a blunt instrument to his temple or a loaded syringe. In any case, when we landed, he, along with another guy, was arrested. No one should mess with these flight people. They may appear all smiley and wimpy, but they have special powers.

After we landed and cleared Customs, I made the mistake of trying to take a picture of Schwarck's suitcase, which had burst open and had to be duct taped. A very large, uniformed woman wearing two shiny badges and carrying a gun, yelled loudly, "You! No cameras!"

I had really wanted that picture for THE BOOK, but instead waited until we got to baggage and took a picture of the suitcase, plus a picture of two beaming and tanned husbands heading our way.

We were at long last back on Michigan soil after five weeks of toil and travel. After polite little pecks on the cheek, the men declared they were starving and wanted to stop and eat on the way home. We, of course, had seemingly eaten every hour for the past five weeks. Both of us were experiencing a heavy brain fog, but we took our laptops into the restaurant so that we could do a slide show for the men.

While we were eating, Hugh's cell phone rang. He answered and handed it over to me. I was anticipating a welcome home message, but it was our youngest daughter asking if I would babysit the two-year old tomorrow. I was stunned. I have not slept in at least two days…maybe three, and I have been out of the country for over five weeks on a life changing mission. I am a totally different person than the babysitting Grandma that left home so long ago. Hugh shared another bit of news:

"Your sister still can't find a job and probably has to live with us for at least another year. I didn't change the bed sheets while you were gone. Nancy offered to wash them, but they looked okay to me."

"Well, ya know, I suppose we needed a new bed anyway." I replied numbly.

As we headed for our homes, the two men up-front were talking very animatedly about their scores in the recent golf tournament. We were not ready to listen to conversation regarding the mundane humdrum lives of these two, but we sighed and nodded, attempting to look engrossed with their explanation of how many dimples were on their new balls. Reentry is definitely going to be iffy at best! When there was a lull in their conversation, Schwarck jumped in:

"Guess what, Crawford? When we were in the restaurant, I was flipping through the brochure rack in the lobby and there was a pamphlet lying on the floor, so I picked it up. It is a sign for us, really! It's all about an amazing three-week Alaskan tour for women only. It's by dog sled, can you believe it? We would sleep in Eskimo Tupiks and harness our own dog teams. They probably stay in the Tupik with us. You love dogs. We should go and then we could do workshops for seniors on "Adventure Travel and The Older Adult". Maybe we could write A BOOK about it. It's amazing that I ever saw that pamphlet. I think the Spirit Guides led me to it. Let's sign up for it right away!"

"Schwarck, my Spirit Guides, George and Hazel are telling me right now not to talk to you anymore for at least a month. Oh yeah, and they are also reminding me how chapped I get when it's forty degrees below zero and I'm living in a Eskimo Tupik with a Siberian Husky."